Why did Shakespeare write *drama?* Did he have specific and significant reasons for his choice of this art form? Did he have clearly defined aesthetic aims in what he wanted drama to do – and why? Pauline Kiernan opens up a new area of debate for Shakespearean criticism in showing that a radical, complex defence of drama which challenges the Renaissance orthodox view of poetry, history and art can be traced in Shakespeare's plays and poems.

This study examines work from different stages in the canon to show that far from being restricted by the 'limitations' of drama, Shakespeare consciously exploits its capacity to accommodate temporality and change, and its reliance on the physical presence of the actor in an attempt to replace both the artifice of mimetic art and the belatedness of historical record. She discusses the influence of Ovid's artistic concerns with poetic originality and immortality and the compelling power of fiction.

Shakespeare's Theory of Drama shows how Shakespeare rejected many of the theories of his age to create an original theory of drama. Kiernan provides a lively, readable but scholarly examination with a deliberately eclectic approach, covering less obvious texts in detail. She demonstrates that the non-dramatic works are about poetry in relation to Shakespeare's own role as a dramatist.

This is an important book: it offers an original and scholarly insight into what Shakespeare wanted his drama to do and why.

SHAKESPEARE'S THEORY
OF DRAMA

SHAKESPEARE'S THEORY OF DRAMA

PAULINE KIERNAN

University of Reading
and
The Globe, Bankside

Published by the Press Syndicate of the University of Cambridge
The Pitt Building, Trumpington Street, Cambridge CB2 1RP
40 West 20th Street, New York, NY 10011-4211, USA
10 Stamford Road, Oakleigh, Melbourne 3166, Australia

First Published 1996

Printed in Great Britain by Redwood Books, Trowbridge, Wiltshire

A catalogue record for this book is available from the British Library

Library of Congress cataloguing in publication data

Kiernan, Pauline.
Shakespeare's theory of drama / Pauline Kiernan.
p.   cm.
Includes bibliographical references and index.
ISBN 0 521 55046 7 (hardback)
1. Shakespeare, William, 1564–1616 – Aesthetics. 2. English drama –
Early modern and Elizabethan, 1500–1600 – 17th century – History and criticism –
Theory, etc. 3. English drama – 17th century – History and
criticism – Theory, etc. 4. Aesthetics, Modern – 16th century.
5. Aesthetics, Modern – 17th century. I. Title.
PR2986.K54   1996
822.3'3 – dc20   95–8533 CIP

ISBN 0 521 55046 7 hardback

For Colin Robson

Contents

Acknowledgements

I would like to thank Emrys Jones for reading this work in draft and offering judicious advice and much-needed encouragement during the stages of its development. Helen Cooper has provided constant support from the beginning of the project, and gave many helpful suggestions for which I am especially grateful. I would like to thank Lyndall Gordon for her timely words of encouragement at an early stage, and Robert Smallwood and Dennis Kay for their helpful comments. To Roy Park and University College, Oxford, I owe a special debt of gratitude.

I would like to give special thanks to the two anonymous readers for Cambridge University Press for giving up their time to provide me with extremely constructive reports: their comments and suggestions have been valuable. Needless to say, the errors and inadequacies that remain are all mine. I thank Sarah Stanton at Cambridge University Press for her faith, hope and charity to enable the book to get out into the world.

Some of my deepest obligations are to the fine Shakespeare critics who inspired me to pursue and sometimes challenge their views, particularly the late Muriel Bradbrook, and Anne Barton. I have endeavoured to record acknowledgements of published criticism in notes and in the bibliography, and I apologise for any omissions.

A version of Chapter 3 appeared in *Review of English Studies* November 1995. I would like to thank the editor and publisher for permission to reprint material.

My greatest debt is to Colin Robson for encouragement, support, interminable discussions and productive criticism; and to him this book is dedicated.

A note on references

Quotations from Shakespeare's plays and narrative poems are from the Arden editions, general editors Harold F. Brooks, Harold Jenkins, Brian Morris and Richard Proudfoot, unless otherwise specified. Quotations from Shakespeare's Sonnets are from *Shakespeare's Sonnets*, edited by W. G. Ingram and Theodore Redpath, London: Hodder and Stoughton, 1978; reprinted 1982.

Quotations from Ovid's works are from the Loeb Classical Library editions, Cambridge, Mass.: Harvard University Press. English translations are from these editions except where otherwise stated.

Quotations from Sidney's *A Defence of Poetry* are from Jan Van Dorsten's edition, Oxford: Oxford University Press, 1966; reprinted 1982.

Quotations from Plutarch's *Lives* are from *Plutarch's Lives of the Noble Grecians and Romanes*, translated by Sir Thomas North, 8 vols., Oxford: Basil Blackwell, 1928.

ABBREVIATIONS

All journals cited are given their title in full, except for *Publications of the Modern Language Association of America* (*PMLA*).

Titles of Shakespeare's plays are given in full, except in the notes, where they follow the abbreviated form recommended in the MLA Handbook.

CHAPTER I

Introduction

Critics have been curiously reluctant to explore the possibility that Shakespeare might have developed a theory of drama. We find discussions of stage technique, audience manipulation, the reflexivity of the plays, their dramatic structuring, Hamlet's advice on acting. We are given analyses of Shakespeare's poetry and uses of language, and considerations of his allusions to art, poetry and fiction. But the question of what might lie *behind* all this evident concern in the plays and poems with drama and aesthetics has prompted surprisingly little examination.

Traditional criticism has tended to view Shakespearean drama as a primarily literary poetic endeavour, and while recent studies have shifted the emphasis towards a pronounced concern with the playwright's theatrical practice, little enquiry has been made into whether he concerned himself with a coherent dramatic theory, or, indeed, had a theoretical position at all.[1] This swing from 'literary' to 'theatrical' approaches to Shakespeare has a puzzlingly seamless aspect to it, in that the question which might have been asked in that transition failed to emerge, and the assumptions of the old approaches were carried into the new: the question of a specifically *dramatic* theory was left out. Hence, studies which focus on Shakespeare's attitude to drama talk of his 'poetics', and 'his Renaissance conception of poetry as a superior kind of truth', on which assumption it is possible to claim that Shakespeare, working as an idealising Renaissance poet in the commercial, transitory world of theatre, reveals a 'scepticism about the value of his art as a model of human experience'. Influential studies have put forward the view that Shakespeare worked against the 'limitations' of his art in its capacity both to represent reality and to deliver a higher

1

kind of truth, or that he used the play as a metaphor for life, to turn
'the world itself into a theatre, blurring the distinctions between art
and life'.[2] Much recent 'metadramatic' criticism has sought to elu-
cidate and explore this idea of Shakespeare's plays as metaphors
for 'life-as-drama', focusing on dramatic reflexivity, the play-
within-the-play, and characters seen as actors, stage-managers and
playwright-directors.[3]

Studies which have included discussions of Shakespeare's concerns with dramatic art (usually focusing on *The Tempest* and *A
Midsummer Night's Dream*) have tended to make a straightforward
equation, or contrast, between the art of the dramatist and the art
of his characters. Traditional interpretations, for example, have
equated Prospero's 'so potent art' with that of Shakespeare;
Quince's 'Pyramus and Thisbe', as its antithesis.[4] The underlying
assumption shared by all these approaches is that Shakespearean
drama is an essentially mimetic art, whether it is seen as imitating
life, or as imitating the theatricality of life, or/and, that it is based
on a Renaissance conception of poetry, aspiring to deliver a higher
kind of truth.

This book pursues a line of enquiry which began by asking 'Why
did Shakespeare write *drama*?' to consider whether he might have
specific and significant reasons for his choice of this particular art
form, with clearly defined aesthetic aims in what he wanted that
drama to do, and why. A central aim is to show why we need to
replace the term 'Shakespeare's poetics' with 'Shakespeare's
theory of drama' to challenge traditional criticism's fundamental
assumption that Shakespeare equates the theoretical and moral
purposes of literary poetry with those of his own art. It argues that
this theory of drama involves a denunciation of literary poetics
and the mimetic concept of art, a challenging of history's claim to
truth and its capacity to accommodate temporality, and an insistence on the fictitiousness of Shakespearean drama. It is what leads
Shakespeare to a repudiation of literary (and historiographical)
representations of truth that provides the main focus of my
enquiry into his theoretical concerns as a dramatist.

Chapter 2 examines the interrelated issues which make up what
I take to be Shakespeare's theory of drama, and the ways in which
it can be seen in the poems and plays to be functioning as 'A

Defence of Drama', challenging the views expressed in Sidney's *A Defence of Poetry* to form, in effect, a refutation of Renaissance aesthetics.

Chapter 3 explores Shakespeare's prevalent concern with the 'de-humanising' processes of mimetic art, by examining *Venus and Adonis* and the Sonnets as highly self-conscious enquiries into the sterilising effects of poetry's rhetorical 'dyes' in relation to his own role as a dramatist, and demonstrates how these literary works provide significant insights into his dramatic theory. It also offers a redefinition of the term 'Ovidian' in Shakespeare by showing how the dramatist's creative responses to the Latin poet's artistic concerns with myth, fiction, poetic originality, and the complex relations between false illusion and substantial reality act as a significant and pervasive Ovidian presence in the canon. The underlying importance for Shakespeare's theory of drama of these strands of Ovidian influence is reflected throughout the book.

Chapter 4 examines *The Rape of Lucrece*, *The Winter's Tale* and *The Tempest* in the light of Renaissance aesthetic theory as examples of Shakespeare's repudiation of neoclassical verisimilitude and conceptions of art as the perfecter of nature; and chapter 5 considers the related question of mimesis, offering a reassessment of what 'fiction' and 'illusion' mean in Shakespearean drama. It distinguishes *mimetic* illusion, which is treated within the plays as an activity which falsifies human life, from *dramatic* illusion, the self-proclaimed fiction which paradoxically explores realities and compels belief. The broad argument of the chapter, which is that the playwright's frequent emphasis on the fictitiousness of his art is of precise and fundamental significance to his dramatic theory, is supported by readings of *Love's Labour's Lost*, *A Midsummer Night's Dream* and *Hamlet* and, more briefly, *As You Like It*, *Twelfth Night*, *Much Ado About Nothing* and *Measure for Measure*.

Chapter 6 argues that Shakespeare replaces historical accounts of past events with a self-proclaimed fiction in order to challenge history's claim to truth. It examines *Richard III*, *Henry VIII*, *Henry V*, and *Richard II* in the context of Shakespeare's responses to the humanist concept of anachronism and his sense of drama's capacity for accommodating temporality and change.

Chapter 7 examines *Antony and Cleopatra* as Shakespeare's most explicit challenge to the claims to truth of both poetry and history, and his most confident proclamation of his drama's powers of self-renewal; its three sections examine the languages of Octavius, Enobarbus and Cleopatra as they reflect the thematic and structural pattern of rivalry set up within the play between the belated narratives of history and poetry on the one hand, and the physical immediacy, performative action and fictitiousness of drama on the other.

This is a necessarily exploratory study on a large and complex topic. The initial plan was to try to be as comprehensive as possible, but to have attempted to cover a more wide-ranging selection of texts and pursue more fully the lines of enquiry it proposes would have resulted in too unwieldy a book. My aim, throughout, has been to suggest a way into a subject and show why it is worth critical debate. But the book makes a large claim, and some explanation of my procedures is necessary. The approach has been deliberately eclectic, and uneven: I devote, for example, one chapter to a long and detailed analysis of a narrative poem because it seemed important to try to substantiate as fully as possible the proposition that a Renaissance writer was attacking some of the most fundamental aesthetic concepts of his time, and *Venus and Adonis* provides some of the strongest evidence for this. The texts I have chosen to examine in detail are probably the more unexpected ones, and those I have ignored or treated less fully, or cursorily, have tended to be the plays which are more usually discussed in relation to Shakespeare's attitude towards his drama. Discussions on *A Midsummer Night's Dream* and *The Tempest*, traditionally considered to be the two central statements about his own art, for example, may seem to some blasphemously brief. I have found that the less obvious texts yielded so many interesting, often complex, insights into Shakespeare's theory of drama that they ended up almost demanding to be analysed at the expense of the more critically familiar works. The extensive coverage of the non-dramatic works might strike the reader as surprising in a study of Shakespeare's dramatic theory, but it is in these works that we find so many of the important ideas being explored, and even tested out. As I hope the study demonstrates, the dramatic theory which I am suggesting can be discerned in Shakespearean drama is concerned with the development of an art form which can overcome what it sees as the inadequacies of literary poetry, and the non-dramatic works are as much about poetry in relation to Shakespeare's own role as a dramatist, as they are about their ostensible subject matter.

It is, then, very much an exploratory and partial study, but I hope it will suggest further lines of enquiry into Shakespeare's theoretical concerns as a dramatist; that it will lend precision to such critical terms as 'fiction' and 'illusion' when applied to his plays; and that it will help us more confidently to place this writer and thinker in the forefront of English Renaissance aesthetic thought.

CHAPTER 2

Shakespeare and Sidney. Two worlds: the brazen and the golden

When we look for criticism on Shakespeare's aesthetic views we find the many references to poetic and artistic theory found in the plays and poems examined, and usually summarily consigned to 'the common thought of his age'; or, where a given statement does not seem to correspond with a contemporary view, or results in interpretative difficulties, commentators are more often than not content to leave the matter unexplored, giving no suggestion that the reason for their confusion might be worth investigating.[1] One example of such critical neglect concerns one of the most significant statements on art to be found in the canon: 'Artificial strife / Lives in these touches, livelier than life', spoken by the Poet in *Timon of Athens* (I.i.37–8). One editor of the play glosses the line, or rather, admits he is incapable of doing so, by taking issue with the gloss of a previous editor: 'This notion of *art at strife with* nature is common enough but "artificial strife" can hardly mean "the strife of art to emulate nature" . . . nor is it clear how that strife could be "livelier than life"'.[2]

The question we would expect to find being asked here is not raised. If the line does not make any sense, which is what we are left to infer from this editor's refusal to make any attempt to interpret it, why is it there? Are we to suppose that a dramatist who has had no apparent difficulty in the structuring of coherent sentences for nine comedies, nine history plays, two Roman plays, three 'problem' comedies, four major tragedies and a sonnet sequence of unprecedentedly complex, intricately structured reasoning, is here suffering a momentary lapse in clarity of expression? Or is it merely taken for granted that we share the critic's assumption that if Shakespeare is not adhering to the prevailing views of

6

Renaissance theorists, it is beyond the bounds of possibility that he might have an intellectually motivated reason for placing within a play a deliberate and uncommon challenge to a common notion about art? Whatever the reason for not enquiring further into the meaning of the line, the gloss provides us with an example of the ways in which criticism traditionally has been wary of attributing to Shakespearean drama any coherent theoretical position on aesthetics.

Why, with this writer, is there a resistance to the idea that there might be specific theoretical issues being raised in such statements, and that these may have far-reaching implications for our understanding of Shakespeare's concerns as a dramatist? It is not the purpose of this study to speculate on the reasons for this resistance, but it might help to bear in mind two critical attitudes. Is it possible that even now the centuries-long tradition which has seen him as the 'natural' genius who came from a provincial country town with his grammar-school education, stumbled into a career in the theatre and, by some inexplicable process of the brain, provided drama of unsurpassed mastery and formidable powers of original thought, continues to act as a subliminal influence on Shakespeare scholars, whatever their critical predilections? Combine this with an equally consciousness-embedded idea of the dramatist's powers of 'negative capability' which makes it 'impossible' for us to determine what he really thought about the matters that are treated in his plays, and it becomes less surprising to find comparatively little evidence of detailed enquiry into the dramatist's views on his art. To argue for greater attention to the theoretical concerns of Shakespearean drama, is not to suggest a return to traditional criticism's quest for immanent meaning, but to insist that these concerns deserve to be explored at the level of enquiry on which modern theorists conduct criticism of, say, Spenser, Milton and the Romantic Poets, and before that can be attained, we need to dispense with the paradoxical attitude that licenses the disclosure of immanent meaning while disavowing access to central aesthetic aims.

If we start out with a different set of assumptions, then, and allow that references to theory in Shakespeare's work might tell us something about his attitude towards imitation in relation to his own role as a dramatist, we might look again at the Poet's line in *Timon* and start by entertaining the possibility that a statement might mean what it says. We find that, though made to seem difficult, which is part of its meaning, the statement is both precise and lucid. It is actually very simple. The 'difficulty' arises if you try to place it within the rigid framework of Renaissance aesthetic theory which leads one to think, like Oliver, that 'it can hardly mean' what it says. It is saying that 'the struggle of art against nature (with the suggestion that the struggle is unnatural) lives in these brushstrokes, and is livelier than life'. If we do not think it makes any sense it is because it is not saying what we would expect it to say. In the mimesis concept of art, the ideal is a skilled imitation of nature that is so life-like we are deceived into thinking the imitated subject is the real thing. In the painting described in *Timon*, it is the *artificial strife* which is livelier than the subject. What lives in this painting is the unnatural struggle against nature, which we can see in the brushstrokes. The dramatist has made a Poet unwittingly expose the absurdity of all art forms which imitate life so skilfully, that it is the skill of the artist which we notice, not the life that he has imitated.

Why is the mimesis concept of art ridiculed? What might be the significances of this statement for Shakespeare's attitude towards imitation? Where else in the canon do we find this concern with the processes by which life is transformed into an imitation of itself, where the copy supersedes the original? What are the implications of this for a writer who spent most of his career choosing to write plays, to write them for performance and not, apparently, for publication? Did he have a particular reason for writing drama, as distinct from poetry or prose, that is related to this concern with imitation?

Where, exceptionally, a critic points out that Shakespeare reverses many of the attitudes of Renaissance aesthetics, it is not in order to explore the possibility that this might indicate a conscious attempt by the playwright to establish a theory of his own. Ekbert Faas writes, 'Shakespeare can be blithely oblivious of some of the hotly debated issues of Renaissance criticism', and 'rarely commits himself to an established theoretical attitude', to conclude that, 'more often than not, [he] reveals an eclectic versatility in subscribing to whatever ideas best serve his immediate demands'.[3] We are given the familiar image of the 'natural' poet with no central aesthetic purpose imposing constraints on what he will or will not accommodate in his art, and who is therefore free to adopt whatever theoretical viewpoint seems most useful for his present requirements.

Is this really all we are able to offer in the way of critical attention to the artistic aims of a dramatist who, throughout his work, is preoccupied with the relations between insubstantial image and corporeal substance, the real and the unreal; a dramatist who explores the physical consequences of deeds prompted by acts of the imagination: the blood that will not be washed away from Lady Macbeth's hands; the coupling of nothing with nothing inside Leontes' head that produces the monstrous command to have a new-born baby murdered; or that comparable union of imaginings in Othello's mind which results in his transforming the white flesh of his beloved into a senseless statue? Is Jonson's poet of nature who 'wanted Arte' still the most we can say about a playwright who persistently shows us why the disembodied language of rhetoric is dangerous, and all forms of de-materialising representation are to be distrusted; who repeatedly demonstrates what happens when we ask symbol to be congruent with meaning, whether it is rhetoric's treachery of value which turns Helen of Troy into a pearl and perpetuates the killing and bloodshed of war in the name of an abstraction named honour, where words and their meanings have become so dislocated, discourse is madness; or whether it is rhetorical poetry's de-corporealising process which turns Adonis into disembodied fragments of dead metaphors so that when he tries to escape suffocation by rhetorical trope he ends his life with his flesh gored by the tusk of a boar?[4]

When we ask symbol to be congruent with meaning, we lose the body, which is what many of Shakespeare's protagonists come to learn, whether it is the metonymic confusion of Richard II which will turn him into no-thing when he is deprived of his name; whether it is the total and absolute identification of individual identity with a code of honour which allows a Roman soldier to put on a new name as unthinkingly as if it were another suit of armour in *Coriolanus*; whether it is Shylock's transmutation of the barren metal which represents abstract fiscal value into a pound of human flesh, and the price that must be paid for turning flesh and blood into a cash nexus is to be robbed of your daughter, your own flesh and blood, and of your spiritual creed; or whether it is the con-crete-into-abstraction process which makes Lear think he can cut into three a cartographical representation of his kingdom with impunity and leaves him, finally, cradling the corpse of his daughter, and asking his heart to break.[5]

This concern with the processes by which life is turned into a representation informs both the subject of the dramatist's art and the form with which he creates it. The two are interdependent, not simply related.

Examples are found throughout the canon of the ways in which flesh and blood are turned into a symbol or an abstraction; fecundity is transformed into sterility; some-thing turned into no-thing, and no-thing turned into some-thing: the problematic relations of the insubstantial and the substantial are embedded in the theoretical foundation on which Shakespearean drama is based.

A 'DEFENCE OF DRAMA'

When we start to enquire into Shakespeare's concerns as a drama-tist, several interrelated issues emerge which suggest a theory of drama which involves:

* complex responses to contemporary artistic and poetic theories, in which the repudiation of the mimesis concept of art is central;
* the primacy of the human body in his art;
* an insistence on the fictitious status of his drama;
* a highly developed sense of the humanist concept of anachronism, expressed in the plays in an acute awareness that his present will become our past;
* an inviolable demand that his drama accommodate temporality and change.

Within Shakespeare's plays and poems there can be traced a 'Defence of Drama' which redefines the parameters of contemporary debate on the rival claims to truth of poetry and history by introducing the question of temporality's effects on the representation and transmission of 'truth'. This 'Defence' rests on three fundamental and inextricably related arguments:

(1) Mimetic art is sterile

All representations of the human body fail to deliver the living, corporeal (present) presence of the subject that is being represented. In poetry, history and art, the subject is rendered inaccessible and lost to the present; such representations cannot restore to us the 'original'. Art which attempts to create a perfect imitation twice removes the subject from itself by firstly, producing a copy of the original, and secondly, making this imitation so 'life-like' that it is the means by which this verisimilitude is achieved that becomes important: the brush work, the painter's 'touches', is 'livelier than life'.

Shakespearean drama does not attempt to represent the original subject or original moment in history, nor does it seek to deliver a Sidneyan 'golden world' in which art attempts to outdo nature in the timeless perfection of artifice, but is concerned with finding ways of creating an art which can exist within the mutable, 'brazen world' of nature. Sidney claims: 'Nature never set forth the earth in so rich tapestry as divers poets have done . . . Her world is brazen, the poets only deliver a golden'.[6] Shakespeare's drama privileges the living human body, the organic matter on which it is created. What is needed to counteract the sterilising process of rhetorical poetry in which the subject is made life-less in a life-like imitation is the Shakespearean reinstating of the body, where art does not aspire to the absurdity of being 'livelier than life'. In place of the painter's 'touches' and the 'strainèd touches rhetoric can lend' to poets (Sonnet 82.10) to make the subject appear to live, there will be the dramatist's cutting of breath: his instrument, the actors' bodies who speak and breathe and move indeed.

A Poetry which seeks to transcend the 'brazen world' must negate nature's organic process: the subject – nature – dies when it is 'dyed' in rhetoric. In future ages all that will be available of what once had unique life, warmth and movement in an immediate presence, will be the skilful application of the painted rhetoric in the iconographical stasis of the written word.

(2) History lies but claims to tell the truth

While poetry uses imitative constructs that have been promiscuously bestowed on previous subjects, and fails to deliver the immediacy and corporeal presence of the subject it imitates, history's belated transmission of knowledge, dependent on relativity of judgement, renders the 'truth' of an original event or character irrecoverably lost to the present. Poetic, artistic and historical representations of persons and events are trapped in a spurious present because these forms do not allow for time, process and change to which all living things are subject.

A history which seeks to represent past events in a contemporaneous present is ignoring history itself, and failing to acknowledge that the past is different from the present. A history which purports to be a truthful representation of past events lies: it is impossible to determine what happened in the past, even if we have access to eye-witness accounts, because the unreliability, instability and relativity of judgement and interpretation of truth mean that history's 'recórds and what we see doth lie' (Sonnet 123.11). Shakespearean drama exploits the fundamental fact of mutability, confronts the inevitable anachronism of historical time by attempting to accommodate temporality and change, and by an insistent refusal to try to persuade its audience that the actors 'are' the actual people of history, or that what it shows is what 'really' happened.

(3) All drama should do is lie

Against the charge that poetry lies, Sidney claims that the poet 'nothing affirms, and therefore never lieth'.[7] Shakespearean drama declares itself unashamedly a liar in order to affirm one unassailable truth, which is the impossibility of determining the truth. It is for this reason that its fictitiousness is the foundation for all that it attempts to achieve.

The argument offered here is that this 'Defence' can be discerned in the plays and poems, and is an integral part of the way in which Shakespearean drama works. It proposes that a fundamental aim of this drama is to reinstate the 'brazen world' of nature, which Sidney's ideal poetry was required to abjure, and that for Shakespeare, this means art must accommodate both the substantiality of matter and the mutability to which all matter is subject. It requires, therefore, a reinstating of the human body and an admitting of temporality. To this end, drama's capacity to accommodate time and change can be exploited, and the importance of the physical presence of the actor made paramount. In place of the secondariness and belatedness of mimetic representation, it will be argued, Shakespearean drama attempts to offer the physical immediacy and present-centredness of Orphic presentation.

FROM ORPHEUS TO MIMESIS; *MAGIKĒ* TO *LOGOS*

In *Modern Poetry and the Idea of Language*, Gerald L. Bruns distinguishes two 'broadly antithetical conceptions of poetic or literary language', the hermetic and the Orphic, both of which, he says, 'assert the primacy of language'. The hermetic, which 'seeks to establish the transcendence of language in the face of a universe of meaning . . . in which words take on value as realities in their own right'; and the Orphic, which, 'by contrast, seeks its transcendence not in isolation but in relation to the world of natural things'. It is an idea 'which finds poetry to be the condition of the world's possibility', in which language is said to 'form the ground of the world, and not the world only but "Welt und Ich": the becoming of man's world, that is to say, is predicated upon the movement of the word'.[8]

These two antithetical conceptions of poetic language, it seems to me, provide us with a helpful framework within which to explore the Shakespearean and Sidneyan theoretical positions. Hermetic language is characterised, Bruns says, by 'a desire to be free of the world', so that the poem is a 'closed' form, analogous to Flaubert's imaginary book about nothing, a book dependent on nothing external, which would be held together by the strength of its style . . . a book which would have almost no subject, or at least in which the subject would be almost invisible.[9]

This has significant parallels with the description of the portrait in *Timon* where, we are told, attention is directed at the skill, artifice or style of the painting, so that the original subject is rendered 'almost invisible'. Style, or 'artificial strife', is what lives in the painting; it is 'livelier than life', that is, livelier than the subject.

Distinct from the idea of hermetic language which is pure form, is the conception of a poetry 'whose power extends . . . beyond the formation of a work toward the creation of the world', whose origin lies in the myth of Orpheus and his power to summon things into his presence.[10] This, Bruns writes, is 'an activity which brings the world into being for the first time and which maintains it there as the ground of all signification'; and he goes on to quote Albert Hofstadter's description of it as 'genuinely creative, for in it man's world and self are originated and maintained, not found already finished'.[11] This poetic act, then, achieves an ideal unity of word and being. Instead of re-creating, or re-presenting the world, the world is brought into being. It is these distinguishing characteristics of Orphic speech that I wish to explore in relation to Shakespearean drama; the idea of working with, and not in isolation from, nature, and of originating the world by means of the movement of the word.

The sense of the poet working through and with 'defective' nature is emphasised in *The Merchant of Venice*, where it is associated with the music of the spheres. Lorenzo describes the effect of music on nature's wild, uncontrollable and savage creatures:

> If they but hear perchance a trumpet sound,
> Or any air of music touch their ears,
> You shall perceive them make a mutual stand,
> Their savage eyes turn'd to a modest gaze,
> By the sweet power of music: therefore the poet
> Did feign that Orpheus drew trees, stones, and floods,
> Since naught so stockish, hard, and full of rage,
> But music for the time doth change his nature . . .
>
> (*The Merchant of Venice*, V.i.75–82)

The significance of the Orpheus myth for Shakespeare is that the poet's power resides in, and works on, nature; a nature which is explicitly shown, in this allusion, to be postlapsarian, or 'brazen', as it is in the earliest allusion that appears in the plays:

> For Orpheus' lute was strung with poets' sinews,
> Whose golden touch could soften steel and stones,
> Make tigers tame, and huge leviathans
> Forsake unsounded deeps, to dance on sands.
> (*The Two Gentlemen of Verona*, III.ii.77–80)

Here, the instrument with which the poet subdues leviathans, the monstrous sea beasts that are a manifestation of nature's defects, is said to have a corporeal physicality: his lute is strung with sinews. Elizabeth Sewell, in her study of *The Orphic Voice*, makes the important observation: 'In that splendid, painful metaphor [Shakespeare] unites himself, as poet, immediately with the Orphic power and becomes the myth he is describing, that inclusive myth . . . where instrument and agent are one'. For Shakespeare, she says, 'Orpheus' instrument is the poet's body'.[12] And we might also add that in Shakespearean drama the artist's instrument is the body of the actor: a flesh-and-blood presence on the stage.[13] The dramatist works with, and not in isolation from, the organic processes of nature.

In Ovid's account of the dismemberment of Orpheus (*Metamorphoses*, XI.1–84) it is while the poet sings of Pygmalion, Myrrha, and Venus and Adonis, drawing all of nature under his spell, that he is assaulted by the crazed women of the Cicones hurling their spears and stones at his mouth. At first, the song of Apollo's bard makes their missiles fall at his feet: 'cunctaque tela forent cantu mollita' (15) 'And all their weapons would have been harmless under the spell of song'. But the mighty uproar of the Berecyntian flutes, mixed with the discordant horns, drums, and breast-beatings and howlings of the Bacchanals, drowned the sound of the lyre: 'tum denique saxa / non exauditi rubuerunt sanguine vatis' (18–19) 'and then at last the stones grew red with the blood of the bard whose voice they could not hear'.[14] Shakespeare alludes to this episode in *A Midsummer Night's Dream* when one of the entertainments offered to Theseus for the nuptial celebrations is

'the riot of the tipsy Bacchanals, / Tearing the Thracian singer in
their rage' (V.i.48–9).

Ovid then describes how the birds and beasts were savaged by
the Maenads, how peasants, ploughing the hard earth, were driven
off their land, their oxen torn in pieces, until the fields were
deserted but for the implements of their toil which lay scattered
across the earth. When the savage women rush back to slay the
poet, Orpheus' voice has lost its power. He is unable to move them,
and they strike him down (10–40). All of nature goes into mourning. The poet's limbs lay scattered all around, but his head and lyre
floated in the stream, and Orpheus' song issues from his lifeless
tongue.

> (mirum!) medio dum labitur amne,
> flebile nescio quid queritur lyra, flebile lingua
> murmurat exanimis, respondent flebile ripae. (51–3)

(a marvel!) while they floated in mid-stream the lyre gave forth some
mournful notes, mournfully the lifeless tongue murmured, mournfully
the banks replied.

The historical dismemberment of Orpheus is described by Bruns
as 'that process of demythologization that marked the gradual dissociation of word and being'. In this process, '*Magikē* . . . gave way
to the *Logos* as the principle of the world's intelligibility, and as it did
so the figure of the poet-magus lost its reason for being'. Instead of
the poet working with and in nature, the poet works against nature.
Bruns writes:

In place of the identity of poetry and reality that gave life to Orpheus,
poetic theory instituted the doctrine of mimesis, which established the
poet over and against the world as a mere onlooker. The magic of poetry,
in turn, came to be understood in terms of a psychology of rhetoric: by
skilled imitation, or perhaps by imagining a more perfect world, the poet
could persuade his audience to follow nature in conduct and in thought;
but no longer could his song build up the world.[15]

Shakespeare's repudiation of the mimesis conception of poetry is
an argument against this idea of the poet's strife against nature to
achieve, by means of rhetoric, a skilled imitation, or to construct
'a more perfect world'; what Sidney described as growing 'in

effect another nature, in making things either better than nature bringeth forth, or, quite anew, forms such as never were in nature'. It is mimesis in this specific sense which I am suggesting Shakespeare's theory of drama is concerned with, not as the term has been used, by A. D. Nuttall, for example, as 'connoting any deliberate relation to the real, as opposed to epiphenomenal or "betrayed" relation'.[16]

What Shakespeare praises in Orpheus is the power the drama-tist gives to Cleopatra, to 'make defect perfection'. Orpheus' song builds up the world. It is a world built on nature, a nature which Sidney would term 'brazen'. In Ovid, the power which moves nature is destroyed not by the weapons which the crazed women hurl, but by the cacophony of flutes, discordant horns and drums which whips up the Bacchanals into a howling frenzy. It is *other* music which, drowning the poet's song, causes the dismemberment of Orpheus. Shakespeare's Adonis has the power to make birds, beasts and trees move into his presence, and his song, which tamed tigers, is threatened to be drowned by the 'shrill-tongu'd' cacoph-ony of Venus' rhetoric, a significant Ovidian parallel which is dis-cussed in the following chapter.

In considering Shakespeare's responses to the Orpheus myth, it is important to keep in mind one very obvious significance of the primordial poet's activity. It is non-textual. Orphic power cannot exist other than as a sound, and other than a sound uttered in the present. Walter Ong's explanation of the priority of the spoken word over the written, which Bruns discusses in his study, describes what I take to be an underlying impulse behind Shakespeare's exploitation of drama's Orphic possibilities:

Sound is more real or existential than other sense objects, despite the fact that it is also *more evanescent*. Sound itself is related to present actuality rather than to past or future. It must emanate from a source *here and now discernibly active*, with the result that involvement with sound is involvement with *the present*, with *here-and-now existence* and *activity*. (my emphasis)

Ong also states, 'None of the other senses gives us the insistent impression that what it registers is necessarily *progressing through time*' (my emphasis).[17]

Bruns writes:

For its part, the spoken word, the word as sound, involves us not only with present time but with *presence* in the phenomenological sense, that is, the mutually determining presence of person and world. It is this involvement with presence that is muted or (as Ricoeur says) interrupted by writing, for writing isolates speech from sound, person and actuality: it creates its own world – a textual universe which compensates for absence by seeking the perfection of form.[18] (Bruns' emphasis)

It is this very loss of existential presence during transcription from speech to writing I am suggesting Shakespearean drama is concerned to pre-empt, which is why poststructuralist criticism's challenging of traditional theories of mimesis cannot take us very far in our understanding of the dramatist's aesthetic aims. But the reason that the question of Shakespeare and mimesis proves resistant to the new theories is itself profoundly significant. Deconstruction's textual-based concerns with exposing the fallacy of an originating presence in language seem redundant when confronted with drama which has Orphic aspirations, intent on exposing the ways in which the derivative signifiers of literary texts render their original subjects lost and inaccessible, turning them into absence.[19] It is precisely the text-centred, literary-defined ground, on which deconstruction studies are conducted, that Shakespearean drama argues against, and the Poet of the Sonnets, with audacious irony, employing literary writing's most formalised form, its most finite interruption and erasure of existential presence, exposes as duplicitous.

While it is not possible within the scope of this present study to examine the question of 'Print *versus* Performance' in English Renaissance drama, or to speculate on Shakespeare's attitude towards the publication of his plays, the significance of drama's dependence upon the spoken word involving the audience with the present time, and also with the human presence of the actor who is uttering it, informs all that is here argued. Jonson, in keeping with his theory of drama as mimesis, in which the poet stands outside nature, holding up a mirror, carefully prepares a collection of plays, improved, altered, augmented, to divorce them from the presence of the live audience and actors and evanescent circumstances of their performance. The transcription of speech into writing creates a 'textual universe' of literary verses, English and

Latin, the heavily edited plays (but not the early hack-work for Henslowe) and a Latin motto. He calls it *The Workes of Beniamin Jonson*, the title elaborately engraved, and the volume appears when all of his plays (apart from the four 'Henslowe' ones which he never mentioned in the innumerable references to his own works) have already been published individually, and soon after their performance.[20] It is a Flaubertian 'closed' book. The spoken word which involves the audience 'not only with present time but with *presence*' has been 'interrupted' by writing which has 'isolated speech from sound, person and actuality'. *The Workes*, published in 1616, marks an extra-ordinary moment in the history of transcription of speech into writing. Where the textual basis of drama had been produced only so that it may be spoken aloud in the presence of a theatre audience, here the text has become all that matters. It has been turned into literature to be read. Jonson's meticulously executed act of transforming the transient presence and movement of the spoken word into the iconographical silence and stasis of the frozen word is an inverse paradigm of Pantagruel's melting of the sugar-plum-coloured frozen words in Rabelais' *Quart Livre*. The significance of Rabelais' description of the written and printed word for the parallels I am here drawing with Jonson's remarkable publication, is that with the coming of spring, the frozen words begin to melt, and when Pantagruel and his friends warm them in their hands, the words can be heard again. But they cannot be understood. 'It was a Barbarous Gibberish.' What Rabelais seems to be suggesting is that when spoken words are taken *out of time* they cannot be put back into time without a loss of meaning. Once consigned to the manuscript or printed page, even nature's miraculous powers of renewal cannot restore the loss. The frozen words are described as being 'of many colours, like those us'd in Heraldry'.[21] The spoken words, then, had already been transformed into rhetorical, literary devices, so what is being suggested here is both the secondariness and belatedness of the written or printed word. From what we know of his preparation of the *Workes* for the press, it would seem that Jonson's aim was to take his plays out of time; out of the mutable world of here-and-now activity and immediate presence. Jonas A. Barish writes that Jonson's

reform aims precisely to detheatricalize the theatre, to strip it of just those
attributes which, in the eyes of most of its votaries, made it theatre in the
first place: not only its gaudiness, its bustle and splendour, but also – what
Jonson deeply objected to – its licentious ways with time and place, and its
sovereign command of the astonishing and the marvellous.

Jonson's escape into print, he says, was a way to achieve 'an ideal of
stasis in the moral and ontological realm' and 'banish' the movement that is one of the mainsprings of 'whatever exists in time' and
'unfolds in time'.[22]

    Shakespeare, as far as we know, did not prepare his plays for the
press.[23] He does seem to have taken great care, however, with the
preparation for the publication in 1593 of a highly rhetorical
poem, *Venus and Adonis*, which was clearly written as a piece of literature to be read.

CHAPTER 3

Shakespeare and Ovid. 'What strainèd touches rhetoric can lend': poetry metamorphosed in 'Venus and Adonis' and the Sonnets

SEMINAL PURITY *VERSUS* RHETORICAL PROMISCUITY

Shakespeare's careful insistence that *Venus and Adonis* is 'the first heir of my invention' has been frequently explained away as the playwright's attempt to dismiss the worth of his dramatic achievements to date, fearful of offending the poem's dedicatee by a reference to his vulgar craft. According to this view, the narrative poems published in 1593 and 1594 become testimony to a quickly abandoned flirtation with literary, as distinct from dramatic, ambitions, and are taken to represent either a desire to begin a new career as a narrative poet or an enforced momentary departure from a life-long commitment to dramatic art.[1]

The practical reason offered by most commentators that the poems were written in a period of enforced idleness when the theatres were closed, as a precaution against the plague, between August 1592 and the end of 1593, does not, of course, explain what kind of artistic motivations were occupying the writer's mind during their composition.[2] There has, however, been a tendency for critics to suppose that financial considerations were primary determinants in the choice of form and subject and this has, perhaps, helped to prevent us from exploring fully their precise significances as a dramatist's responses to Renaissance concerns with literary imitation and rhetorical history. F. T. Prince, for example, seems happy to conclude that if we accept that these poems were written to help compensate for losses incurred by the theatre shutdown, 'we have an explanation both of why the rising young dramatist turned to "narrative" verse, and of why he chose first such a subject as that of Venus and Adonis'.[3] Shakespeare success-

21

fully gauged the taste of his readers by producing a risqué Ovidian romance he knew would be a best-seller and, along with Marlowe, started the popular craze for erotic epyllion. All of which is probable, and embarrassing for those critics who have had trouble reconciling their image of the great artist happy to starve for his art with the idea of a commercial writer responding to market forces: 'Despite the presentation of *Venus and Adonis* and *Lucrece* as the works of a conscious artist, Shakespeare probably sat down to write them in the hope that they would bring him some immediate practical reward'.[4] The problem that arises from this kind of righteous sensitivity is that it muddles critical judgement. Commentators have sought to find ways of defending the poem by concentrating on the beauty of the language and verse as if this will somehow compensate for the supposedly unseemly reason it was written, only to find themselves feeling uncomfortable with its rhetorical excesses.

It has long been recognised, if not always approvingly, that *Venus and Adonis* possesses a high degree of self-conscious artistry and elaborate rhetoric. Richard Wilbur concedes that its 'main and steadiest sources of pleasure' are 'its elaborate inventiveness, its rhetorical dexterity, its technical éclat', and in the next sentence regrets that 'mostly one is reacting to an ostentatious poetic performance' of 'artful variety'. F. E. Halliday complains that the stanzas are 'rigid with rhetorical constructions and studded with compound and decorative epithets', and the diction 'studiously artificial and "poetical"'. Robert Ellrodt thinks that 'Through the poem the artist seems at once hesitant about tone and too confident in the power of rhetoric'.[5]

Richard Lanham has provided a helpful corrective to such discomfort with the poem's rhetorical artifice, in arguing that *Venus and Adonis* and *The Rape of Lucrece* 'are poems about rhetorical identity and the strategies of rhetorical style'. Shakespeare, he says, 'often describes and exemplifies at the same time; he writes about the form he writes in'. I would like to pursue further this point and consider why the dramatist seems to have felt it important to conduct his interrogation of rhetorical poetics employing rhetorical strategies in a narrative form, and to prepare this written narrative poem for the press. Is there some further, and related, significance in his choosing to foreground the literary and textual status of rhetorical poetry, and the medium of print to 'write about the form he writes in'?[6]

Before we can begin to explore the ramifications of the dramatic consciousness working in a narrative, non-dramatic form, perhaps we need to look again at the problematic status of the statement that *Venus and Adonis* is the first heir of Shakespeare's invention, and try to work out a more satisfactory explanation than the 'dyer's hand' theory: the 'vulgar' playwright aspiring to coterie literary fame, which assumes a primary narrative impulse behind the poem at odds with an essentially dramatic creative urge.[7] Both the narrative poems have tended to be placed in a marginalised position in relation to the main body of Shakespeare's work, but even when critics have argued that the poems possess pivotal importance in Shakespeare's development as a dramatist, they have usually been content to examine their relation to the plays in terms of technical experimentation.[8]

The statement begins to invite a quite different reading if we can ignore – for the moment – questions of chronology, of whether or not it means the poem is a first composition or a first published work, and start by trying to take it at face-value.[9] We would then have to ask different questions about this poem. Is it about origins? About the genesis of an original poetic identity? In what way does its author see it as being seminal? Is the dramatist announcing his intention, in this poem, to deliver an original self-authorising poetic authority, uncontaminated by the seminal chaos of previous literary conceptions? If he regards it as the first heir of his invention, why does he choose an 'overhandled theme', and one, moreover, that has received an apparently definitive treatment by the most influential classical poet on the Renaissance, and which has itself engendered imitative texts? Spenser's treatment of the myth, for example, was published as recently as 1590 when the first three Books of *The Faerie Queene* appeared in print. If we now reinstate the importance of chronological considerations and assume, for our present purposes, that four history plays and three comedies precede the writing of *Venus and Adonis*, we may become yet more sceptical of taking the statement at any kind of literal level, but our refusal to do so is dependent upon a prior assumption that the author is aspiring to a specifically literary fame.[10] Confronted with the statement's stubborn insistence that it is there, uncharacteristically carefully prepared for publication and bearing its author's signature, loudly proclaiming his début in print, we would seem to have conclusive evidence that the poem represents a new ambition to achieve recognition as a literary poet who would not want to draw attention to his presumed ignominious status as a dramatist.

But what if we attend to the artistic concerns which the poem itself examines? If, as I hope to demonstrate, the narrative poems are a dramatist's means of working out his relationship to non-dramatic poetry, to the printed texts of his literary precursors, the printed proclamation can begin to take on a rather more complex significance. What I want to argue is that in *Venus and Adonis* Shakespeare is conducting a highly self-conscious exploration of the nature of poetic identity, and of his own role as a dramatist in rhetorical history, and that this involves an enquiry into the differences between poetic literature and drama, between written narrative and enacted performance, and perhaps, even, an examination of the constraints which print itself imposes on the performative capabilities of rhetorical language.

That Shakespeare chose the consummate practitioner of rhetorical poetics to be the source inspiration for what he himself describes as this seminal moment of his career has, I suggest, a significance beyond that which the poem's criticism traditionally acknowledges.[11] That most imitators of Ovid in the Renaissance seem to have been primarily concerned with emulating the classical poet's wit and style and/or exploiting his amatory themes, is borne out by criticism's use of the term 'Ovidian' (taking its cue from Francis Meres' famous comparison of Shakespeare and Ovid) as a convenient and loose definition of a poetic style to cover almost any example of mellifluous rhetoric and verbal wit, and often one, or more, or all of the following: self-conscious artistry, an ostentatious disregard for structural and formal narrative continuity, a particular tone of detachment, moral levity, psychological realism, titillating eroticism and metamorphic transformation.[12]

But I would want to argue that Shakespeare's narrative imitations of Ovid involve a complex set of responses, requiring a more carefully delineated definition of the term 'Ovidian', and less willingness to assume that his poems register the same kind of responses to the style and content of Ovid's work as the poems of his literary contemporaries do.[13] The Ovidian presence which underlies *Venus and Adonis* at its deepest and most significant level is acting in response to certain, specific implications which its artistic and thematic concerns offered to a dramatist who is exploring questions of poetic originality and the workings of literary imitation. Namely, Change as the thematic, formal and structural narrative principle of the *Metamorphoses*, the self-proclaimed originality and immortality of that poem; the various ways in which the poem presents metamorphosis as integral to identity and, what I wish to examine here, the way in which the *Metamorphoses* explores the complex interrelations of identity and identification, insubstantial image and corporeal substance.

SHAKESPEARE AND OVID: INSUBSTANTIAL SHADOWS AND THE DOUBLY UNREAL

'Nova' is the second word of Ovid's *Metamorphoses*: 'In nova fert animus mutatas dicere formas corpora' (I.1–2) 'My mind is bent to tell of forms changed into new bodies'. As Karl Galinsky has observed, the word is placed right at the beginning of the poem, separated from 'corpora', its syntactical complement, in an 'unusual and deliberate arrangement', which suggests that it is alluding to the 'novelty of Ovid's undertaking'.[14] Ovid's innovatory aims with his poem have, I suggest, important parallels with the creative impulses which led Shakespeare to write *Venus and Adonis*. Galinsky makes the point that one of Ovid's sources of inspiration for the poem was the Hellenistic genre of metamorphosis poetry: the poet demonstrates that he had read the versions of his predecessors in order to show that he could treat the myths 'in his own way'.[15] He does so, Galinsky says, by making three important innovations: in the poem's ambitious scope, in placing it within a chronological framework to suggest the universality of myth and, most original of all, in making it a poem not about metamorphosis, but about myth. He was able to 'metamorphose myth' by adopting the strategy which the poet himself gave to Odysseus in *Ars Amatoria*: to tell a story *aliter* – differently, or in a different way.[16] Throughout his study, Galinsky demonstrates the importance of recognising that the *Metamorphoses* 'cannot be properly understood without the realisation that they were meant to be Ovid's answer to Virgil's *Aeneid*' and that it is the literary implication of *referre idem aliter* which constitutes the poem's reason for being.[17]

Charles Martindale draws attention to the ways in which the *Metamorphoses* 'seem implicitly to raise questions about the nature of narrative', and describes the poem's series of tales within tales as creating 'a "Chinese box" effect which dissolves the normal stable authority of story-telling'. The obtrusive stylishness of the writing, he says, 'reminds us that we are dealing with a sceptical, sophisticated mind playing in the world of myth, which is seen not as a mirror of reality, as it was in the main by Greek tragedians, but as *the creation of a fictive world*' (my emphasis). Martindale suggests that while the *Metamorphoses* 'is nothing so crude as an anti-Aeneid', it is possible to see that the style, content and tone of Virgil's epic 'is deconstructed in the *Metamorphoses*'; and that 'formally too Ovid deconstructs the unified Aristotelian form of epic to provide an alternative model for narrative poets . . .'[18]

It is within this specific Ovidian context – Ovid's allusion to the novelty of his poem to announce the originality of his treatment of earlier metamorphosis myths and to provide an alternative model for narrative poets – that I wish to place Shakespeare's 'first invention' statement which prefaces *Venus and Adonis* (and 'The Argument' which precedes the poem proper in *The Rape of Lucrece*).[19] For with this poem, I want to argue, Shakespeare is using Ovid to raise questions about the genesis of an original poetic language, and about drama's creation of a fictive world as an alternative to mimetic poetry.

For a writer who has been concerned with making the bodies of actors change into 'new bodies', the first words of the *Metamorphoses* would have had a particular resonance. The dramatist does not have to rely solely on the medium of words to 'tell of' (*dicere*) 'forms changed into new bodies'. Ovid's *carmen perpetuum*, his continuous song about bodies changing their shapes in a world that is in a constant state of flux and mutability, remains fixed in the written signs of his verse, however daringly he defies the structural and formal principles of epic narrative. If a dramatist wants to identify his powers with the song of Orpheus he does not have to describe how the first poet made the trees and beasts move, and then give Orpheus some of the stories to tell, as Ovid does in Book X of his poem, where his story of Venus and Adonis appears. When Ovid invokes the Orphic power of reordering creation to draw attention to his own skill at creating a fictive world of mutability and change, it remains an identification, not an ideal identity. The dramatist possesses the power to make real bodies change their shape, and to make the 'song' itself become a dynamic process of metamorphosis: the same story, not told, but enacted, *aliter*, differently, every time it is performed.

It is clear that at an early stage in his development, Shakespeare is exploiting the protean potential of the corporeal presence of the actor, has discovered how to move his audience with displays of rhetorical manipulation through the sensual and visual immediacy of the voices and the bodies of his actors (changing Burbage the Bouncer's body into new forms; the deformed shape of Richard Gloucester, for example).[20] He has also begun to consider the theoretical implications of an art form which seems to defy the permanence of print: – editions of plays by other dramatists have been published – Marlowe's *Tamburlaine I* and *II*, and Kyd's *The Spanish Tragedy* are two obvious examples – but no written or printed representation accurately delivers what has been performed on a given afternoon, or conveys how its reception may have subtly altered the playing of it on that particular day.[21] What you first wrote is transformed as soon as you start to rehearse it with the actors (or the moment you realise there are not *enough* actors to speak the parts!)[22] One performance is different from the next; as soon as one is over its 'present' has become the past. It is the very mutability of your medium that makes any attempt at transfixing it to a page seem futile or, if that mutability is the very thing you want to exploit, undesirable. That Shakespeare was explicitly raising such questions in his drama about literary representation at an early stage in his career is apparent from *The Two Gentlemen of Verona*, a play much concerned with the transmission of texts, the troubled relations between rhetorical tropes and sexual desire, and the problematising mediation of 'black ink' and 'print'.

Perhaps such a dramatist, turning to an ancient text which has been re-presented in countless editions, translated, imitated, analysed and moralised, in yet further printed texts, is about continuous mutability and yet has itself survived the effects of a continuous cultural mutability, found in Ovid's *Venus and Adonis* something more than a witty, wanton theme, and a useful model for a self-conscious literary exercise.[23] If wantonness and wit and an imitative model for displaying a dazzling rhetoric to overgo the poetic eloquence of immediate predecessors and contemporaries is all that is required, why combine the story of Venus and Adonis with two additional myths from the *Metamorphoses* in which the problem of identity and loss of corporeal autonomy are prominently emphasised?[24] One answer may lie in examining the implications of the thematic continuity which links Narcissus and Hermaphroditus with the story of Phaethon, the longest episode in the *Metamorphoses* which comes early on in the poem, where the attempt to establish identity is thwarted by a naïve confusion of symbol and reality, and causes catastrophic damage to the universe.

Ovid's story of Phaethon is an example of the kind of material which does not offer simple, logical parallels to which traditional source criticism attends, but which can be demonstrated to deserve consideration as a significant influence on the dramatist's development, and the growth of a work's origins. The relation of a Shakespeare poem or play with its precursors being complex, irregular and disorderly, it is the tracing of the hidden transformations of its origins that can reveal profound significances. The response to Ovid which I am here suggesting can be discerned in *Venus and Adonis* is a characteristic, and by no means isolated, example of Shakespearean 're-sourcefulness'. The loss of corporeal autonomy, the physical consequences of taking for real that which is symbol, or a false semblance, or without body, are interrelated in Ovid. Hermaphroditus suffers physical emasculation when confronted with an enervating other which leaves him no more than half a man.[25] Narcissus falls in love with an insubstantial image, mistaking a mere shadow for a real body, and ends with his real body's evanescence into symbol, but not before he has caused Echo's corporeal substance to waste away, and has turned her into a disembodied voice. Phaethon believes that the instrument of his father's power, the chariot of fire, is Phoebus' actual power, so in a sense Phaethon confuses symbol with reality: as a result he brings destruction upon himself.

Shakespeare makes three explicit allusions to the boy who had aspired to the sun-god's power in two of his early plays – twice in *Henry VI Part Three* (I.iv.33–4; II.vi.12–14) and once in *The Two Gentlemen of Verona* (III.i.152–6) – which suggests that this particular myth is exerting some kind of imaginative influence on the playwright during the period to which we have assigned *Venus and Adonis*. Ovid had changed the meaning of the myth he found in Euripides' play by making it a story about the catastrophic consequences of attempting to establish a self-identity by an identification with an image.[26] When his divine origins are called into question, Phaethon demands proof that he is 'sprung from heavenly seed', and when his mother assures him that Phoebus is his real father, Phaethon, 'already grasping the heavens in imagination', believes that the sun-chariot will give him divine power (I. 761, 777). Ovid emphasises the dangers of Phaethon's metonymic confusion (a subject which will become a central concern of *Richard II*) in the ambiguous wording with which Epaphus accuses the boy of being 'tumidus genitoris imagine falsi' (I. 754). Golding translates this, 'Thou shalt perceyve that fathers name a forged thing to beene'. F. Justus Miller in the Loeb edition gives 'swelled up with false notions about your father'; Galinsky, 'puffed up with the illusion of a false father'; and Innes, 'giving yourself airs on the score of a father who is not your real father at all'.[27] But none of these quite registers the deeper significance of Ovid's use of 'imagine falsi' which has the effect of doubling the force of each word to suggest a 'false semblance', a 'false comparison', a 'false illusion', a 'mere shadow which is false'. Phoebus is Phaethon's real father, but what is not real is the son's image of him: an image which is itself based on an image – the chariot, itself real, is the *symbol* of divine power. When Phaethon realises that he cannot control the chariot, he wishes he had never touched his father's horses, and repents that he had discovered his true origin. The fiery steeds break loose from their course and burn up the skies. The earth bursts into flames and splits into deep cracks. The seas shrink up, the trees are consumed, the ripe grain furnishes fuel for it own destruction, and the vast conflagration reduces whole nations to ashes. The symbol of the sun-god's power, the 'false comparison' on which Phaethon had sought to establish his identity, is torn apart and lies scattered far and wide in fragments. Phaethon's body is set on fire and is hurled through the air far from his native land. His mother wanders over the earth, seeking first his lifeless limbs, then his bones. She finds them buried on a river-bank on the far side of the globe. His sisters in their grief are turned into weeping trees, their tears hardening into amber by the sun which are borne by the river, one day to be worn by the brides of Rome (II. 153–366). He who asks symbol to be congruent with meaning, does, indeed, lose the body.

The false image which Narcissus creates is of himself: 'imaginis umbra est: nil habet ista sui' (III. 434–5). Like 'imagine falsi' in Phaethon's story, 'imaginis umbra' suggests something that is doubly unreal: 'but the shadow of a reflected form and has no substance of its own', or 'only shadow, only reflection, lacking any substance'.[28] Ovid's use of the pronoun *ista*, suggesting, in its conflation of 'that' and 'your', Narcissus' confusion over how to address the image in the pool which both is and is not an Other, reinforces the emphasis he places on what has caused the youth to fall in love with his own reflection. It is the reflection or echo of his own voice which Narcissus first encounters, thinking it another's words. It is important, when examining Shakespeare's responses to this myth, to realise how much Ovid makes of Narcissus' encounter with Echo to reinforce this point.

Galinsky points out that Ovid uses the story which had been presented as 'a simple paradox in Graeco-Roman legend, and as a banal morality fable of merited punishment in one of its famous Greek versions', in order to explore the complex relations of identity and desire, and he does so by combining it – being the first to do so – with the story of Echo.[29] When Echo first encounters Narcissus, we are told, she still had a body. Juno had punished the nymph for preventing her from catching Jupiter in his adulterous philanderings, so that Echo could only repeat the last words she heard spoken. The nymph, robbed of her power of originating words, falls in love with Narcissus, but having lost all linguistic autonomy, she can only woo the love object by echoing the love object's words. But the meaning of Narcissus' words changes in the process of repetition. In Echo's echo, his words are made to mean the opposite of what he has said: the same words signifying antithetical meanings.

> 'ante' ait 'emoriar, quam sit tibi copia nostri';
> rettulit illa nihil nisi 'sit tibi copia nostri!' (III.391–2)

'I'll die before I'll let you have me', he says. She answers nothing but 'I'll let you have me'.[30]

Echo's reply is an imitation that does not tell the truth, in the sense that it falsifies what Narcissus has said even though it makes an exact repetition of his last words. The tone of tragicomedy and Narcissus' persistent refusal to be touched can be discerned in Shakespeare's presentation of Venus' wooing of Adonis, but it is hard to imagine that something of Ovid's emphasis on this problematic exchange of words is not also finding its way into a poem in which almost everything the lover says is presented as an imitation of others' words, and who makes 'verbal repetition of her moans' twenty times so that 'twenty echoes twenty times cry so' (834).[31] It would be surprising if the encounter were not exerting some kind of significant pressure on a poem by a dramatist who has just written (or is writing) a play in which exchanges in the language of love are fraught with misinterpretations and unwitting deceptions. Silvia, we remember, makes Valentine write a love letter to himself (*The Two Gentlemen of Verona*, II. i).

But Echo's reply is an imitation which also tells the truth. She cannot originate language, but she can take another's words and turn them into an expression that to her own feelings is true, original to herself. Her truth-telling words of love are rejected and her body wastes away: 'et aera sucus corporis omnis abit' ('all moisture fades from her body into the air'), and only her voice and bones remain. Then even her skeleton dislimns and is turned into a stone, so that all that is left is her voice (III. 396–401). Narcissus' cruelty is avenged by the goddess Nemesis: now he will be unable to gain that which he loves. Worn out by the heat and the chase, Narcissus comes across a clear, sunless pool and lying down to drink from it, becomes enchanted with the insubstantial reflection of himself which he takes to be the real body of another: 'spem sine corpore

amat, corpus putat esse, quod umbra est' (417) 'He loves a bodiless
hope, thinks that body which is shadow'.[32] The fluid bodiless image
seems to turn Narcissus into a speechless, motionless statue:

> adstupet ipse sibi vultuque inmotus eodem
> haeret, ut e Pario formatum marmore signum. (III.418–19)

He looks in speechless wonder at himself and hangs there motionless in
the same expression, like a statue carved from Parian marble.

What has warmth, substance, speech, movement and life is turned
into an insubstantial image. The image which has disembodied
Narcissus turns him into substance again – but an incorporeal substance, a lifeless stone. Notice the kind of verbal imagery the *image*
of Narcissus prompts, emphasising this de-corporealising process:

> spectat humi positus geminum, sua lumina, sidus
> et dignos Baccho, dignos et Apolline crines
> inpubesque genas et eburnea colla decusque
> oris et in niveo mixtum candore ruborem. (III.420–3)

Prone on the ground, he gazes at his eyes, twin stars, and his locks, worthy
of Bacchus, worthy of Apollo; on his smooth cheeks, his ivory neck, the
glorious beauty of his face, the blush mingled with snowy white.

Eyes are turned into stars, flesh into ivory. Narcissus longs to touch
the image, and stretches out his arms to embrace it. Ovid's use of
the Echo story serves now to strengthen and complicate the
paradox that obtains in the confusion of object and subject, image
and substance, lover and beloved. Trying vainly, as Echo had done,
to clasp the thing he loves, Narcissus starts to speak to the image.
The devastating recognition 'iste ego sum' (III.463) 'I am he!'
comes not with the sight of his beloved stretching out his arms
when Narcissus does, nor laughing and weeping when he does, but
with the realisation that the object of his desire answers his words
with words which do not reach his ears. 'Sensi, nec me mea fallit
imago' (III.463) 'I have felt it, I know now my own image'. But at
the moment when Narcissus is able to distinguish between image
and substance, real and unreal, he is prompted to utter the most
imagistic 'unreal' trope in the literary lover's repertoire: 'uror
amore mei' (III.464) 'I burn with love of my own self'. His new-
found knowledge is unbearable, and he cries out for self-division: 'o

utinam a nostro secedere corpore possem!' (III.467) 'Oh, that I might be parted from my own body!'. The boy wants death and prays that the object of his love will outlive him, a literary convention which here has no place at all (and one, we might add, that is being used in a new and original way, as Ovid does not fail to remind us): 'votum in amante novum, vellem, quod amamus abesset' (III.468) 'Strange prayer for a lover, I would that what I love were absent from me!' But at the moment we are made fully aware of this paradox, the tragic joke of his wishing that which he loves would outlive him, Narcissus produces another conventional amatory hyperbole. This one, however, is surprisingly close to a literal description of what would physically take place at Narcissus' death: 'nunc duo concordes anima moriemur in una' (III.473) 'we two shall die together in one breath'.

He turns again to the image, and his tears ruffle the water so that the shape in the pool keeps moving, becoming indistinct, losing its visible shape (III.474–6). A. D. Nuttall, in a fine essay comparing this moment with the mirror scene in *Richard II* when Richard smashes the image of his face, makes the important point that 'Narcissus inadvertently destroys the vision by the mere physical effect of his grief'.[33] I want to suggest that the deeper significance of this is that in the story of Narcissus, as in so many of Ovid's myths, it is the physical, the corporeal, the 'flesh-and-bloodness' of human existence that can never be 'mere'. Ovid draws attention to the tears shattering the static, bodiless image in the pool to give a climactic force to what has been emphasised throughout. An organic, physical process of the human body destroys the insubstantial illusion. The image of himself reflected in the pool had turned Narcissus into someone *other than himself*, had made him like Bacchus, like Apollo, had turned his flesh into ivory and snow, the kind of de-individualising, de-humanising transformation we find examined again and again in Shakespeare's works. In the reflection the human body is metamorphosed into a deity, a transformation which the poet of the Sonnets refuses to perform on his beloved ('I grant I never saw a goddess go, – / My mistress when she walks treads on the ground . . .' Sonnet 130. 11–12). But it is precisely this de-corporealising process in which Shakespeare's Venus and the rival poets of the Sonnets excel. Narcissus loses his body because it was turned into an insubstantial imitation. The tears which destroy what Narcissus had once thought was a real body, but was 'sine corpore', and' imagine falsi', come not from stars, but from eyes. It is a real body which is weeping, not a marble statue, or a substance-less shadow. Narcissus longs to see again the image he may not touch (III.478–9), but the substanceless shadow has gone from sight. He strikes his breast so hard it starts to glow and is slowly consumed by its hidden fire (III.480–90). The outrageously fanciful hyperbole, 'uror amore mei: flammas moveoque feroque' (III.464) 'I burn with love of my own self. I both kindle the flames and suffer them', has become, within Ovid's fictive world, a physical enactment, a literal truth.

The pyre which his sisters prepare for his dead body is not needed because there is nothing left to burn: 'nusquam corpus erat; croceum pro corpore florem / inveniunt foliis medium cingentibus albis' (509–10) 'His body was nowhere to be found. In place of his body they find a flower, its yellow centre girt with white petals'. Narcissus has been metamorphosed into a symbol of his flesh and blood, into a flower that bears his name.

'TO GROW UNTO HIMSELF WAS HIS DESIRE': THE NEW ORPHEUS

Shakespeare's *Venus and Adonis* begins, as it were, where Ovid's story ends. The classical writer's story *ends* with Venus turning the *dead* body of Adonis into a flower: Shakespeare's poem *begins* with Venus turning the *living* body of Adonis into flower. In Ovid, Venus finds Adonis 'lying lifeless and weltering in his blood', and then tells his corpse that her grief shall have an 'enduring monument':

> 'luctus monimenta manebunt
> semper, Adoni, mei, repetitaque mortis imago
> annua plangoris peraget simulamina nostri;
> at cruor in florem mutabitur.'   (X.725–8)

'My grief, Adonis, shall have an enduring monument, and each passing year in memory of your death shall give an imitation of my grief. But your blood shall be changed to a flower.'

She sprinkled the blood with sweet-scented nectar, and a flower of blood-red hue sprang up (732–5). The blood of Adonis is replaced by a symbol, an imitation ('simulamina'). In Shakespeare, Venus' first metaphor turns the flesh and blood of Adonis into a flower three times more beautiful than herself. This second stanza is packed with hyperbolic comparisons, her characteristic wooing mode throughout the poem. Shakespeare turns Ovid's happily compliant Adonis into a recalcitrant love object who refuses to mate with a Poet who can offer only the praise of 'false compare' in 'strainèd touches' of derivative rhetoric:

> 'Thrice fairer than myself', thus she began,
> 'The field's chief flower, sweet above compare;
> Stain to all nymphs, more lovely than a man,
> More white and red than doves or roses are': (7–10)

The succeeding stanzas begin to suggest why such couplements of proud compare must be resisted. She threatens to smother him with kisses, make his lips red-sore, and drain them of their colour ('Making red, and pale, with fresh variety'), so that a summer's day will seem but short: 'Being wasted in such time-beguiling sport' (21–4). 'Being' suggests that Adonis himself, as well as the day, will be 'wasted', spent, sapped of strength. Here, the narrator interrupts Venus to insist on the boy's organic corporeality and to mock the enervating effect of her metamorphic displacement which robs the human body of its energy and strength:

> With this she seizeth on his sweating palm,
> The precedent of pith and livelihood,
> And trembling in her passion, calls it balm. (25–7)

Prince's gloss on 'pith and livelihood' reads: 'strength and energy. "Pith" means "marrow", the full development of which signifies maturity and hence strength.'[34] What is being presented here is not the simple paradox of an immature, coldly chaste young virgin bearing what is traditionally thought of as the physical mark of sexual desire. The flesh that is sweating, which arouses Venus' desire and makes her flesh tremble with passion, prompts her to use a language which robs the object of her desire of the very organicism and physicality which has made it desirable, and which has set in motion an organic process in her own body. The biological movement of sweat coming though the pores of Adonis' flesh which, by definition, is subject to time and process and change, is arrested in a stopped momentum by the metaphor 'balm', and turned into a sense-less, life-less figure of speech.

It is a technique which is repeated throughout the poem. Two kinds of language are juxtaposed, placed in conflict with each other, to point up the contrast between a poetry which stresses corporeal substance and seeks to accommodate organic process, mutability and time, so that the body may be summoned into something like an immediate physical presence; and a poetry which dematerialises flesh and blood and seeks to transcend time and change and therefore succeeds only in making the body absent, lost to the present. Here is the narrating voice again stressing the biological, dynamic process of Adonis' body to demonstrate how Venus' use of metaphor deprives fleshly existence of its vital principle:

> Panting he lies and breatheth in her face,
> She feedeth on the steam as on a prey,
> And calls it heavenly moisture, air of grace. (62–4)

Venus' rhetoric disembodies the body she desires: a metaphor has taken Adonis' breath away. But when this heavenly goddess praises her own body to Adonis, it is the sensuous warmth and life of her flesh which her words emphasise:

> Mine eyes are grey and bright and *quick* in *turning*.
> My beauty as the *spring* doth yearly *grow*,
> My *flesh* is *soft* and *plump*, my *marrow burning*.
>   My smooth *moist* hand, were it with thy hand felt,
>   Would in thy palm *dissolve*, or seem to *melt*.
>   (140–44, my emphasis)

Fluidity and change, organic process, physical growth and renewal, all that she has removed from Adonis' body in the metaphor 'air of grace', are here brought into a visual and sensual immediacy. Several stanzas later, she accuses Adonis of being a life-less image:

> 'Fie, lifeless picture, cold and senseless stone,
> Well-painted idol, image dull and dead,

Statue contenting but the eye alone,
Thing like a man, but of no woman bred!' (211–14)

But it is Venus who has turned Adonis' flesh and blood into a cold and senseless statue, she who has turned life into art. Ovid's story of Venus and Adonis is placed in a sequence in which an artist, prompted by a revulsion against the real bodies of women, creates a cold and sense-less statue of his ideal woman's body. In the *Metamorphoses*, when Pygmalion becomes inflamed with desire for this semblance of a body, 'simulati corporis' (X.253), he prays to have a wife like his statue. And it is important to notice the precise use Ovid makes of his expressions of similitude and corporeal substance:

> 'si, di, dare cuncta potestis,
> sit coniunx, opto,' non ausus 'eburnea virgo'
> dicere, Pygmalion 'similis mea' dixit 'eburnae'. (X.274–6)

'If ye, O gods, can give all things, I pray to have as wife – ' he did not dare add 'my ivory maid', but said, 'one like my ivory maid'.

But Venus, Ovid says, knew what the prayer really meant, and brings the statue to life. When Pygmalion returned from the altar of the goddess, he sought once again the 'image of his maid', 'simulacra suae petit ille puellae', and bending over the couch he kissed her:

> visa tepere est;
> admovet os iterum, manibus quoque pectora temptat:
> temptatum mollescit ebur positoque rigore
> subsidit digitis ceditque, ut Hymettia sole
> cera remollescit tractataque pollice multas
> flectitur in facies ipsoque fit utilis usu.
> dum stupet et dubie gaudet fallique veretur,
> rursus amans rursusque manu sua vota retractat.
> corpus erat! saliunt temptatae pollice venae. (281–9)

She seemed warm to his touch. Again he kissed her, and with his hands also he touched her breast. The ivory grew soft to his touch and, its hardness vanishing, gave and yielded beneath his fingers, as Hymettian wax grows soft under the sun and, moulded by the thumb, is easily shaped to many forms and becomes usable through use itself. The lover stands amazed, rejoices still in doubt, fears he is mistaken, and tries his hopes again and yet again with his hand. Yes, it was real flesh! The veins were pulsing beneath his testing finger.

In Shakespeare, Venus' hand touches the malleable cheek of Adonis and turns active, fleshly warmth into a passive, cold white-ness:

> Now was she just before him as he sat,
> And like a lowly lover down she kneels;
> With one fair hand she heaveth up his hat,
> Her other tender hand his fair cheek feels:
> His tend'rer cheek receives her soft hand's print,
> As apt as new-fall'n snow takes any dint. (349–54)

The simile of the last line jars, as it is intended to. It demonstrates the mimetic inadequacy of figurative similitude by giving a particularly lame and inappropriate example of such literary poetic expression (the use of 'apt' here wittily reinforces the point). It is an example of the ways in which Shakespeare in this poem writes about the form he writes in in order to make an implied criticism of the way the poetic written word turns everything which has life, warmth and movement in its immediate presence into an icono-graphical stasis, irretrievably lost to the present. Adonis' life, in Venus' hands, becomes a dead, literary image so that the only progeny he will be capable of begetting is sterile rhetorical tropes. For a stanza later not just the cheek, but Adonis' hand has become a metaphor, then his whole body. The supplicating Venus kneeling before him like a lowly lover, is now overpowering him. Adonis himself becomes an inaccessible original, trapped inside a literary device:

> Full gently now she takes him by the hand,
> A lily prison'd in a gaol of snow,
> Or ivory in an alabaster band:
> So white a friend engirts so white a foe. (361–4)

A lily, or ivory – it does not matter which. Choose whatever tired trope comes to mind, and simply tack it on to the subject. A lily? That will do. The poem already has Venus turning Adonis into a cold, senseless statue: when her 'arms infold him like a band' he struggles to be gone, and she 'locks her lily fingers one in one', so that two lines later her linked arms become a 'circuit' of 'ivory

pale' (225, 228, 230). Before that, she has described her encircling
arms making Mars 'a prisoner in a red rose chain' (110). Adonis'
cheek has just been turned into 'snow', so: 'A lily prison'd in a gaol
of snow, / Or ivory in an alabaster band'.

So this is how rhetorical poetry gets written. Take a conceit from
Spenser, a figure from Marlowe, a hyperbole from Lyly and Sidney,
and the poem has begun. Turn hot, pulsating cheeks into a rose,
compare them with the 'purple-coloured face' of the sun taking his
leave of 'the weeping morn' (1–3).[35] Metamorphose the beloved
into the field's chief flower whose superior beauty casts a 'stain' on
all others (8, 9).[36] Say, as everyone else does, that the face is 'More
white and red than doves or roses are' and there are your first two
stanzas. But once you start you find you cannot stop. Make human
sweat a 'balm' (27) and hot breath an 'air of grace' (64). Turn a
blushing cheek into a 'crimson shame' and cold anger into something 'ashy pale' (76); tumescent female pudenda and pubic hair
into 'Round rising hillocks, brakes obscure and rough' (237).[37]
Make eyes 'two blue windows' up-heaved so that they may be compared to the sun at dawn (482–6).[38] Play with an extended
metaphor which makes lips red sealing-wax and a thousand kisses
the price of a human heart (511–22). Turn all that is red, which you
make not red, but something else such as 'ruby-colour'd portal' or
'red morn' instead of a mouth, into white. But make sure you do
not simply say white. Flesh can be a dove, a lily, white sheets,
alabaster or snow. What it cannot be is . . . flesh.

Take the human body and turn it into something being written
in a poem, and the poet's writing hand seems to find itself involun-
tarily steeped in rhetorical dyes:

> The forward violet thus did I chide:
> 'Sweet thief, whence didst thou steal thy sweet that smells,
> If not from my love's breath? The purple pride
> Which on thy soft cheek for complexion dwells   4
> In my love's veins thou has too grossly dyed.'
> The lily I condemnèd for thy hand,
> And buds of marjoram had stol'n thy hair;
> The roses fearfully on thorns did stand -   8
> One blushing shame, another white despair;
> A third nor red nor white, had stol'n of both,
> And to his robbery had annex'd thy breath,

> But for his theft in pride of all his growth   12
> A vengeful canker ate him up to death.
> More flowers I noted, yet I none could see
> But sweet or colour it had stol'n from thee. (Sonnet 99)[39]

As in Sonnets 98 and 53, the Friend is made an original, a kind of seminary of all created forms and their substances. As 98 insists: the lily's white and the deep vermilion in the rose 'were but figures of delight, / Drawn after you, you pattern of all those' (9–12). But look how Shakespeare exploits this sonneteering convention to introduce the idea that when the Friend is absent, the original of the world's beauty is inaccessible. The odour and hue of all the flowers means it must be summer, 'Yet seem'd it winter still' (13), and the Poet has to make do with looking at poor imitations of the original: 'and, you away, / As with your shadow I with these did play' (13–14).

If we pause now to examine 98 in relation to 53, we may begin to detect how Ovid's preoccupation with the relations of image and substance, unreal and real, helps to shape Shakespeare's exploration into the mysterious workings of poetry's rhetorical dyeing process both in the Sonnets and in *Venus and Adonis*. We may also begin to discover some further significance in why the forward violet is so firmly castigated in Sonnet 99. Here is Sonnet 53 quoted in full:

> What is your substance, whereof are you made,
> That millions of strange shadows on you tend?
> Since every one hath, every one, one shade,
> And you, but one, can every shadow lend: 4
> Describe Adonis, and the counterfeit
> Is poorly imitated after you;
> On Helen's cheek all art of beauty set,
> And you in Grecian tires are painted new: 8
> Speak of the spring and foison of the year, –
> The one doth shadow of your beauty show,
> The other as your bounty doth appear;
> And you in every blessèd shape we know: 12
>   In all external grace you have some part,
>   But you like none, none you, for constant heart.

This seems to be peculiarly responsive to the exactness of Ovid's expressions of corporeal substance and false semblance, and their problematic relations to individual identity. In Ovid's story of Narcissus and Echo, Narcissus 'spem sine corpore amat, corpus putat esse, quod umbra est' (falls in love with that which is 'imaginis umbra . . . nil habet ista sui'). He falls in love with a bodiless hope, thinking that shadow is a body, with that which is but the shadow of a reflected form and has no substance of its own. Ingram and Redpath's gloss on 'shadows' in lines 2 and 4 of Sonnet 53 reads: 'Here . . . presumably not *umbrae*, in which colour, texture and detail are *absent*, but *imagines*, as the examples in lines 5ff show, though the phrase "on you tend" would more naturally apply to *umbrae*'.[40] But if the central idea of this sonnet is approached with Ovid's extremely precise sense of something doubly unreal in mind, we can see that it is *because* the Friend's substance, the 'colour, texture and detail' of his living body are absent in *umbrae*, and because all other beauty is but a bodiless semblance of the Friend's substance, that the word 'shadows' is used. The shadows are bodiless, false illusions of the real thing, like the reflection in the pool upon which Narcissus gazes and which Ovid calls 'imaginis umbra' and 'sine corpore'. Similarly, in answer to Ingram and Redpath's question about the use of the word 'shade' at line 3 – 'Does the word here mean *umbrae* or *imago*, or neither with any precision? It is hard to say' – I would want to argue that each shade is both 'umbra' and 'imago' in the Ovidian sense of it being a likeness of a form in which the body is absent. We need to reassess criticism's traditional view that in this sonnet Shakespeare is deliberately employing such vocabulary without precise connotation and comprehensiveness.[41] When we examine just a few of the ways in which Ovid, throughout the *Metamorphoses*, exploits the words 'imago' and 'corpus' to explore distinctions between that which has corporeality and is real, and that which is without bodily substance and is unreal, it becomes clear that Shakespeare's use of substance, shadow and shade, far from being vague and undelineated, is both precise and paradoxical in the strictly Ovidian sense found in the Latin which describes Narcissus falling in love with that which is 'imaginis umbra' and Phaethon being puffed up with 'imagine falsi', with their precise connotation of something doubly unreal. Ovid's Venus, we remember, replaces the blood of Adonis with 'simulamina', an imitation of her grief, an *imago* of his dead body.

Pygmalion asks for a wife who is like his false semblance of a body.

It is significant that in Sonnet 53 Nature's organic renewal process and its fruitful progeny, 'the spring and foison of the year', are made but shadows of the Friend's beauty (9–11). As Ingram and Redpath point out, 'the antithesis is not between Spring and Autumn simply as seasons of the year, but between the active properties which characterise them, the concreteness of association being characteristically Shakespearean. The "spring" is freshness and vitality, as the "foison" is abundance of produce.'[42]

If the Friend's beauty is the source of nature's beauty and its powers of renewal and fecundity, it must not be allowed to fade until its life-giving essence is distilled by something that will ensure its perpetual presence and immortality. Nature cannot do this: though it is summer when the Friend is absent, 'Yet seem'd it winter still'. The flowers are merely reminders of what is absent, and the world has to make do with a semblance of the original: '. . . and, you away, / As with your shadow I with these did play' (98.13–14). Indeed, nature's flowers are castigated for being passive dissipators of the Friend's strength and vital energy, and the repeated insistence in Sonnet 99 that the conventions of poetic similitude and comparison are pointless because the Friend's beauty cannot be compared to anything but itself takes on a new and sinister significance.

In Sonnet 21 another Muse is described as 'Making a couplement of proud compare / With sun and moon, with earth and sea's rich gems, / With April's first-born flowers and all things rare' (5–7), and is accused of merely repeating what others have said before: 'And every fair with his fair doth rehearse' (4). But the other poet's praise becomes an act of double theft. He steals someone else's words and because such praise has already been bestowed on other subjects, it robs the subject of present praise of his individuality and true worth – something which Adonis seems particularly enraged by when he condemns Venus' 'device in love / That lends embracements unto every stranger' (789–90). This is why the Poet keeps insisting that his verse is 'so barren of new pride, / So far from variation or quick change', why he keeps 'invention in a noted weed' (76.1–2, 6), and why the Friend must be 'most proud of that which I compile, / Whose influence is thine and born of thee' (78.9–10).

The 'rival' poet in 79 is accused of robbing the Friend in order to give back what the Friend already possesses: 'Yet what of thee thy poet doth invent, / He robs thee of, and pays it thee again . . . beauty doth he give, / *And found it in thy cheek*' (7–8, 10–11, my emphasis). The 'true plain words' of the Poet are explicitly contrasted with the 'gross painting' of other poets:

> yet when they have devis'd
> What strainèd touches rhetoric can lend,
> Thou, truly fair, wert truly sympathiz'd
> In true plain words by thy true-telling friend;
> And their gross painting might be better us'd
> *Where cheeks need blood* – in thee it is abus'd
> (82. 9–14, my emphasis)

Such poets, then, are like the violet chided in 99 who is 'forward', which suggests precocious, presumptuous, but also flowering before its time; forced, because fed on the blood and breath it has stolen from the fecund source of the world's organic growth. The violet has 'too grossly dyed' (5) the fresh blood flowing through the veins of the Friend's cheek, and what is being suggested here is that the violet causes the Friend's blood to 'die' – to stop flowing through the veins, with the same enervating effect of the rhetorical dyes in which the rival poets *grossly* paint the beauty of the Friend in 82. Ingram and Redpath gloss 82's 'gross painting': 'In addition to the obvious sense of "laying it on thick" . . . there may also be a reference here to "larded" rhetoric. Cf. "Colours" = rhetorical figures.'[43] This idea that rhetoric's gross painting stops the life flow of the human body is made explicit in 83 which begins: 'I never saw that you did painting need, / And therefore to your fair no painting set' (1–2). There is more glory, the Poet says, in his silence, 'being dumb' (9–10), because when the 'rival' poets try to capture the vital presence of the Friend's beauty, their painting 'kills' it:

> For I impair not beauty, being mute,
> When others would give life and *bring a tomb*.
> There lives more life in one of your fair eyes
> Than both your poets can in praise devise.
> (11–14, my emphasis)

In Sonnet 99 all the flowers of nature are implicated in the life-destroying theft. 'The roses fearfully on thorns did stand', because conscious of their guilty thefts, but the pink rose is the most guilty because not showing shame like the red, nor despair like the white, it steals the Friend's breath as well as his colour ('And to his robbery had annex'd thy breath', 11). The pink rose is punished for robbing a living human organism of its life-force: 'But for his theft in pride of all his growth / A vengeful canker ate him up to death' (12–13), so that, in the words of 54, nothing of the original vital essence can now be distilled.

It is significant that the sonnet which claims that the Poet's verse will immortalise the Friend's truth and beauty associates the life-preserving effect of the verse with the sweet odour of the rose, whose essence may be preserved when the rose perishes, in contrast to the canker blooms which have no perfume, to make a distinction between that which has colour and an essence which can be made to live on after death, and that which has 'as deep a dye' (54.5), but nothing that can be made to last once it has decayed. The verse of the 'rival' poets is like the canker bloom: 'But for their virtue only is their show / They live unwoo'd and unrespected fade –/ Die to themselves' (54.9–11). The 'rival' poets of 82 cannot make the Friend live after death: their rhetorical dyes 'kill' him while he still is alive. Their verse is like the pink rose which, in feeding on the Friend's flesh and blood, deprives him of the very thing which could ensure the survival and perpetuation of his vital essence (99). The verse of these other poets is like both the canker, the pale pink dog-rose, whose colour is a short-lived display and has no potentially enduring essence, and the canker-worm which eats up its blossoms (54). The 'rival' poets, then, eat up the Friend 'to death', like the vengeful canker-worm who eats up the pink rose 'to death', because the shameless pink rose had robbed the Friend of his colour and his breath (99). Being both canker and canker-worm, the other poets are responsible for the decay of their own verse.

This, then, is the price poets have to pay for turning flesh and blood into a rhetorical trope. This is why the Poet keeps defending the 'poverty' and 'silence' of his Muse, insisting that his 'argument all bare is of more worth / Than when it hath my added praise beside!' (103.3–4). 'I think good thoughts, whilst others write good

words . . . In polish'd form of well-refinèd pen' (85.5,8).
Throughout the sonnets which ridicule the painted rhetoric of
other poets, we find an almost obsessive concern with the idea of
writing, pen, quill, pencil being repeatedly used to suggest that it is the
colours of rhetoric *written down* which deserves the greatest con-
demnation.[44] It is a 'modern quill' (*'modern:* "commonplace, trite,
ordinary", as always in Shakespeare') which comes too short of the
Friend's worth in 83, where, as we have seen, the writers who
'would give life . . . bring a tomb'. The 'rival' poets of Sonnet 85
write 'In polish'd form of well-refinèd pen', in contrast to the Poet
who is silent: 'Me for my dumb thoughts, speaking in effect'. The
mistrust of polished written poetry evident in these sonnets suggests that what appears to be merely the conventional 'modesty' of
a poet in Shakespeare's dedication in *Venus and Adonis*, 'I know not
how I shall offend in dedicating my *unpolished lines* to your Lordship
. . .', is more an ironic claim to the poet's truthfulness rather than
prompted by a fear of offending the dedicatee because the poem's
author is a 'vulgar' playwright.[45] That the lines are 'unpolished' is
presented, then, as a virtue. Speaking in effect, Shakespeare is
implicitly criticising the polished form of the well-refined pens of
other poets whose work Henry Wriothesley would have been used
to reading. Transcription thus becomes equated with death of the
subject, with destroying life. The only way to summon that life into
presence is to compare it to nothing else, because it exceeds the
'barren tender' (fruitless offering) of a poet's debt (3–4), and simply
say 'you are you':

> Who is it that says most which can say more
> Than this rich praise, – that you alone are you,
> In whose confine immurèd is the store
> Which should example where your equal grew? (84, 1–4)

Ingram and Redpath think that the image in lines 3–4 here 'certainly seems to be biological' rather than a treasury. 'The sense
would be that the only stock from which one could learn under
what conditions a person of the Friend's excellence could develop
is to be found in the Friend himself.'[46] The only way we can understand how the Friend developed his unique excellence is to attend
only to what we see now: the biological physical presence of what

he *is*. This is why we find, in *Venus and Adonis*, so many passages itemising parts of the body in 'true plain words'. Why, for example, we find a conventional extended metaphor being paradoxically employed for a bare, literal description of the different parts of Adonis' face:

> Even as an empty eagle, sharp by fast,
> Tires with her beak on *feathers, flesh and bone*,
> Shaking her wings, devouring all in haste,
> Till either gorge be stuff'd or prey be gone:
>> Even so she kiss'd *his brow, his cheek, his chin*,
>> And where she ends she doth anew begin.
>>> (55–60, my emphasis)

When Venus feigns death, Adonis 'wrings her nose, he strikes her on *the cheeks*, / He bends her *fingers*, holds her *pulses* hard, / He chafes her *lips* . . .' (475–7, my emphasis). It is why, in the poem's description of the horse, each part of the animal's body is carefully delineated:

> Round-hoof'd, short-jointed, fetlocks shag and long,
> Broad breast, full eye, small head, and nostril wide,
> High crest, short ears, straight legs, and passing strong,
> Thin mane, thick tail, broad buttock, tender hide:
>> Look what a horse should have he did not lack,
>> Save a proud rider on so proud a back.   (295–300)

Dowden, in his famous comment on this passage, spoke truer than he knew when he asked with heavy sarcasm: 'Is it poetry or a paragraph from an advertisement for a horse sale? It is part of Shakespeare's study of an animal and he does his work thoroughly.'[47] Touchstone could have told him that the 'truest poetry (that which is most poetic) is the most feigning'. Such a reversal of the poetry of false compare is placed in the poem in order to demonstrate that the poet who can say a horse is a horse is a horse is the one who tells the truth. As the Poet of the Sonnets says: 'he that writes of you, if he can tell / That you are you, so dignifies his story' (84.7–8), unlike Venus who, far from making Adonis 'the onlie begetter' of her poetry, succeeds only in saying that Adonis is everything but *himself*. She has no power to preserve Adonis' distilled self because like the pink rose in Sonnet 99

she feeds on his flesh and blood. It is the threat of the self being
overwhelmed in a plethora of derivative rhetorical tropes that
Adonis, in refusing union with Venus, is trying to resist. When she
traps him within her 'circuit of ivory pale' so that he becomes 'a
lily . . . /Or ivory in an alabaster band', the now inaccessible
original essence that was Adonis has been turned into a literary
figure borrowed from a prior literary text, so that Adonis is no
longer *Adonis* as an ideal poetry would present him – a unique,
original essence capable of being perpetually renewed like the
rose essence which endures after the rose perishes, but the
Hermaphroditus of Ovid's poem, trapped in Salmacis' enervating pool, flashing with gleaming body through the transparent
flood, 'ut eburnea si quis / signa tegat claro vel candida lilia vitro'
(*Metamorphoses*, IV. 354–5) 'as if one should encase ivory figures or
white lilies in translucent glass'.[48] Venus is like the rival poet who
'every fair with his fair doth rehearse'. She merely repeats what
other poets have written and deprives Adonis of his individuality
and vital presence.

But Shakespeare's use of Ovid here is characteristically more
complex than even this. Adonis, in Venus' entrapping and
paralysing embrace, becomes Ovid's Hermaphroditus to provide a
paradigm for the poet confronted by a seductive enervating other
which threatens to overwhelm, enfeeble and emasculate his fertile
powers of invention:

> Was it the proud full sail of his great verse,
> Bound for the prize of all-too-precious you,
> That did my ripe thoughts in my brain inhearse,
> Making their tomb the womb wherein they grew?   4
> Was it his spirit, by spirits taught to write
> Above a mortal pitch, that struck me dead?
> No, neither he, nor his compeers by night
> Giving him aid, my verse astonishèd: 8
> He, nor that affable familiar ghost
> Which nightly gulls him with intelligence,
> As victors of my silence cannot boast, –
> I was not sick of any fear from thence: 12
>   But when your countenance fill'd up his line,
>   Then lack'd I matter; that enfeebl'd mine. (Sonnet 86)

The poet's verse, ripe for birth, dies unborn, is forever buried in the womb where it was conceived. Why? The Poet takes eight of the sonnet's ten remaining lines to say what has *not* aborted this embryo. But we find that the false starts and changes of direction in this sonnet lead us to believe that it is the other poet's verse which killed the Poet's embryonic thoughts. We do not know *as we read* lines 5 and 6 that the answer to the questions in lines 1 to 6 will be 'No'. We are made to imagine the Poet's verse dying before it is born, buried by the verse of another poet which is itself an imitative text ('his spirit, by spirits taught to write', 5) and this remains in our minds even after line 7's refutation 'No, neither he', because 'compeers by night' in that line has the effect of reinforcing the image of the spirits in line 5. The other poet, aided by *compeers*, other books or their authors, and/or a coterie of literary associates, has *astonished*, paralysed, his verse into silence.[49] Trope begets trope, literary text begets literary text. Line 12 obliterates all that has preceded it, so that the concluding couplet can reveal what has really struck him dead. But the couplet does not fully contradict all that has been said before. The Friend's countenance 'fill'd up his line' takes us back to 'the proud full sail of his great verse' in the opening line, and we imagine the Friend's countenance swelling the sails of the other poet's verse. 'Then lack'd I matter' faintly recalls, by contrast, 'his spirit, by spirits taught to write', and the Friend's countenance is something being written in a poem which itself is swelled with the written words of other poets. By the time the Poet comes to write his verse, there is no substance of the Friend left for him to write about. The line which would have been able to bring 'all-too-precious you' into being cannot now be born.

That is why Shakespeare's Venus must be punished, why Adonis resists her enfeebling rhetoric, is determined not to be crushed in the huge expanse of her bosom ('Fie, fie, fie . . . you crush me; let me go', 611), which is the rhetorical excess of other poets and their books, the surfeit of literary texts which 'fill up' the space where new poetic creation should take place. Venus is denied any part in Adonis' metamorphosis because she has been made to function as a poet whose 'gross painting' turns life into art, by robbing flesh and blood, as the forward violet and pink rose steal the colour and odour of the Friend's beauty. She is incapable of an Orphic lan-

guage which can bring life into being for the first time. Her verse
cannot bring fleshly existence into an eternal present. She cannot
renew him because all along her rhetoric has turned its object into
a literary figurative device, as Adonis well knows: 'I hate not love,
but your device in love' (789); and she must make way for the
dramatist who alone can reverse the flesh-and-blood-into-symbol
process of such sterile rhetoric. Venus' kisses will destroy time itself,
'A summer's day will seem an hour but short, / Being wasted . . .'
(23–4). But it is time itself that Adonis needs if he is to reach maturity with his fertility intact. Venus repeatedly tries to persuade him
that it is his duty to procreate and fructify the world when it is her
persuasion, her rhetoric itself, which is threatening to emasculate
his potential fecundity. The sterile fate which she prophesies will
befall him if he does not mate with her, is precisely what will
happen to him if he does:

> 'What is thy body but a swallowing grave,
> Seeming to bury that posterity,
> Which by the rights of time thou needs must have,
> If thou destroy them not in dark obscurity?
> ...
> 'So in thyself thyself art made away.'   (757–63)

But, as her subsequent list of conceits testifies once again, it is
Venus' self-propagating proliferation of figurative devices that has
'made' Adonis 'away'. Adonis resists what by this stage of the poem
have become heavily ironic entreaties to 'Be prodigal' in 'despite of
fruitless chastity' (755, 751), because copulation with her will prove
a fruitless union. It is her rhetoric, which as Adonis points out is
merely a sterile imitation of another poet's words, that must be
rejected if he is to produce a fertile language of his own. Venus
warns him that his body and all the life that it is capable of repro-
ducing will be buried in a grave of his body's own making, which is:
'"Foul cank'ring rust the hidden treasure frets, / But gold that's put
to use more gold begets"' (767–8).

Adonis recognises Venus' last metaphor as deriving from
another text. She has turned him into Marlowe's Hero and once
again, he is tossed on to the vast stock-pile of literary convention to
be buried in what is his real *swallowing grave*: '"Nay then," quoth

Adon, "you will fall again / Into your idle over-handled theme"'
(769–70).[50] We might note in passing how this allusion to the interchangeability of Renaissance poetic texts is associated with the
idea of 'foul cank'ring' which 'frets' (eats away) 'hidden treasure',
in the way that the pink rose of Sonnet 99 is eaten away by the
canker.

The Adonis who keeps disappearing under the weight of Venus'
rhetorical glut is allowed to re-emerge to utter an impassioned cri-
tique of her kind of poetry. He must not allow her words to enter
his ear, fearing contamination:

> 'If love have lent you twenty thousand tongues,
> And every tongue more moving than your own,
> Bewitching like the wanton mermaid's songs,
> Yet from my heart the tempting tune is blown;
>　　For know, my heart stands armed in mine ear,
>　　And will not let a false sound enter there'. (775–80)

He knows that the 'false sounds' of Venus' poetry will not be true to
him, because they are used on everyone else:

> 'I hate not love, but your device in love
> That lends embracements unto every stranger.
>　　You do it for increase.'　　　　　　　　(789–91)

Breeding with Venus promises only an infinite proliferation of the
eloquent 'figures' beloved by the Renaissance rhetoricians: the
increase they meant by the term 'copia'.[51] His distinction between
love and lust is a plea for poetic chastity which can produce a perpetually renewing truth which has the power to bring forth new life
after the surfeit of rhetorical images has gorged itself to death:

> 'Love's gentle spring doth always fresh remain,
> Lust's winter comes ere summer half be done;
>　　Love surfeits not, lust like a glutton dies;
>　　Love is all truth, lust full of forged lies.

> 'More I could tell, but more I dare not say:
> The text is old, the orator too green.
> Therefore in sadness, now I will away;
> My face is full of shame, my heart of teen,
>　　Mine ears that to your wanton talk attended,
>　　Do burn themselves, for having so offended.' (799–810)

In trying to express the difference between a poetry bred by a union with the rhetorical past which is doomed to perish, and a poetry that is self-created and uncontaminated by such rhetoric and which will, therefore, 'always fresh remain', *Venus and Adonis* seems to be going beyond a pointing to the inadequacy of rhetorical strategies to reproduce an object, to consider what means a poet might use to ensure that his invention possesses its own powers of self-renewal. Adonis demands to be allowed to ripen in his own good time:

> 'Who plucks the bud before one leaf put forth?
> If springing things be any jot diminish'd,
> They wither in their prime, prove nothing worth.' (416–18)

'If the first heir of my invention prove deformed', William Shakespeare writes in the poem's dedication, 'I shall be sorry it had so noble a godfather, and never after ear so barren a land, for fear it yield me still so bad a harvest'. The truly dangerous threat which Venus poses is that of the proud full sail of the 'rival' poet in Sonnet 86 which buries the ripe thoughts in the Poet's brain 'Making their tomb the womb wherein they grew'. Adonis is identified as both poet and poem. He is the poet's embryonic poem 'springing', growing, in the creative womb which Venus is threatening to 'diminish' by stunting its growth. But he is also the poet trying to protect the embryonic heir of his invention from anything that might cause it to be deformed at birth. Venus' rhetoric, like the 'gross painting' of the 'rival' poets in the Sonnets, who 'would give life' but 'bring a tomb', robs him of the biological, organic processes needed for the creation of new life. Her 'tedious' song that outwore the night because spent with 'idle sounds resembling parasites, / Like shrill-tongu'd tapsters answering every call, / Soothing the humour of fantastic wits' (841, 848–50), is merely second-hand rhetoric, stolen from other literary texts, and used indiscriminately to lavish praise on everyone.[52] Her 'compeers by night' have given her aid, taught her to write her 'idle over-handled theme' in the strainèd touches rhetoric can lend 'unto every stranger'.[53] The neighbouring caves 'Make verbal repetition of her moans; / Passion on passion deeply is redoubled'. Twenty times she cries '"Woe, woe,"/ And twenty echoes twenty times cry so'

(831–4). The night resounds with a cacophony of shrill parasitic sounds and becomes a nightmare vision of poetry's incestuous interchangeability. Union with Venus would produce only one more parasitic echo of other poets' words, and merely add to the seminal chaos of previous literary embryos.

> If there be nothing new, but that which is
> Hath been before, how are our brains beguil'd,
> Which labouring for invention bear amiss
> The second burthen of a former child! (Sonnet 59.1–4)

The image of pregnancy and birth has remarkably close affinities with the way Shakespeare describes *Venus and Adonis* in the dedication to Henry Wriothesley, and perhaps we can now suggest why. We might begin by noting that the sonnet opens with a conditional *If* to suggest that novelty is not a certain impossibility. But *if* repetition is all that a poet can hope for, how are our brains beguiled when they labour for invention, the first process of rhetoric defined in the Renaissance as 'the finding out of apt matter . . . a searching out of things true or things likely; the which may reasonably set forth a matter'.[54] Shakespeare uses 'beguile' elsewhere to mean: (1) to deprive or rob of; (2) to cheat, disappoint (hopes); (3) to divert attention in some pleasant way from (anything disagreeable); to while away (time); and (4) to disguise.[55] In this sonnet, the primary sense is of disappointed hopes, being cheated or deluded, but perhaps there is also a suggestion of the brain being robbed of something *and* of sense (3) whiling away time, which, incidentally, is a Shakespearean neologism, and could therefore be a subtle refutation of the idea that there is nothing new, reinforcing the conditional 'If'. In *Venus and Adonis*, as we have seen, the goddess tells the youth that her kisses will make the summer's day but short, 'Being wasted by such time-beguiling sport', which the poem presents as a threat, something that will *rob* Adonis of his vital strength and energy.

The image in 59 of labouring to carry out the first of rhetoric's five processes, *inventio*, becomes, as we reach *bear*, an image of pregnancy, and imaginative creation is now the dominating sense of *invention*, so that at *amiss* we are holding in our minds the idea of an embryo growing in some way imperfectly inside the womb. At line

4 the sense of the pain of a heavily pregnant womb is doubled by the word 'second' but then we are confronted with the mental exertion of trying to grasp the sense of 'The *second* burthen of a *former* child'. Ingram and Redpath think that without the word 'amiss' the sense would be perfectly clear:

'If everything is merely a repetition of what has happened before; how our brains are deluded, when they toil and labour to give birth to new matter, and only bring forth what has been created before!' But what is the sense of the word 'amiss', modifying 'bear'? If we took it to mean 'wrongly', then 'bear amiss' might suggest an abortion, which clearly does not fit the sense, since if there is an exact repetition, either the new birth is not an abortion or the old one was also.[56]

But what if we imagine the embryo being deformed as it develops in the womb because there is not enough space there for its body to be perfectly formed? 'If springing things be one jot diminish'd', Adonis says, 'They wither in their prime, prove nothing worth'. Is the 'former child' the heir of some other poet's invention, squashing the embryo, restricting and stunting its growth, so that what is being carried in the womb is an unwelcome extra weight, a second burden which should not be there? What is being borne 'amiss', *wrongly*, is this second burden which itself was once a child. The sense would then be: 'If everything is a repetition of all that has been before, how are our brains deluded, when they try to originate new matter, and find that their thoughts are being stifled by the oppressive weight of all that has been created before. Our brains, being filled up with what has already been reproduced by others, are deprived of the means of creating anything that *is*.'

Perhaps what is being suggested in this quatrain is the idea of a poet trying to create a new and original poetry in a biological process by making that which is *is*, and not lost to the present, but who is confronted by the seminal chaos of literary imitation where nothing new can be born because that which is 'hath been before'. The Poet tries to bring something into being for the first time, but before it can get born it is crushed under the weight of previous creations. The Poet then has to carry a double weight in the creative womb: his own embryonic thoughts, and the second burden, another poet's poem which was once a child being borne in another womb. When it is time for the new child to be born it has been deformed, like the Poet's verse in Sonnet 86 – enfeebled and paralysed.

When Adonis finally manages to break from Venus' paralysing embrace, he runs 'homeward through the dark laund' (813). *Laund* is an open space of untilled ground in a wood, land that has not yet been cultivated for the raising of crops – virgin ground where new seeds can be sown uncontaminated by previous crops. There, in the 'pitchy night', Adonis is safe from his predatory wooer. The night did 'Fold in the object that did feed her sight' (821–2). Now it is Venus' turn to be paralysed:

> Whereat amaz'd, as one that unaware
> Hath dropp'd a precious jewel in the flood,
> Or 'stonish'd as night-wand'rers often are,
> Their light blown out in some mistrustful wood:
>   Even so confounded in the dark she lay,
>   Having lost the fair discovery of her way. (823–8)

In the words of Sonnet 86, the proud full sail of Venus' great verse, bound for the prize of all-too-precious Adonis, is astonished. She has never been capable of saying to him 'You alone are you', but has kept turning him into a precious jewel – de-corporealised inert matter. But the poem now reverses the effect of those 'glutton-like' kisses insatiably feeding on his flesh and blood to 'draw his lips' rich treasure dry' (548, 552), when she finds Adonis' blood on the boar and is made to confront the stark physicality of a 'frothy mouth bepainted all with red, / Like milk and blood mingled both together' (901–2). Venus had turned the living flesh and blood of Adonis into an image 'dead and dull' when she steeped him in rhetoric's colours to make him 'too grossly dyed'. We remember how the sweat on Adonis' palm made her body tremble with passion, the biological process of his body setting in motion an organic change in her own, and how her metaphor 'balm' stopped time, process and change and turned organic substance into a sense-less figure of speech. Now she must be made to suffer the sight of the truly gross dye of real blood, and her 'gross painting' poetic techniques must be replaced by a poetic language which can accommodate time, process and change. The narrating voice takes over to demonstrate how poetry can be made to *reinstate* the body in all its sensuous and organic power. The language which tells us that the blood which Venus sees makes her body tremble with fear becomes an active moving process summoning the goddess' fear into a physical presence: 'A second fear through all her sinews spread' (903).

> A thousand spleens bear her a thousand ways,
> She treads the path that she untreads again;
> Her more than haste is mated with delays
> Like the proceedings of a drunken brain. (907–10)

It has the power to move nature's beasts into an immediate present. Here are the narrator's true, plain words describing the animals Venus encounters:

> And here she meets another sadly scowling,
> To whom she speaks, and he replies with howling.

> When he hath ceas'd his ill-resounding noise,
> Another flap-mouth'd mourner, black and grim,
> Against the welkin volleys out his voice;
> Another and another answer him,
>> Clapping their proud tails to the ground below,
>> Shaking their scratch'd ears, bleeding as they go. (917–24)

Venus finds terrible omens in 'these sad signs', and is prompted to 'exclaim on death' (925–30). She 'chides' death:

> Grim-grinning ghost, earth's *worm*, what dost thou mean,
> To *stifle beauty and to steal his breath*?
>> Who when he liv'd, his breath and beauty set
>> Gloss on the *rose*, smell to the *violet*. (933–6, my emphasis)

But it is Venus who stifled Adonis' beauty and stole his breath when he lived, just as the forward violet and the pink rose, chided in Sonnet 99, robbed the Friend of his beauty and breath.

When Venus finds Adonis dead, the eyes which had fed on his living flesh and blood are unable to bear the sight of the substance her kind of rhetoric has turned into lilies and roses, doves and ruby-coloured portals, red sealing-wax and snow:

> her eyes as murder'd with the view,
> Like stars asham'd of day, themselves withdrew.

> Or as the snail, whose tender horns being hit,
> Shrinks backward in his shelly cave with pain,
> And there all smother'd up in shade doth sit,
> Long after fearing to creep forth again:
>> So at this bloody view her eyes are fled
>> Into the deep dark cabins of her head. (1031–8)

The punishment for turning the human body into a literary stylistic trick must be a *prolonged* torture. When she opens her eyes again the cruel light shows the wound in shocking and vivid immediacy. Notice how rhetoric's colours are now made to reinstate corporeal substance to stress what Venus' eyes must be opened to:

> And being open'd threw unwilling light
> Upon the wide wound that the boar had trench'd
> In his soft flank, whose wonted lily-white
> With purple tears that his wound wept, was drench'd.
>> No flower was nigh, no grass, herb, leaf or weed,
>> But stole his blood and seem'd with him to bleed. (1051–6)

Venus' eyes are so dazzled, her sight 'makes the wound seem three' and 'makes more gashes, where no breach should be. / His face seems twain, each several limb doubled' (1064–7). And at once, Venus starts to use language which brings the uniqueness and individuality of Adonis to life, to capture the freshness and vitality she had taken from him when he was alive. 'The flowers are sweet, their colours fresh and trim, / But true sweet beauty liv'd and died with him' (1079–80). When Adonis lived, 'sun and sharp air / Lurk'd like two thieves to rob him of his fair' (1085–6). All of nature, she says, responded to his presence. The sun and wind would compete for the privilege of drying his tears, the lion would walk behind a hedge so that he could see Adonis without frightening him. Adonis' song tamed tigers. To hear him speak, wolves would leave their prey. He made the birds sing and they would bring the fruits and berries of the trees to feed him:

> 'When he beheld his shadow in the brook,
> The fishes spread on it their golden gills;
> When he was by, the birds such pleasure took
> That some would sing, some other in their bills
>> Would bring him mulberries and ripe red cherries:
>> He fed them with his sight, they him with berries.' (1099–1104)

In Ovid, it is Venus who transforms Adonis into a flower, but Shakespeare's Adonis, having Orpheus' power to make the birds and the beasts and the trees move, can effect his own metamorphosis:

> By this the boy that by her side lay kill'd
> Was melted like a vapour from her sight,
> And in his blood that on the ground lay spill'd,
> *A purple flower* sprung up, checker'd with white,
> *Resembling well his pale cheeks and the blood*
> Which in round drops upon their whiteness stood.
>
> (1165–70, my emphasis)[57]

This purple flower will *not* be 'too grossly dyed'. Its colour and odour have not been stolen from the blood and breath of another. The false rhetorical exercise of comparing Adonis to a flower, with which Venus opened the poem, to produce a sterile, life-less image, that could beget only barren verse, has undergone an exact reversal. Adonis has refused to be compared to anything else, an insistence paralleled by the Poet of the Sonnets, who spurns couplements of 'proud compare' (21.5) in repeated refusals to compare his subject with anything else and in reiterated injunctions that everything else must be compared to his subject. The blood with which Venus has smeared her cheeks is no metaphor, but the congealed substance that once flowed through the veins of Adonis' body (she 'stains her face with his congealed blood', 1122), and which is now flowing as nourishing green sap through the stalk of the flower. Comparing the flower to Adonis' flesh and blood is no rhetorical exercise. The 'new-sprung' flower has grown to vigorous strength from an original seed sown in an open space of untilled ground, fed by its own vital body fluid. If it is picked, the self-renewing power which has created it can produce another.

> She bows her head, the new-sprung flower to smell,
> Comparing it to her Adonis' breath,
> And says within her bosom it shall dwell,
> Since he himself is reft from her by death.
>   She crops the stalk, and in the breach appears
>   Green-dropping sap, which she compares to tears.
>
> 'Poor flower,' quoth she, 'this was thy father's guise, –
> Sweet issue of a more sweet-smelling sire, –

For every little grief to wet his eyes;
To grow unto himself was his desire,
  And so 'tis thine; but know, it is as good
  To wither in my breast as in his blood.'
                    (1171–82, my emphasis)

Venus may place the self-created heir of Adonis in her bosom where it will wither, but its vital essence has been distilled. Her sterile rhetoric has been metamorphosed into an organic Orphic language that can bring everything into new life. She hies home to Paphos, where she 'Means to immure herself and not be seen', taking the flower with her – but leaving Shakespeare's poem behind.

CHAPTER 4

'In scorn of nature, art gave lifeless life': exposing art's sterility. 'The Rape of Lucrece', 'The Winter's Tale' and 'The Tempest'

THE RAPE OF LUCRECE

A year after *Venus and Adonis* Shakespeare published another narrative poem, choosing again a subject which had inspired numerous literary representations. At the centre of *The Rape of Lucrece* we find a long and detailed examination of a piece of mimetic art; the 'skilful painting made for' (made to stand for, to *re-present*) 'Priam's Troy', upon which Lucrece stares for two hundred lines in a poem where rape is motivated not by the sight of the victim's body but by a description of it which transforms her flesh and blood into heraldic symbols ('This heraldry in Lucrece's face was seen . . .'), and where the rapist turns breasts into 'ivory globes', lips into coral, and skin, as Desdemona's body would be, into alabaster (*Lucrece*, 64, 407, 419–20).

After she is raped, Lucrece spends over six hundred lines unpacking her heart with words, before she grows weary of sighing, weeping and moaning and, looking for 'means to mourn some newer way', remembers the painting of Troy. There she finds 'conceit deceitful' and 'wondrous skill' (1365, 1423, 1528). The description of this painting consists entirely of the ingenuity and skill with which the artist has imitated grief and suffering. To imitate humanity is to deprive the subject of its life so that art might live (my emphasis throughout):

> In scorn of nature, art gave *lifeless* life. (1374)

> The red blood reek'd *to show the painter's strife*. (1377)

An idea that is given the same syntactically ironic treatment in *The Taming of The Shrew*:

> As *lively painted* as the deed was done. . . .
> So *workmanly* the blood and tears are drawn. (Ind.ii.57; 61)

in *Venus and Adonis*:

> Look when a painter would surpass the life
> In limning out a well-proportion'd steed,
> *His art with nature's workmanship at strife,*
> *As if the dead the living should exceed.* (289–292)

in *Cymbeline*:

> it was hang'd
> With tapestry of silk and silver, the story
> Proud Cleopatra, when she met her Roman,
> And Cydnus swell'd above the banks, or for
> The press of boats, or pride. A piece of work
> So bravely done, so rich, that it did *strive*
> In workmanship and value; which I wonder'd
> Could be so rarely and exactly wrought,
> Since the true life on't was – . . . . (II.iv.68–76)

and twice in *Timon of Athens*:

> It tutors nature; *artificial strife*
> Lives in these touches, *livelier than life* (I.i.37–8)

> Thou draw'st a counterfeit
> Best in all Athens: th'art indeed the best;
> *Thou counterfeit'st most lively* (V.i.79–81)

The effect of the painting in *Lucrece* is of a laboured skill, not a natural one:

> In him the painter *labour'd* with his skill
> To hide deceit and give the harmless show
> An humble gait, calm looks, eyes wailing still. (1506–8)

> The *well-skill'd* workman this mild image drew . . . (1520)

Mimetic seeming always operates in the 'as it were' mode: something which Hamlet thinks a virtue, but which the narrator of *Lucrece* seems to have much ironic fun playing with. It 'holds as 'twere the mirror up to nature' to deliver something doubly unreal. The subject is twice removed from itself: *as if it were*, not nature, but *a reflected image* of nature. Everything in the painting of Troy described in *The Rape of Lucrece* is what seems, or *might* be seen:

Which the conceited painter drew so proud,
As heaven, *it seem'd*, to kiss the turrets bow'd. (1371–2)

Many a dry drop *seem'd* a weeping tear. (1375)

There *might you see* the labouring pioner
Begrim'd with sweat and smeared all with dust;
And from the towers of Troy there *would appear*
The very eyes of men through loop-holes thrust:
Gazing upon the Greeks with little lust:
   Such sweet observance in this work was had,
   That *one might see* those far-off eyes look sad. (1380–6)

In great commanders grace and majesty
You might behold, triumphing in their faces . . .
. . .
And here and there the painter interlaces
Pale cowards marching on with trembling paces,
   Which heartless peasants did *so well resemble*,
   That *one would swear he saw them quake and tremble*. (1387–93)

There pleading *might you see* grave Nestor stand,
As *'twere* encouraging the Greeks to fight . . .
. . .
In speech *it seem'd* his beard all silver white
   Wagg'd up and down, and from his lips did fly
   Thin winding breath which purl'd up to the sky.

About him were a press of gaping faces,
Which seem'd to swallow up his sound advice. . .
. . .
As if some mermaid did their ears entice . . .
   The scalps of many almost hid behind,
   To jump up higher *seem'd*, to mock the mind. (1401–14)

Another smother'd *seems* to pelt and swear . . .
   It seem'd they would debate with angry swords. (1418,1421)

In Ajax and Ulysses, *O what art*
Of physiognomy *might one behold*! (1394–5)

Lucrece studies 'this well-painted piece' to find a face where all
sorrow is represented. The narrator tells us that she despairs of
finding one, until she comes to Hecuba staring on Priam's wounds
bleeding under Pyrrhus' proud foot. The irony with which the narrator stresses the perfect verisimilitude achieved by the artist's strife
against nature here reaches its most forceful – and most subtle –

definition. While ostensibly describing the painter's representation of the pitiful ruin which Hecuba had become, the stanza guides us through the life-destroying processes by which the artist achieves his life-like verisimilitude. 'In her the painter had anatomiz'd', that is, 'dissected', 'Time's ruin, beauty's wrack, and grim care's reign'. The sense of a human body being dissected beneath the painter's scalpel-like brush leads into the suggestion of a face replaced by a mask, and the complete obliteration of the original subject: 'Her cheeks with chops and wrinkles were disguised: / *Of what she was no semblance did remain*'. Hecuba has been drained of her very life's blood: 'Her blue blood chang'd to black in every vein, / Wanting the spring that those shrunk pipes had fed, / *Show'd life imprison'd in a body dead*' (1450–6, my emphasis). She has been steeped in painting's equivalent of poetry's rhetorical dyes:

> Why should false painting imitate his cheek
> And steal *dead seeming of his living hue*?
> Why should poor beauty indirectly seek
> Roses of shadow since his rose is true?
> Why should he live, now Nature bankrupt is –
> Beggar'd of blood to blush through lively veins . . . ?
>
> (Sonnet 67.5–10)

Lucrece, who 'shapes her sorrow' to Hecuba's woes, takes this painted image to be real (1458). She thinks she can tear Helen's beauty with her nails (1471–2), and finally 'She tears the senseless Sinon with her nails', until she realises the subject in the painting is not actually present: '"Fool, fool," quoth she, "his wounds will not be sore"' which suggests that even at this point, Lucrece has not quite grasped the distinction between art and life (1564, 1568). To speak of the effect of nails tearing a sense-less painted figure as *wounds*, is to invest it with a flesh and blood existence which it does not possess.

In *Titus Andronicus*, Marcus performs an action which is the exact reverse of Lucrece's. He treats human blood flowing from the torn flesh of a living body as though it were art:

> Speak, gentle niece, what stern ungentle hands
> Hath lopp'd and hew'd and made thy body bare
> Of her two branches, those sweet ornaments,
> Whose circling shadows kings have sought to sleep in . . .
> . . .

Alas, a crimson river of warm blood,
Like to a bubbling fountain stirr'd with wind,
Doth rise and fall between thy rosed lips,
Coming and going with thy honey breath.
But, sure, some Tereus hath deflow'red thee,
And, lest thou should'st detect him, cut thy tongue.
Ah, now thou turn'st away thy face for shame,
And, notwithstanding, all this loss of blood,
As from a conduit with three issuing spouts,
Yet do thy cheeks look red as Titan's face
Blushing to be encount'red with a cloud.
Shall I speak for thee? shall I say 'tis so? (II.iv.16–33)

It is a remarkable moment in Shakespearean drama. The actor's physical presence on stage, her body compelling us to believe in the fiction that her flesh is torn and bleeding and her mind is mutilated, cannot be healed by Marcus' poetic description of the former wholeness of her body and mind, however much he calls on the resources of metaphorical language to make the pitiful sight of her bearable for himself, and for us. We, helpless spectators of this harrowing scene, are made to experience for ourselves the terrible inadequacy of poetic language in the face of insupportable human suffering. Marcus' attempt to deal with it becomes all the more poignant because we are made to realise that poetry is all he has.

Where the painter's representation of Hecuba's sorrow

Her blue blood chang'd to black in every vein,
Wanting the spring that those shrunk pipes had fed,
Show'd *life imprison'd in a body dead.* (*Lucrece*, 1454–6)

the playwright's presentation of Lavinia shows life imprisoned in a body *alive*.

It is an important distinction, both for our understanding of what this scene tells us about Shakespearean drama's use of the human body of the actor in relation to its treatment of Renaissance aesthetic theory early in his career, and for the light it sheds on how the playwright exploits this distinction to such dazzlingly theatrical effect towards the end of it, in *The Winter's Tale*.

Where Marcus is twice compelled to remove the blood seeping from a severed tongue from its original, human source, by turning it first into a crimson *river*, then, by a figurative simile, comparing this river to a bubbling *fountain*, issuing from lips, again, no longer human, but *roses*, to find comfort in the confusing of real and unreal, Lucrece looks at the painted image of Hecuba in the picture of Troy, and finds comfort confusing an artificial representation with a real human body. There is the further parallel between the play and poem of course, in that both raped women turn to artistic representations of physical and mental trauma after they have been attacked: Lavinia remembers the printed story of Philomel in Ovid's *Metamorphoses*; Lucrece the painted story of Troy. Lavinia is compelled to distance the event from herself even as she must insist on the physical effect on her body (IV.i.77). The truly macabre irony as Marcus places the writing instrument, the pole, into her mouth, is that the victim is forced to re-live, and the audience to imagine, the unspeakable acts she has been made to perform with the hands and tongue which have been cut off. We watch as her broken body struggles in a physical effort to block from her mind what her body is at that moment refusing to allow that mind to do. Marcus, having turned her physical and mental torment into a disembodied abstraction, a literary poem, a stylistic symbol, is asking her to take this abstracting of physical experience even further, and turn it into something *written down*. Not the refinèd pen of the rival poets in the Sonnets. Lavinia's need to tell makes her collaborate in this flesh-and-blood-into-symbol process. She *transcribes* the experience, and writes it in Latin, thereby three times removing the primary experience of the rape from itself. The brute physical fact of rape and mutilation has become a written sign. That, rather, is what it would have become in a poem or in a painting. But this is Shakespeare's stage, and the physical mutilation, the insupportable mental torment of this broken body, is not allowed to be turned into the abstraction of art. One simple dramatic device saves the experience of human suffering from being reduced to a symbol: the unignorable presence of Lavinia's body on stage for the rest of the play. It is the effect which Shakespeare might have felt Ovid was attempting in the very story Lavinia is referring to here, when the Latin poet describes Philomel's severed tongue still palpitating, its mangled root quivering, after her 'death' as a human being and metamorphosis into an animal.

Lavinia, then, goes to poetry; Lucrece, to art. In the poem, not having the human body of the actor present on a stage to remind us that a woman is suffering physical and mental torment, it is the narrator who has to point up the contrast between primary experience and an artistic representation of it. Hence, Lucrece tries to tear the painted image of the flesh of a human body in the Troy painting. But throughout, the narrator has alerted us to Lucrece's confusion of the real and the unreal, absence and presence, blood and red dye, in the face of this exemplary mimetic representation.

Where the narrator says 'seems', she says, 'Lo here weeps Hecuba, here Priam dies . . .' (1485), even when she has just spent two stanzas chastising the painter for failing to make Hecuba speak: 'The painter was no god to lend her' words, 'And therefore Lucrece swears he did her wrong, / To give her so much grief, and not a tongue' (1461–3). The subject of *imitatio vitae*, then, cannot speak. What this artist lacks, is 'eternity', which '*could put breath* into his work', a deficiency shared by that other perfect 'ape' of nature, 'Julio Romano' (*The Winter's Tale*, V.ii.96–9). To remedy this 'wrong', Lucrece decides to lend the picture words, and imitates the imitation: 'So Lucrece set a-work, sad tales doth tell/ To pen-cill'd pensiveness and *colour'd* sorrow: / She lends them words, and she their looks doth borrow' (1496–8, my emphasis). Sidney's metaphoric Speaking Picture thus becomes comically actualised:

Poesy therefore is an art of imitation . . . that is to say, a representing, counterfeiting, or figuring forth – to speak metaphorically, a speaking picture . . .[1]

But it is Sidney's source for this definition which seems to have prompted Shakespeare's irreverent exposure of the incestuous conflation of art and poetry which would be required to make good their respective defects. In his advice on how to study poetry, Plutarch insists not only on an acquaintance with:

the hearing of that vulgar speech so common in every mans mouth, that Poesie is a speaking picture, and picture a dumb Poesie: but also we ought to teach him, that when we behold a Lizard or an Ape wel painted, or the face of Thersites lively drawne, we take pleasure therein & praise the same wonderfully; not for any beautie in the one or in the other, but because they are so *naturally counterfeited*.[2] (my emphasis)

The painting of Troy in Lucrece is a supreme example of the life-like illusion so much praised in the England of the late 1590s and early 1600s.[3] The skill with which the deception was achieved was what mattered. The spectator's sight is 'so bewitched that its then most delighted, when tis most deceived, by shadowings, and land-skips and in mistaking counterfaits for truths'.[4] A true work of art was one which feigned: the more it feigned the more it was true art, and the more inorganic the life it created, the more *lively* painted it would be.[5] The painting of Troy is an exemplary product of the mimetic manufacturing process which Sidney's *Arcadia* both describes and is, where the artist as maker substitutes the real with the unreal, 'forms such as never were in nature'. If we examine Sidney's famous definition in the light of Shakespeare's syntactically expressive denunciations of mimetic art, the irony in the dramatist's statements becomes even clearer:

Only the poet . . . lifted up with the vigour of his own invention, doth grow in effect another nature, in making things either better than nature bringeth forth, or, quite anew, forms such as never were in nature . . . he goeth hand in hand with nature . . . Nature never set forth the earth in so rich tapestry as divers poets have done: neither with so pleasant rivers, fruitful trees, sweet-smelling flowers, nor whatsoever else may make the too much loved earth more lovely. Her world is brazen, the poets only deliver a golden.[6]

Sidney's alternative creation takes the living, the organic, the fertile and self-renewing, and turns it into an inorganic sterile tapestry of life-less artifice, or, as the *Lucrece* poet's witty syntax puts it: 'In scorn of nature, art gave life-less life' (my hyphenation).

In *Venus and Adonis*, the idea of art striving to deliver a nature of a higher order, in which artifice is set over and above that which is real, is made to seem ridiculous by a deft syntactical stroke: 'As if the dead the living should exceed' (292). We are suddenly confronted with what the neoplatonic ideal of the artist as maker of a world more perfect than nature actually *means*. You try to make the thing more *real*. As we have already seen, even when praise of this idea of art outdoing nature is given to buffoons to say, critics have difficulty in pursuing the full implications of Shakespeare's irony. If we attend more closely to the choice of words given to the Poet and Painter in *Timon*, we find that they, too, have just been reading

Sidney's definition of 'poesy' as 'a speaking picture'. The Poet, a zealous advocate of the theory, exclaims: 'How grace / *Speaks his own standing!* What a mental power / This eye *shoots forth!*'

The Poet, by being given such ludicrously hyperbolic language to utter, is made to demonstrate what a 'speaking picture' would mean. In it, abstract ideas and concepts perform activities which only the organs of the body can do: hence, grace can speak! But there is more. In a 'speaking picture', the imitation of a real human eye can *shoot forth* an abstraction: 'What a mental power / This eye shoots forth!' And further, an abstraction can be made to *move* in a counterfeited image of a bodily organ: 'How big imagination / Moves in this lip!' (I.i.30–3, my emphasis).

A speaking picture, then, provides a nonsensical confusion of art and nature, abstract and concrete, real and unreal, and begs the question: 'Do we want to hear grace speaking? Or see imagination moving in a slash of red paint?' But then, the Poet (unknowingly) demolishes the whole speaking-picture argument:

> *Poet.* To th'dumbness of the gesture
> One might interpret.
> *Paint.* It is a pretty mocking of the life.
> Here is a touch: is't good?
> *Poet.* I will say of it,
> It tutors nature; artificial strife
> Lives in these touches, livelier than life. (I.i.33–8)

The Poet is marvelling that one might easily provide the words to accompany the gesture which *cannot speak itself.* This picture, then, is silent. It cannot speak at all. It is only a 'pretty mocking of the life'. 'Mockery' is always, in Shakespeare, a word with derogatory connotations. Usually, it means 'imitation, counterfeit, representation, unreal appearance', but in Hamlet's 'our vain blows (are) malicious mockery', it means 'ludicrously futile action' (I.i.151).[7] This idea of life being *mocked* by art is given its most forceful definition in a play where the body of the actor is placed on the stage to perform the part of a statue, so that the golden world of mimetic art is superposed on to the brazen world of Shakespearean drama, only for that golden world to be made to vanish under the pressure of warm, living flesh which moves and breathes and speaks.

THE WINTER'S TALE

In *The Winter's Tale*, the *ars simila naturae* concept, cherished by Renaissance theorists, so elaborately described in *Lucrece*, is subjected to the same disparaging scrutiny, this time in a play, and in order to demonstrate the superior powers of the dramatist's art. 'Prepare / To see the life as lively mock'd as ever / Still sleep mock'd death', Paulina warns Leontes as she 'draws a curtain and discovers Hermione standing *like* a statue'. This stage direction does not appear in the Folio, where there is none, but an editor or director of the play has to provide this direction because of its significances for our understanding of the playwright's meaning in what follows. 'Would you not deem it breath'd? and that those veins / Did verily bear blood?' Leontes exclaims. Polixenes replies, 'Masterly done: / The very life *seems* warm upon her lip'. Leontes marvels a second time that he thinks he sees the statue move: 'The fixure of her eye has motion in't, / As we are *mock'd* with art' (V.iii.18–30, 64–8, my emphasis).

Close attention to the choice of words and syntax reveals an attitude that is the antithesis of the Renaissance aesthetician's praising of an imitation so life-like that the painting seems to live. The theorist, Henry Peacham, in defining *hypotiposis*, speaks of the 'cunning Paynter [who] paynteth all manner of thinges most lyvely'.[8] In Shakespeare's play, 'life' is 'lively mock'd' as sleep mocks death. The first of several points to be made about this line is that *lively* and *mock'd* are juxtaposed. Onions notes three meanings for *mock* in Shakespeare. One is 'to defy, set to nought'. Hermione's life is counted as nothing in the statue. The real Hermione, the subject of the imitation, is reduced to nought. She is life-less. What is 'lively' is the mocking itself: the act of depriving life of . . . life. The second meaning Onions gives is 'ridicule'. In the statue of Hermione, a human life is ridiculed by the artist: nature is *mock'd* by art. The third meaning for the word which, Onions notes, is 'peculiar to Shakespeare', is 'to make a false pretence of'.[9] Shakespeare's works reveal an almost obsessive preoccupation with the idea of mimetic art as something doubly false. In the previous chapter, we examined the influence of Ovid's precise use of such phrases as *imagine falsi* on Shakespeare's enquiry into the ways in which art twice removes the subject from itself. The sculptor described in *The Winter's Tale* we are told has created with his statue a pretence, or illusion of Hermione which is itself false.

The second significance to be noted in Paulina's line is the carefully selected simile. The lively mocking of life, which requires the death of that life, is *compared* to something else. To convey the extent to which art has triumphed over nature, art has to be compared to . . . an act of nature. The artist's triumph is completely undermined: his achievement instantly belittled. Every human being performs as wondrous a miracle every day. We just shut our eyes. It requires no skill; sometimes it happens without our having to will it to. In sleep, the living body can make an illusion of death, a resemblance, a counterfeit, a representation of it. But it cannot make a *false* illusion, a *false* semblance, a *false* comparison: there is no art involved. The imitation is achieved, not by 'artificial strife' against nature; it is made by nature.

When art is not 'with nature's workmanship at strife', that which has life, warmth and movement does not need to be compared to anything other than itself. In a statue, a painting or a poem, the human body *seems* warm, *appears* to move, is *like* life, but the original is absent because its death is the prerequisite for the artist's lively mocking of it. Nature must die, that art might live. The redemption of life means that art must die so that nature might live. Paulina tells the statue: 'Bequeath to death your numbness; for from him / Dear life redeems you' (V.iii 102–3). At the moment when art dies into life, Paulina warns Leontes: 'Do not shun her / Until you see her die again; for then / You kill her double' (V.iii.105–7). Leontes had condemned Hermione to death. The audience is about to find out that she did not die, but in the context of the scene the death means that Hermione was killed by art when she became a statue. The equating of art with death of the human body is made again when Polixenes asks Hermione to tell them how she was 'stolen from the dead!' (V.iii.115).

The intricate layers of irony here are suggesting that when Leontes sees what he thinks is a manufactured painted image of an original flesh-and-blood presence, the human body *seems* warm. For him, this is a straightforward expression of praise for what he believes is the artist's achievement of mimetic perfection. Then Leontes (and the theatre audience) are shown that this is not an imitation of a human body at all. In Shakespeare's play, in the person of his actor, the body *is* warm: 'O, she's warm!' Leontes cries when he first touches Hermione, 'If this be magic, let it be an art / Lawful as eating'. 'She embraces him!' Polixenes marvels. *This* human body moves. It is Camillo who asks whether this art can pass the greatest test: 'If she pertain to life, let her speak too!' (V.iii.109–11,113). We do not have to provide the words to explain the gesture which cannot speak with this work of art. Unlike the *Timon* painting, *this* 'speaking picture' speaks!

When Leontes saw the statue, he said: 'Methinks / There is an air comes from her'. His response is that of John Lyly who said, more than twenty years before, 'Tushe there is no paynting can make a pycture sensible,' and is a repudiation of the Renaissance idea of an art so life-like that one is deceived into thinking the image is alive: 'What fine chisel / Could ever yet cut breath?' (77–9).[10] The answer, as we shall see, is that no sculptor's, or painter's, or poet's 'chisel' can ever 'cut breath'. Shakespeare's chisel can. It is the very substance which makes the body live, and keeps it alive: breath. The dramatist has prepared us for this triumphant boast earlier in the play, just before the Statue scene, in a comment which describes the statue as a perfect imitation of nature. Again, we need to look at what the dramatist is making his character say without assuming, as most critics have, that this is yet another straightforward reaffirmation of the 'lively art' argument.[11] The Third Gentleman tells the First that:

Julio Romano, who, had he himself eternity and could put breath into his work, would beguile Nature of her custom, so perfectly he is her ape: he so near to Hermione hath done Hermione that they say one would speak to her and stand in hope of answer . . . (V.ii.96–101)

This is the 'perfect imitation' argument again, and with characteristic Shakespearean irony what is being stressed is what this work of art *lacks*: breath. What it promises, it does not actually deliver. The artist's achievement is described in the conditional: *if* he had the power, he could make the subject live. 'So near to Hermione' is his imitation, which has the effect of emphasising how far from her it is. The artist can perfectly *ape* her: '*Imitari* is nothing', Holofernes says in *Love's Labour's Lost*, 'so doth the hound his master, the ape his keeper, the tired horse his rider' (IV.ii.121–2). *If* this 'sculptor' possessed the power to put 'breath' into his statue, he would have been able to do what nature does, to create life. The ostensible praise for the work of art becomes, though the speaker does not know it, an expression not of its perfection, but of its defect. Compare mimetic art with nature, and however skilfully art apes her, nature will show up its one overriding failure: such art delivers life-less life. Jean H. Hagstrum writes that Shakespeare 'has reversed the situation that usually prevails in the art epigram. Art has not defeated nature, nature has defeated art.' This, Hagstrum says, 'turns *The Winter's Tale* into a negation of art'.[12] Yes, a negation of the *mimesis* concept of art, the 'speaking picture' art that destroys nature. But it is a celebration of that other art which does not turn all that has life, warmth, movement and sensuous presence into a static, silent, sterile image.

The statue said to have been carved by Julio Romano is dumb and cannot speak, or move. In the scene in which Leontes' reunion with Perdita is described, we are not allowed to see what the First Gentleman tells Autolycus he has witnessed, but so vividly is the meeting re-created for us, we are 'deceived into thinking' we can see it:

they seemed almost, with staring on one another, to tear the cases of their eyes: there was *speech in their dumbness, language in their very gesture*; they looked as they had heard of a world ransomed, or one destroyed: a notable passion of wonder appeared in them; but the wisest beholder, that knew no more but seeing, could not say if th'importance were joy or sorrow; but in the extremity of the one it must needs be. (V.ii.11–19, my emphasis)

Here, the living bodies of Leontes and Perdita are described as looking like a 'speaking picture': an imitation so life-like that they *seem* to speak. Real human beings, then, can do what speaking pictures do. They can be dumb and yet speak, they can be motionless and yet move. But the second point the speech is making is that however evocative this description of the moment when father and daughter find one another may be, it is not the original moment. And there is a third significance in the speech, which is its allusion to the unreliability of eye-witness report. The spectators of the scene could not tell whether the two people were happy or sad, only that whether it was sorrow or joy, it was an extreme emotion. It can be argued, with some justice, that if a report of an event cannot determine the truth about that event's most important aspect, then its value as a record of what actually happened is questionable.

When the Second Gentleman arrives, poetry is added to history in the play's refutation of all transmission of knowledge that does not provide the 'original performance': 'the king's daughter is found: such a deal of wonder is broken out within this hour, that ballad-makers cannot be able to express it' (V.ii.23–5). He asks the Second Gentleman whether he has seen the meeting of Leontes and Polixenes. When the Second Gentleman replies 'No', he is told: 'Then have you lost a sight which was to be seen, *cannot be spoken of*' (V.ii.43–4). And we are placed in the position of the Second Gentleman, told of the wonder we *would* have seen, if we had actually been there.

> There might you have beheld one joy crown another, so and in such manner that it seemed sorrow wept to take leave of them, for their joy waded in tears. There was casting up of eyes, holding up of hands, with countenance of such distraction . . . *I never heard of* such another encounter, which lames report *to follow it*, and *undoes description* to do it.
>
> (V.ii.43–7, 57–9, my emphasis)

The scene continues with a description of Paulina's learning of her husband's gruesome death, and her reunion with Perdita to the cumulative exasperation of the play's audience. When the Third Gentleman gets to the moment when Perdita is told of her mother's death, he says:

> she did, with an 'Alas', I would fain say, bleed tears, for I am sure my heart wept blood. *Who was most marble, there changed colour;* some swooned, all sorrowed: if all the world could have seen't, the woe had been universal.
>
> (V.ii.87–91, my emphasis)

We are told that the human body can look like a statue, something we are about to be shown. The true miracle is that the body can change colour voluntarily, does not need paint. With this implied criticism of the sculptor's art, the name of Julio Romano enters the dialogue to be described as an 'ape' of nature.

The dramatist is carefully building up suspense, so that the audience is impatiently waiting to witness for itself an 'original performance'. When it comes, all that we are allowed to see at first is a meeting of life with death, with a mockery of life. Leontes is not even reunited with the real corpse of his wife, but a painted, carved imitation of her. It is so life-like, Leontes' first words when he sees it are: 'Her natural posture! / Chide me, dear stone, that I may say indeed / Thou art Hermione'. Then comes the startling observation that hints at the possibility that this mockery of life is not what it seems, cannot be a mockery at all, since it partakes of nature's process of time and change: 'But yet, Paulina, / Hermione was not so much wrinkled, nothing / So aged as this seems'. An art that can accommodate temporality and mutability, the organic process of human life, is the more worthy of praise. Paulina replies: 'So much the more our carver's excellence, / Which lets go by some sixteen years and makes her / As she liv'd now' (V.iii.23–5, 27–9, 30–2).

As yet, of course, the audience does not know that this is Hermione 'indeed'. But it reminds the audience that the first time we saw Hermione indeed was when she was carrying new life, and the last time, fainting at the news of her son's death, before time had 'carved' these wrinkles. Has art, then, done nature's work for her? At this moment in the play, we may believe that it is the 'sculptor' who has performed this miracle of defying the belatedness of art. But we are soon made to realise who has really 'carved' these wrinkles, and let go by 'some sixteen years', to summon Hermione into our presence, not *as if* she were living now, but Hermione living now.

It is this insistence on art that has the power to include in its creations nature's organic processes through time that lies behind the unusually long time-spans of the Final Plays. Loss and restoration, the process of death and rebirth, of decay and renewal, are seen to partake of the eternal and the infinite, through the vital power of 'great creating nature', and only an artist who has 'himself eternity' can 'beguile Nature of her custom'. Such an artist includes within his art the rhythms of natural growth, decay and renewal. If these are excluded, nature is artificially mocked, made unnatural by an art that is 'with nature's workmanship at strife'.

This is why the preoccupation with age is to be found in a play in which two lovers find immortality in death. It is why Cleopatra tells the absent Antony: 'Think on me, / That am with Phoebus' amorous pinches black, / And wrinkled deep in time' (I.v.27–9). Her language is always grounded in nature, stressing the organic process of fleshly existence in which time and change are not only acknowledged, but insisted upon. She tells Antony to think of her not as some abstract, idealised image of flawless youthful perfection, but as a body whose flesh is bruised black by amorous pinches and wrinkled deep in time. The syntax here conveys the sense of organic process taking place within time, and time moving within an organic process: *deep* modifies *wrinkles*, to suggest the extremity of the ageing, decaying process, but it also modifies *in time*, so that we imagine the wrinkles being furrowed in process, in time, but also *by time itself* as physical marks that were made a long time ago, and have made her body what it is now: 'Think on me, / That *am* . . .' What she is now is nature's work: 'Phoebus' amorous pinches'. The sun, each day's beginning, makes love to Cleopatra, which means that time has made love to her with *amorous pinches*. To reinforce this recognition of temporality, Cleopatra addresses another absent lover, one who is now dead: 'Broad-fronted Caesar, / When thou wast here above the ground, I was / A morsel for a monarch . . .' (29–31), and at the end of the scene, she reminds us again of the passing of time: 'My salad days, / When I was green in judgment, cold in blood . . .' (73–4).

Cleopatra's acute sense of the human body's continuous subjection to time, process and change, part of a nature that exists in a state of endless flux and mutability, aligns her with the Poet of the procreation sonnets: 'When forty winters shall besiege thy brow,/ And dig deep trenches in thy beauty's field . . .' (2.1–2). But whereas in Cleopatra this recognition leads to a celebration of all nature's mutability, in the Poet, it is a source of anxiety. 'That face should form another', the young man is told, 'So thou through windows of thine age shalt see / Despite of wrinkles this thy golden time' (3.2, 11–12). In these sonnets, though, time is both enemy and ally of immortality; or, to put it another way, time can only be defeated by time. 'And nothing 'gainst Time's scythe can make defence / Save breed to brave him when he takes thee hence' (12.13–14).

Significantly, the triumph over time recommended here fully

acknowledges and accommodates temporality; indeed, has to collude with the enemy, for what is being proposed is biological process which takes place within and by means of time. Decay and death of the flesh is to be pre-empted by conception, birth and youth, a process that is made possible only by time. What is being suggested is not a resistance to time, but a submission to it. Nowhere in his pleas to the Friend to get a son does the Poet say that the wrinkles will be prevented. The recurrent image is of the Friend's inevitable old age which must be compensated for by a 'copy' of his present beauty and youth before they fade. In Sonnet 3, the concluding couplet warns 'But if thou live remember'd not to be, / Die single, and thine *image* dies with thee!' In Sonnet 6, we find the interesting phrase '*refigur'd* thee' (10), which Ingram and Redpath gloss, 'repeated in facsimile'. Sonnet 8 uses the image of the musical harmony of strings '*Resembling* sire, and child, and happy mother' (11); and in Sonnet 11, this idea of youth and beauty being reproduced as an imitation of an original, is most explicitly expressed. Since nature has bestowed so bounteous a gift on him, the Friend 'should'st in bounty cherish: / She carv'd thee for her seal, and meant thereby / Thou shouldst print more, not let that *copy* die' (12–14, my emphasis).

Strikingly, in the sonnets which promise the Friend immortality in the Poet's verse, his youth and beauty will not decay. Instead of being copied, the original is to be preserved, and will not die. This art has power against death, unlike the 'statue' of 'Julio Romano', or the paintings described in *Timon*, *Venus and Adonis* and *Lucrece*, which all suggest the golden world referred to by Sidney as an art which surpasses nature: which makes 'things either better than nature bringeth forth, or, quite anew, forms such as never were in nature'. Sidney's poet:

goeth hand in hand with nature . . . Nature never set forth the earth in so rich tapestry as divers poets have done: neither with so pleasant rivers, fruitful trees, sweet-smelling flowers, nor whatsoever else may make the too much loved earth more lovely. Her world is brazen, the poets only deliver a golden.[13]

Sidney, of course, is suggesting that the poet's task is to transcend the fallen world to deliver a higher order of creation so that we glimpse something of prelapsarian perfection. This suggests that art must somehow be defined against nature. This assertion that poetry says nothing about the real world allows Sidney to defend poetry against the charge of lying: 'Now, for the poet, he nothing affirms, and therefore never lieth'. He 'never maketh any circles about your imagination, to conjure you to believe for true what he writes.' Yet Sidney, like Puttenham and other literary theorists of the period, claims that art works with nature (the poet 'goeth hand in hand with nature'), indeed, imitates it:

There is no art delivered to mankind that hath not the works of nature for his principal object, without which they could not consist, and on which they so depend, as they become actors and players as it were, of what nature will have set forth.[14]

To advance art as a product of man's enlightened intellect which enables him to apprehend the truth that is invisible in the fallen and corrupt world because of his 'infected will', Renaissance theorists were obliged to see nature as imperfect, and the artist's task to perfect nature.[15] Puttenham speaks of art as an 'alterer' or 'surmounter' of nature:

In some cases we say arte is an ayde or coadiutor to nature, and a furtherer of her actions to good effect, or peradventure a meane to supply her wants, by renforcing the causes wherein shee is impotent and defective as doth the arte of phisicke.[16]

It transpires, however, that the art which is said by Puttenham to correct and reform nature is deceit. He describes the figures of rhetoric as 'abuses of common utterance', which are intended 'to deceive the eare and also the minde, drawing it from plainnesse and simplicitie to a certaine doublenesse, whereby our talk is the more guilefull and abusing'.[17] Art, then, falsifies nature, adulterating the very world it is supposed to be rescuing from adulteration. To resolve this dilemma, art must be seen to be part of nature, and follow the *perfect* example she sets in decorum:

This lovely conformitie, or proportion, or conveniencie betweene the sence and the sensible hath nature her selfe first most carefully observed in all her owne workes, then also by *kinde graft* it in the appetites of every creature working by intelligence to covet and desire: and in their actions to imitate and performe: and of man chiefly before any other creature aswell in his speaches, as in every other part of his behaviour.[18] (my emphasis)

Perdita, having apparently carefully examined the central argument in Renaissance aesthetic theory and detected its irreconcilable contradictions, exposes the fundamental defect in all art which seeks to surpass nature, and asks, in effect, 'Why bother?':

> *Perdita.*   Sir, the year growing ancient,
> Not yet on summer's *death* nor on the *birth*
> Of trembling winter, the fairest flowers o'th' season
> Are our carnations and streak'd gillyvors,
> Which some call nature's *bastards*: of that kind
> Our rustic garden's *barren;* and I care not
> To get slips of them.
> *Polixenes.*   Wherefore, gentle maiden,
> Do you neglect them?
> *Perdita.*   For I have heard it said
> There is an art which, in their piedness, shares
> With great creating nature.
> *Polixenes.*   Say there be;
> Yet nature is made better by no mean
> But nature makes that mean: so, over that art,
> Which you say adds to nature, is an art
> That nature makes. You see, sweet maid, we marry
> A gentler scion to the wildest stock,
> And make conceive a bark of baser kind
> By bud of nobler race. This is an art
> Which does mend nature – *change it rather* – but
> The art itself is nature.
> *Perdita.*   So it is.
> *Polixenes.* Then make your garden rich in gillyvors,
> And do not call them bastards.
> *Perdita.*   I'll not put
> The dibble in earth to set one slip of them;
> No more than, were I painted, I would wish
> This youth should say 'twere well, and only therefore
> Desire to breed by me.
>   (*The Winter's Tale*, IV.iv.79–103, my emphasis)

I have given in full the famous debate between art and nature in *The Winter's Tale* because it contains one of the most forcefully expressed repudiations of art as an 'alterer' or 'surmounter' of nature in the canon. The significance for the play's plot of Polixenes' grafting analogy has, rightly, been given much attention, but the passage also involves an important engagement with issues of aesthetic theory which extends beyond the immediate confines of *The Winter's Tale*. [19] Most commentators have argued that it is the speaker who advocates the surmounting of nature as having the better of the argument. The Arden editor, for example, writes:

Polixenes' wider and more philosophical grasp of the principles befits him: but Perdita's resolute sensitiveness and feminine refinement about anything that might savour of sophistication or unchastity befits her. The argument does her no less honour than it does Polixenes, though, *qua* argument, he has the better of it. [20]

But does the passage give Polixenes' argument more strength than Perdita's, or is it the expectation of finding a reinforcement of a Renaissance commonplace in a Shakespeare play that leads critics to this interpretation? If we follow closely the argument Perdita is putting forward and, in particular, the imagery she is using to advance it, we find an uncommon statement about a common notion of art. The exponent of the unorthodox position, in a play in which the young will redeem the mistakes of the old, is at the spring stage of life, as everything in this scene emphasises. The promise of fertility is set against the sexual atrophy of old age. Instead of beginning chronologically with spring, the first season of the year, she talks first of winter, and gives the two old men the flowers of remembrance and repentance, the flowers of winter. Next, comes summer, and she gives out the flowers of midsummer which symbolise the prime of life. Then comes autumn but she has no autumn flowers, which denote artifice and unchastity. She alludes once again to winter with a comment to *old* Camillo, about 'the blasts of January', before, finally, she speaks of the flowers of the spring to the *young* at the feast. This movement, reversing the cycle of seasons so that she is able to end, as it were, with the beginning of new life, is the important context in which the nature–art debate has been placed. There are no carnations and streaked gillyvors to give, Perdita says: 'of that kind' our garden is *barren*, which refers back, by contrast, to nature's self-renewing process, suggested in her opening line – summer's *death*, and the *birth* of trembling winter. She says that some call gillyvors nature's 'bastards', a word which, in addition to its usual sense, is used by Shakespeare to mean *counter-feits*. 'Nature's bastards' are counterfeits of great creating nature. *Counterfeits*, in turn, is a term used by Shakespeare to denote 'false, deceitful'.[21] Polixenes, advancing the position of nature as incomplete, chaotic and defective, requiring art to remedy its defects, corrects himself in mid-sentence: 'This is an art / Which does mend nature – *change it rather. . .*'. His correction of *mend*, and his substitution of *change*, is itself a demonstration of what the artist does when he seeks to perfect nature, and locates the precise point at which Renaissance aesthetic theory falls apart. If you try to perfect nature you cannot escape perverting nature. In that *change*, fecund nature is metamorphosed into sterile artifice. Polixenes justifies this union of art and nature by adopting a position similar to that of Puttenham (and Aristotle), by insisting that it is a 'natural' art: 'The art itself is nature', in that it is made by man.[22] Perdita agrees that since man is of nature, any man-made means ('it') of altering nature is natural: 'So it is'. She is not, as most commentators have silently assumed, agreeing with the assumption in Polixenes' statement that what man does with nature when he changes it is necessarily a good thing; as her next impassioned, defiant words confirm. What she is objecting to is the artifice of this art: the art which produces streaked gillyvors. She insists again – this time more vehemently – that she will not allow gillyvors into her garden; and again, she suggests why: they smack of artifice; the painted nature produced by cosmetics. Her startling image, with its suggestion of artifice being sterile, that it would be as horrible to pierce the earth with a gardening tool to plant one gillyvor as it would be if Florizel would only want to breed with her if she were painted, is a powerful echo of the numerous moments in Shakespeare where we find the idea of art attempting to outdo nature mercilessly mocked: the 'strainèd touches' rhetoric can lend to the rival poets in the Sonnets which kill the subject of their art; the 'artificial strife' of the artist's touches described in *Timon*; the 'painter's strife' in *Lucrece*, the painter who 'surpasses the life' in *Venus and Adonis*; the silk tapestry of Antony and Cleopatra at Cydnus in Imogen's bedchamber, 'A piece of work / So bravely done, so rich, that it did strive / In workmanship and value' (*Cymbeline*, II.iv.68–76).

In *The Winter's Tale* the art which 'adds to nature' is linked with the image of penetrating the earth, by the way in which the images *barren, breed, conceive, bastard, marry* and *race* are modulated through the passage. It is Perdita who prompts the discussion by referring to carnations and gillyvors as 'nature's bastards' and continues the imagery suggested in 'bastards' (illegitimate offspring; counterfeits = images; but also false, deceitful) with the ironic, and witty, use of the word 'barren'. Polixenes then states the Renaissance common-place that art is a creation of nature, and gives as an example the analogy of grafting in which the gentlest root can be married to the wildest stock so that a nobler race can be conceived, and from this premise, concludes that such art, in mending, 'or rather', changing nature, is nature itself. The point needs to be stressed that when Perdita says 'So it is', she is agreeing that the art can be called natural in that the agent – man – is of nature, but in reply to Polixenes' insistence that she make her garden rich in gillyvors and desist from calling them nature's bastards, she takes the debate back to its starting point – to the issue *she* is talking about – where she had associated gillyvors with barrenness. Perdita, it seems nec-essary to point out, controls this debate, and refuses to be side-tracked from the central issue of her argument. She is talking about tampering with nature; Polixenes, with improving it. They are 'debating' at cross-purposes. The parallel Perdita makes here, between the inappropriateness, and pointlessness, of the dibble being put into the earth in order to plant a *streak'd* gillyvor, and Florizel desiring to enter her in a procreative union only because she is *painted*, brings, with its expression of disapproval, the sugges-tion of the antithesis of *breed*. It is the characteristic Shakespearean association of sterility with something painted; the false words which produce sterile, insubstantial images of fleshly existence. It is the 'gross painting' of Sonnet 82, alluded to in 83, and accused in 99 of destroying the life of the beloved, which is the price poets pay for turning flesh and blood into a rhetorical trope, of changing nature into artifice, in the futile desire to improve her. That the gar-dener's art is part of great creating nature does not alter the fact that what he does when he 'perfects' nature is to adulterate her.

Perdita has lifted the nature-art argument to a level of intellec-tual enquiry which Polixenes clearly cannot begin to comprehend.

With one simple analogy, reinforced by her own vibrant presence, Perdita exposes the absurdity of art which arrogantly attempts to imitate, perfect and surpass nature, and rests her case. The evidence is irrefutable. There she stands, the embodiment of budding springtime, of the fertile earth and its future fruits, full of life, warmth, movement and beauty, and asks us to imagine her being mended, or rather, changed, by art into a painted image which Florizel would only desire because she was painted.

It is Perdita who has the last word in this argument, and she has effectively silenced the traditional theorists and adherents of the concept of art as an idealising re-presentation of nature, by showing what a pointless exercise it all is. Adulteration, depravity and sterilisation are the price that must be paid for that improvement of nature whose purpose is to glimpse the perfection created by the First Maker. Perdita's words in this scene provide something like a theoretical basis for what will be shown to the audience in the 'statue' scene where 'defective' nature is made to triumph over painted image, when Shakespeare's 'lawful art' exposes the inadequacy of counterfeit art.

Florizel looks upon one of defective nature's creatures, and says: 'What you do, / Still betters what is done'. Polixenes adds: 'nothing she does or seems / But smacks of something greater than herself' (IV.iv.135–6, 157–8). We do not need artifice, then, to make things 'better than nature bringeth forth'; a point that will be reinforced to breathtaking effect when the warm and wrinkled body of her mother is made to negate the timeless perfection of mimetic art. Perdita is here being made to prepare *The Winter's Tale* audience for the moment where it will be shown the true distinction between Shakespearean art and a painted image: one art is lawful; the other not. Perdita wishes she had some of the first flowers of nature's year to strew over Florizel. In a speech that describes flowers whose self-propagating process reveals nature's miraculous powers of self-renewal, she includes the cyclical death of nature, by alluding to Proserpina whose rape by Pluto brought winter to the world. In revenge, her mother, Ceres, goddess of the earth and fertility, makes the earth barren, because, Ovid says, the world is now unworthy to receive nature's gifts. But when the lost daughter is found, Jove divides the years into two equal parts, and Proserpina spends winter in the underworld, and summer in the upper world (*Metamorphoses*, V.346–571). Proserpina becomes associated, in other interpretations of the myth, with nature's powers of fecundity and renewal: *Proserpina foecunditatem seminum significat.*[23] Thus, Proserpina can be seen as both winter, the death that is the prerequisite for new life, when nature goes 'underground' to receive the power necessary for next year's growth, and spring, the birth of nature, and promise of the earth's fruits.

The lost daughter in Shakespeare's play is explicitly identified with the girl whose myth describes a transition from a 'golden' world to a 'brazen' world. In Ovid, in the wood where Proserpina is gathering flowers when Pluto rapes her *perpetuum ver est* (V.391), 'Spring is everlasting'. Her rape is a de-flowering:

> et ut summa vestem laniarat ab ora,
> collecti flores tunicis cecidere remissis,
> tantaque simplicitas puerilibus adfuit annis,
> haec quoque virgineum movit iactura dolorem. (398–401)

And since she had torn her garment at its upper edge, the flowers which she had gathered fell out of her loosened tunic; and such was the innocence of her girlish years, the loss of her flowers even at such a time aroused new grief.

This de-flowering causes the sterilisation of the earth. Ceres, in a paroxysm of rage, calls the world ungrateful and unworthy to receive the gifts of the earth. The mother of fruits brings destruction to farmers and cattle, breaks into pieces the ploughs, and bids the earth to produce no more of its fruits. She blighted the seed and made the land infertile (V.474–81).

It is Timon's curse come to pass. In a play written just before the Final Plays, and much concerned with the relationship between man's ingratitude to nature and the severing of human ties, Timon asks nature to dry up her womb as punishment for man's unworthiness of her fruits:

> Ensear thy fertile and conceptious womb;
> Let it no more bring out ingrateful man.
> Go great with tigers, dragons, wolves and bears;
> Teem with new monsters . . .
> Dry up thy marrows, vines and plough-torn leas . . .
>   (*Timon of Athens*, IV.iii.189–195)

But there is an important difference between the nature which
Timon is calling upon, and the nature which Ovid's Ceres makes
barren. In Timon's speech, he is addressing fallen, or defective
nature: 'Common mother, thou / Whose womb unmeasurable
and infinite breast / Teems and feeds all' is made of the 'self-same
mettle' as her 'proud child, arrogant man', and engenders 'the
black toad' and 'eyeless venom'd worm' and 'all th' abhorred births
below crisp heaven' (179–85). In *The Winter's Tale*, Perdita alludes to
the time before the fall of the flowers, before the rape of the earth:

> *(To Florizel)*
> I would I had some flowers o' th' spring, that might
> Become your time of day; and yours and yours,
> > *(To Mopsa and the other girls)*
> That wear upon your virgin branches yet
> Your maidenheads growing. O Proserpina,
> For the flowers now that, frighted, thou let'st fall
> From Dis's waggon!   (IV.iv.113–18)

There are no daffodils, violets and lilies at this time of year now. 'O
. . . For the flowers now' Perdita says, making an explicit distinction
between perfect and imperfect nature. She exists in the brazen
world, where the year does grow ancient, and dies, where one must
talk of summer's *death* and winter's *birth*, a division caused, according to pagan myths at least, by the rape of a virgin.

But as the play testifies, nature's wounds are healed when time
and death are admitted, and the cyclical process of birth, fruition,
decay and death begins. Perdita is shown to share such redemptive
powers in what is always referred to as the 'Spring' part of *The
Winter's Tale*. The flowers she would strew over Florizel are to form
a marriage bed, and have the power to revitalise the dead; 'What,
like a corpse?' he asks. Perdita replies: 'No, like a bank, for love to
lie and play on: / Not like a corpse; or if – not to be buried, / But
quick, and in mine arms' (IV.iv.129–32). Spring's potential fecundity must be protected at all costs, an exhortation which finds its
most insistent articulation in Shakespeare's Final Plays, and which
is anticipated, inversely, in Timon's 'To general filths / Convert, o'
th'instant, green virginity!' in a play where the desecration of
chastity, the degradation of human sexuality and the breaking of
familial bonds are associated, by its protagonist, with nature's ster-

ilisation (*Timon of Athens*, IV.i.6–8). Prospero's almost hysterical insistence on the preservation of Miranda's virginity warns that the breaking of her 'virgin-knot' before marriage will make her union with Ferdinand infecund. Their marriage bed will not be strewn with Perdita's life-renewing flowers, but with weeds: 'No sweet aspersion shall the heavens let fall / To make this contract grow; but barren hate, / Sour-ey'd disdain and discord shall bestrew / The union of your bed with weeds . . .' (*The Tempest*, IV.i.15,18–21).

In *Pericles, Cymbeline* and *The Winter's Tale*, the source of nature's protection from sterility is lost, and must be found. Inside the brothel at Mytilene, Marina's speech enables her not only to escape defilement, but also to purify corrupted nature, as an example of the way in which chastity can correct defective nature (*Pericles*, IV.vi). Pericles hears the music of the heavenly spheres, the sound of perfect nature, when he finds his daughter, and tells her that she has brought back to life the father whose fertility gave her life: 'O come hither, / Thou that beget'st him that did thee beget' (V.i.194–5). Once the daughter is restored to Pericles, her mother is found, in the temple of the goddess of chastity, who is also goddess of childbirth, and the play which opens with another daughter's 'defiling of her parent's bed' (I.i.132), ends with fertile chastity reinstated and precious virginity intact.

Marriage, in the Final Plays, is seen to be a celebration of the power Cleopatra is said by Enobarbus to possess, to 'make defect perfection' (*Antony and Cleopatra*, II.ii.231). Fertile chastity is the means by which nature's imperfect and corrupt state may be redeemed. Shakespeare's quarrel with art as the perfecter of nature is that it destroys the very source of nature's redemption. There is no going back to the golden world, to that age before we 'fell' into time, and nature's 'everlasting' spring was ruptured by death and decay. But there is Orphic song, a power which can return nature to her everlasting spring, make 'plants and flowers / Ever sprung' by language that is fertile because chaste, uncontaminated by the rhetoric of other poets' words. Instead of the artist's 'artificial strife' against nature, which succeeds only in sterilising her and creating life-less images, art must accommodate the very element which signalled the transition from a golden to a 'brazen' world. Time, and the cyclical, organic process of nature, are what the neoclassical unities seem precisely invented to exclude from the art which, paradoxically, its adherents call *imitatio vitae*. It is not without significance that the only time Shakespeare adhered to these unities (apart from early on, in *The Comedy of Errors*) was with a play, generally considered to be the culmination of his career, in which his fiction is made to be so transparently fictitious as to be totally surreal. The one occasion when he strictly follows the precepts of neoclassical verisimilitude, it is to stress his play's unlike-lifeness.

It is a joke Ovid would have enjoyed.

THE TEMPEST AND PROSPERO'S INSUBSTANTIAL ART

A golden world is created on Shakespeare's stage in *The Tempest* — by Prospero. Then we see it destroyed when the goddesses of the 'insubstantial' pageant he has created 'heavily vanish' to 'a strange, hollow and confused noise' (IV.i. after 138). The stage direction, which appears in the Folio, is an essential part of the dramatist's meaning in the speech which follows.

The vision Prospero is describing has usually been identified with *The Tempest*, or Shakespeare's art in general, that Prospero is comparing the stage he stands on to the world outside the theatre, and that he is foretelling the dissolution of that world. In this reading Shakespeare is using the theatre we are sitting in as a metaphor for the real world. But what if we consider an alternative, straightforward interpretation and take the speech to mean what it says? What if Prospero is simply describing the masque which he, Prospero, has created? He is telling Miranda and Ferdinand that the fabric of the vision they have seen is baseless, that it is an insubstantial pageant, and that it has faded. The similes in the speech all refer to the 'actors' who, Prospero tells Miranda and Ferdinand, 'were all spirits'; and, to make absolutely sure there can be no misinterpretation of his statement, that they fully understand which actors he is talking about, pointedly reminds them that he told them these actors were spirits before the masque began. The emphasis, then, is on the insubstantiality of the masque's actors: these are not flesh-and-blood beings, but spirits that have been conjured out of thin air. There is no suggestion that this piece of artifice is grounded in the real world. This is the speech as it appears in the First Folio, with spelling and punctuation retained, and the long 's' modernised:

> Our Reuels now are ended: These *our actors*,
> (As I foretold you) were all *Spirits*, and
> Are melted into *Ayre*, into thin *Ayre*,
> And like the baselesse fabricke of this vision
> The Clowd-capt Towres, the gorgeous Pallaces,
> The solemne Temples, the great Globe itselfe,
> Yea, all which it inherit, shall dissolue,
> And like this insubstantiall Pageant faded
> Leaue not a racke behinde: we are such *stuffe*
> *As dreames are made on*; and our little life
> Is rounded with a sleepe. (1819–1829, my emphasis)

Prospero begins with the conventional term 'Our revels', used by 'masquers and audience, in masques and other courtly displays'.[24] The main subject of the sentence from 'Our reuels . . . racke behinde' is 'our actors': 'Our masque is over' (meaning the masque of Prospero, the masquer, and Miranda and Ferdinand, the audience). 'The actors were all spirits and have melted into air; and will dissolve; and like the entire insubstantial spectacle they have performed in, will leaving nothing behind.'

The phrase 'this vision' has done much to encourage traditional interpretations of the speech as an allusion to Shakespeare's own drama, which would have Prospero turning to the audience with a gesture encompassing the theatre and the world beyond it.[25] But it is difficult to see how this can refer to *The Tempest*, or any other play by Shakespeare; 'Clowd-capt Towres, gorgeous Pallaces', and any other kind of spectacular edifice, being conspicuously absent in his drama. If traditional readings which insist on the primary metaphorical status of Prospero's speech can have been allowed to continue unchallenged for decades, there are grounds for considering the validity (and the theoretical implications) of the alternative interpretation suggested here. The vision Prospero is talking about is the one which Miranda and Ferdinand have just seen: a theatrical representation in which goddesses speak in heroic couplets and enjambement lines, and are dressed in cunningly devised costumes of lavish ostentation against a backdrop of mechanically contrived stage scenery. 'Yea, all which it', all which this vision, occupies: 'everything which has been so magnificently artificed for this elaborate, substanceless masque that is now dissolved'. What is left is: 'We'. Prospero, Miranda and Ferdinand are not insubstantial, but 'such *stuff* / As dreams are made *on*.' Dreams as distinct from visions. *Stuff* is placed at the end of the line, to emphatic effect. The substance of Shakespeare's actors is contrasted with the insubstantiality of Prospero's actors. Dreams are 'made on' substance, matter; visions, on 'baseless fabric'. The actors of insubstantial pageants dissolve into nothingness; the 'little life' of Prospero, Miranda and Ferdinand, of two hours' duration, ends when the performance is over, with a break before their next short life begins.

Prospero's kind of art, with its Ovidian insubstantial images, shall dissolve. Which is why it is so rudely interrupted, and made so wittily to heavily vanish. Textual scholars have remarked that since the Folio text of *The Tempest* was prepared with care, 'as befits the opening play in such a volume', one of the stage directions in the masque presents a problem. The Oxford Shakespeare editors note: 'In F the direction "Iuno descends" appears some thirty lines *before Juno arrives on the stage*'; and they point out that if the direction 'is retained where it is marked in F, the range of plausible interpretations consistent with Jacobean stagecraft is limited'. They conclude that there are no reasons for relocating it to the moment when Juno is first acknowledged, 'nor . . . is F's plausibly an anticipatory direction. A long, slow descent is *theatrically awkward*'; and they suggest it can be interpreted in the light of 'theatrical practice elsewhere', in which 'descends' signifies an appearance in the air rather than a descent to the stage (my emphasis).[26]

In common with critics who have sought to find influences of court masques of the period on the structure of *The Tempest*, and on the staging of Prospero's masque, the Oxford editors have resorted to explaining the position of the direction by reference to Jacobean stagecraft practice.[27] Such an approach is based on the premise that the masque in *The Tempest* is intended to be a conventional example of the genre. If we leave the stage direction as it is marked in F, and take it to mean what it says, this is what happens in the masque which Prospero's art has created. Iris, messenger of the gods, goddess of the rainbow, enters, dressed in her dazzling many-coloured costume, to the sound of soft music. She delivers her apostrophe to the unseen Ceres, in which the goddess of fertility, the Giver of Life, Mother of Earth, *is asked to leave the earth* which it is her sacred duty to protect. On the line, 'Bids thee leave . . .', '*Juno descends*', two lines after she has been mentioned, in her chariot, noisily, slowly, cranked down from above. It is going to take thirty lines for this operation to be accomplished: a long, slow descent would be 'theatrically awkward', which is what a dramatist intent on exposing the absurd artificiality of Prospero's kind of art, would want it to be. Iris's poem, which has been interrupted by the distracting sight of Juno suddenly appearing on high (and being now an inch or so lower) comes to an end, and Ceres enters, having abandoned the natural world, to begin her eulogy of Iris, and to be reassured that the wanton goddess of Love will not be coming to this gathering. Meanwhile, as the two deities gossip, the queen of the gods is hanging suspended, tottering and swaying above the clouds which cap the two-dimensional towers, the make-believe temples and the hollow great globe (made, perhaps, to look like the impressive stage-globe of Jonson's *Hymenaei*?).[28]

Thirty lines after our first sight of her, she has finally landed on 'earth'. Ceres bestows her blessing, which banishes *winter* from their world: the season of the necessary death for new life; in which destruction produces creation, and which Shakespeare had recently used for the title of a play in which female redemption is explicitly identified with the myth of Proserpina whose rape by Pluto brought winter to the world, but also the promise of a cyclical spring, an annual renewal of life.

When the three goddesses have bestowed their blessing on the couple, Ferdinand, the ideal spectator of mimetic art forms, tells Prospero: 'This is a most majestic vision . . . May I be bold / To think these *spirits*?' Prospero completes this half-line by repeating its last word: '*Spirits*, which by mine Art / I have from their confines call'd to enact / My present fancies' (IV.i.118–22). It is Prospero who has commanded Ceres to *leave* Nature so that she may *enact* his present *fancies*; Prospero who has made the queen of the gods, the goddess of marriage and of women, hang like an ungainly puppet in the air for thirty lines of his ding-dong poetry. It is, in short,

Prospero who has 'mocked' nature. And it is Shakespeare who makes them 'heavily vanish'. *Heavily* is usually glossed 'sorrowfully'; but it is possible that it is also registering the sense of 'weightily'. Hollow spectacle requires unwieldy stage machinery. Spirits that are supposed to be weightless cannot effortlessly vanish. They have to leave the stage weighed down with all the mechanical paraphernalia that was needed to get them on to the stage in the first place. It is, perhaps, the cleverest and most mischievous joke that Shakespeare plays on all practitioners and adherents of mimetic art, that he makes one of his characters create a 'golden world' only to have him turn round and tell us that it is nothing but an insubstantial image. Ferdinand is made to voice, in characteristic Shakespearean irony, the response of the ideal spectator of a Sidneyan 'golden world' when he calls it a 'most majestical vision'.

The insubstantial actors creak and crank their way off stage, not to solemn music, but to a *strange, hollow and confused noise*. Usually, it is music that is played, to cover the noise of the machinery; and it is further support to the argument that the *Juno descends* stage direction is intended as a comic deflation of courtly masques, that the Folio has no stage direction for music to be played when Juno descends, or when she is first acknowledged by Ceres, thirty lines later, and has reached the stage.

Solemn music is, however, played at the moment when Prospero vows to bury the manual that has taught him how to create such insubstantial art; the unnatural art which has been in 'artificial strife' with nature, has 'bedimm'd / The noontide sun, call'd forth the mutinous winds, / And 'twixt the green sea and the azur'd vault / Set roaring war' (V.i.33–57). It is the inverse of Orpheus' art redeeming nature. Prospero is offered to us an example of what happened when *Magikē* gave way to *Logos*, when the identity of word and being was split after the dismemberment of Orpheus.[29] Significantly, Shakespeare's false magus-poet learns his art from books ('Burn but his books' (III.ii.93) Caliban advises the potential usurpers on the island if they want to seize power); and instead of summoning the world into presence with and through nature, sets himself over against nature as an onlooker, to construct a more perfect world. Such 'potent art' has caused a tempest so 'life-like', the clothes of the shipwrecked survivors emerge from the sea cleaner than they were before (!) This art makes 'things either better than nature bringeth forth, or, quite anew, forms such as never were in nature'.[30] It does not, however, seem to possess what we would term practical use: as Caliban is made to remind us, Prospero's power does not bring him the knowledge necessary for survival on the island; where to find the fresh springs and all the fertile parts of the island, how to catch seafood, get wood for fuel (I.ii.332–46; II.ii.148–9, 160–1,167–70). It does not, then, work with nature, but against her. This power usurps nature. Lear tries to control the elements, but he fails. Prospero decides to whip up a storm and causes a shipwreck, then turns to nature and can boast that he can even clean up her mess. A human magician who can order the goddess of nature to do his bidding with impunity cannot even find fresh water on his island if he is left to his own devices. Ferdinand, of course, does not know this, and sees only the 'majestical vision' of Prospero's spectacular masque.

The Tempest discredits the insubstantial fancy of Prospero's tempest, which 'outdoes' nature, and it banishes the shadows of his absurd masque, those dis-embodied spirits whose movements make so much noise. To suggest that Prospero's masque is like the dramatist's play, *The Tempest*, to suggest that his speech on the masque is comparing the vision to the play, and the play to the real world, seems a curiously reductive reading of an explicit, important statement on art and artifice by an artist in the final period of his career. Shakespearean drama is not Prospero's artificial strife against nature; it is made on *stuff*, substantial matter, or, as Cleopatra says, 'Nature's piece', which strives against *fancy* (*Antony and Cleopatra*. V.ii. 99).

At the end of *The Tempest*, Prospero is made to take responsibility for Caliban, the base nature which is shown to be capable of creating beauty in language and, uniquely in this play, of seeking for grace (V.i.275; III.ii.133–41; V.i.295). Prospero is made to give up his art, as he tells the audience at the beginning of his Epilogue when, as many critics have noted, he comes to the front of the stage to talk to us in character, not as Shakespeare's actor: 'Now my charms are all o'erthrown', he says. The artist who has usurped Nature is now overthrown.

CHAPTER 5

'O'er-wrested seeming': dramatic illusion and the repudiation of mimesis. 'Love's Labour's Lost', 'A Midsummer Night's Dream' and 'Hamlet'

SHAKESPEARE'S STRUTTING PLAYER

The 'Defence of Drama' which can be discerned in Shakespeare's works suggests that through drama it is possible to develop the power possessed by Orpheus of summoning the world into *presence* for the first time. If drama's potential for an Orphic bringing-into-being can be realised, genesis can take place without the seminal taint of previous literary (and historiographical) texts, and the world it presents can be renewed every time a play is performed. Such power lies in its evocation of concrete, physical nature in an immediate presence through the language and the body of the actor, and requires an insistence on the fictitiousness of what is being presented, since to re-present or imitate reality is to 'mock' nature, to ignore temporality and deceive us into thinking that the counterfeit is the truth. The story, the action, the characters, these are all a fiction. What is real is the bodily presence of the actor, breathing, speaking, moving on the stage before us *now*. Through transience, permanence is achieved: the enduring power of renewal in which the play can be repeated within and through time, and is never exactly the same because each performance of this play exists only here and now, its life at an end when it is two or three hours old. When this life is over, the play can be reborn, summoned, Orphic-like, into presence for the first time, whether or not we have seen a performance of it before. The audience is frequently reminded that what is being presented is not the truth, and that the characters are not real people, but fictional creations played by real people. The response it elicits is one in which we believe the fiction, and not, we take the fiction to be truth.

This is not Coleridge's 'we *choose* to be deceived'; his 'true Theory of Stage Illusion' where drama is 'to produce a sort of temporary half-faith, which the spectator encourages in himself and supports by a voluntary contribution on his own part, because he knows that it is at all times in his power to see the thing as it really is'. Coleridge's idea of a kind of 'negative belief', more famously expressed as 'that willing suspension of disbelief . . . which constitutes poetic faith', implies that the audience becomes absorbed in the stage illusion as though it were real life, although he does allow that a certain amount of awareness of artifice is involved in the audience response.

Coleridge rejects both the notion that the spectators are actually deluded into mistaking the illusion for life, and Samuel Johnson's view that they are never at any time deluded.

> the true Theory of Stage Illusion – equally distant from the absurd notion of the French critics, who ground their principles on the presumption of *De*lusion, and of Dr Johnson who would persuade us that our judgements are as broad awake during the most masterly representation of the deepest scenes of Othello, as a philosopher would be during the exhibition of a Magic Lanthorn with Punch & Joan, & Pull Devil Pull Baker . . .[1]

Dr Johnson's comments on the subject take us closer to Shakespeare's attitude to illusion. In a vigorous defence of the dramatist's violation of the unities, he writes:

> The necessity of observing the unities of time and place arises from *the supposed necessity of making the drama credible.* The critics hold it impossible, that an action of months or years can be possibly believed to pass in three hours; or that the spectator can suppose himself to sit in the theatre, while the ambassadors go and return between distant kings . . .[2] (my emphasis)

Such critics, he continues, object that 'The mind revolts from evident falsehood, and *fiction* loses its force when it departs from *the resemblance of reality*' (my emphasis). As for the contraction of place, critics argue that the spectator cannot suppose he has moved from Alexandria to Rome, but 'knows with certainty . . . that what was Thebes can never be Persepolis'. It is time, therefore, Johnson says, to tell such a critic, 'by the authority of Shakespeare', that he must assume 'as an unquestionable principle' that '*It is false*, that *any representation is mistaken for reality*; that *any dramatic fable in its materiality was ever credible, or, for a single moment, was ever credited*' (my emphasis)[3].

In our own century, semioticians have refuted the Coleridgean position. In *The Semiotics of Theatre and Drama*, Keir Elam defines what he terms '*dramatic* possible worlds' as 'hypothetical ("as if") constructs', recognised by the audience as 'counterfactual (i.e. non-real) states of affairs' that are 'embodied *as if* in the actual here and now'. Because 'the spectator's awareness of the *counterfactual* standing of the drama . . . is a necessary constant it is not necessary to accept the Coleridgean notion of the audience's "suspension of disbelief" in the presented world' (Elam's emphasis).[4] According to this theory, 'spectators will conventionally interpret all stage doings in the light of this general "as if" rule', and in words which echo those of Johnson, it argues that 'any member of the audience who does not realize that the interpretation is counter-factual will be *mistaking drama for actuality*' (my emphasis)[5].

Dr Johnson stresses the fictitiousness of Shakespearean drama, and when he insists that the spectators 'know, from the first act to the last, that the stage is only a stage, and that the players are only players', he is denying that the play asks us to take it for real life.[6] Coleridge thinks the spectator – temporarily at least – takes the play for real life. Semiotic theory proposes that a 'spectator familiar with dramatic worlds can become engrossed in the representation without ever losing a detached consciousness that what he is witnessing is simply the way "things could have been"'.[7] The dramatic world is taken to be non-real, but is also, Elam says, 'necessarily *based on* the spectators' actual world' (Elam's emphasis). The semioticians' notion of an 'as if' construct appears to be based on an assumption that the dramatic world is fundamentally one of mimetic representation, which can be either in a realistic or non-realistic way: 'It should not be thought that the "accessibility" of dramatic worlds renders them always and necessarily realistically mimetic'. Such dramatic worlds allow 'any number of invented and even fantastic elements into the drama without destroying the audience's ability to recognize what is going on'.[8] The widespread view in 'metadramatic' criticism that Shakespeare's drama operates on a plane of mimetic illusion which is 'disrupted' by presentational devices, depends upon a prior assumption that it is concerned with re-presenting reality which exists outside the fiction the playwright is creating. In this view, the play at times pretends to be real life, and we believe the illusion to be life, and at other times, the play tells us that it is not life, and is only pretending to be. Or, the two planes operate simultaneously, in what Robert Weimann has called 'the mimesis of mimesis'. By means of the dual perspective of real actor and assumed role with which we see the character, 'the nature of reality is explored by the imitation of imitation'. A. D. Nuttall's view, put forward in his study of Shakespeare, that 'literature can represent reality, but it can also invent, cheat, play and enchant', does not take into account the possibility that in order to represent reality, the dramatist invents, cheats, plays, and therefore enchants.[9]

I want to argue that at no time does the play ask us to see the illusion as if it were life, and at those moments when it draws our attention to its theatrical status it is not, therefore, disrupting an illusion of reality. We need, with Shakespeare, a more precise lexicon of illusion, one which distinguishes between mimetic representation and fiction, and it is difficult to find the precise terms. When we talk of our simultaneous awareness of real actor and assumed role, do we mean that one plane is operating outside the play, and the other inside the play, so that the perspective contains both reality and the illusion of that reality? When Coriolanus says, 'Like a dull actor now / I have forgot my part, and I am out . . .' (*Coriolanus*, V.iii.40–1), are we being taken *out* of the illusion, into the reality outside the theatre? I would argue that the effect is otherwise: at such moments in Shakespeare's plays, we are drawn further into the fiction. Coriolanus is reminding us that he is an actor playing a part in a play. The reinforcing of our recognition that the role is being performed by a real actor does not prompt us to wonder whether the actor loves his mother, or ask, to paraphrase L. C. Knights, how many children does he have? It is worth remarking here that Knights' seminal essay arguing against the novelistic approach of A. C. Bradley, treats the Shakespeare play as a literary poem, and its Elizabethan audience as readers of a literary text, with 'An educated interest in words, a passionate concern for the possibilities of language and the subtleties of poetry'.[10] Jonson's fantasy, in fact.

I am deliberately overstating my case in order to make the point that after almost a century of criticism that has argued against the Bradleyan 'Play as Novel' approach, commentators still discuss Shakespeare's drama as mimetic illusion without fully exploring the possible implications that his frequent denunciations of mimetic forms of art might have for our understanding of what *kind* of illusion he sought to create. The assumption that a Shakespeare play is intended to be an imitation of life, an 'illusion of reality', leads critics to speak of the dramatist's struggle with the 'limitations' of his art, of references in the plays to 'counterfeiting actors' and 'quick comedians' as expressions of Shakespeare's 'disgust with himself' and his craft.[11]

Howard Felperin argues that mimesis arises in Shakespeare from representation of inherited models or constructs of nature or life. Shakespeare 'invalidates older models even as he includes them, supersedes them, in the very act of subsuming them'. The result, he says, is 'a troubled awareness . . . of the simultaneous resemblance and discrepancy between the play and its older models'. While agreeing that Shakespeare 'invalidates' and 'super-sedes' earlier models – this study is suggesting that his plays are intended to cancel out the authority of prior texts – I would want to argue that the means by which he does so prevents any 'troubled awareness' of similarity and difference between his play and inherited models. Felperin's view of Shakespearean drama is that it is a mimetic art. The tone and logic of the argument seem to me to suggest partly why it has been so difficult for criticism to shake off the assumption that Shakespeare shares with Renaissance theorists and practitioners the ideal of the mimesis concept of art, which is why I quote it at length:

the study of Shakespearean mimesis, surely the most compelling *illusion of reality* in world literature, begins, paradoxically, in the study of convention. Any artist, in order to represent life, must resort to the conventions of art, and in so doing, falsify life in so far as art creates a world to rival life's. Yet for art to be moral, to teach as well as delight, it must also be mimetic; we cannot learn from the actions of creatures with whom we have nothing in common, who are not in some degree like us. Shakespeare resolves this paradox by subsuming within his work a recognizably conventional model of life, repudiating that model, and thereby creating the illusion that he uses no art at all, *that he is presenting life directly.*[12] (my emphasis)

The argument starts with the traditional assumption that Shakespeare's drama is an illusion of reality, then suggests that this arises, not from a direct imitation of nature, but from representation of inherited models of nature which the playwright repudiates in his own artful imitation of an imitation, which is made to seem artless.

The word 'mimesis' is entirely absent in Shakespeare's canon. The only time it is referred to is by the metaphor 'mirror' in a play which, it will be argued, seeks to invalidate the Renaissance commonplace of drama as mimesis, a concept which ultimately derived from Plato and Aristotle, and was based on a phrase attributed to Cicero by Donatus: 'Cicero ait Comoedia est imitatio vitae, speculum consuetudinis, et imago veritatis'.[13]

Where Shakespeare uses the word 'imitation' in the sense of mimetic drama, the activity is derided, and it is made quite clear to us why: the actor is condemned for trying to re-present the actual physical presence of real people. Ulysses deplores Patroclus' impersonations:

> And with ridiculous and awkward action,
> Which, slanderer, he imitation calls, –
> He pageants us. Sometime, great Agamemnon,
> Thy topless deputation he puts on;
> And like a strutting player whose conceit
> Lies in his hamstring and doth think it rich
> To hear the wooden dialogue and sound
> 'Twixt his stretch'd footing and the scaffoldage,
> Such to-be-pitied and o'er wrested seeming
> He acts thy greatness in. (*Troilus and Cressida*, I.iii.149–58)

Ulysses, elsewhere in the play, is by no means his creator's mouthpiece (an assumption which has bedevilled interpretations of his 'degree' speech in this play), but we need to be aware that such objections to 'o'er-wrested seeming' are voiced in various forms, throughout the canon, to condemn mimetic representation's struggle against nature (o'er-wrested' is 'strained', but also 'to have perverted' and 'distorted' and 'sprained').[14] Part of the playwright's purpose might well be to show that Ulysses is attempting to sting his auditors into self-awareness, but the way in which he is made to do so is worth examining because it gives us one of the longest and most sustained descriptions of acting in Shakespeare's works, and because the dramatist often says two (or more) things at the same time. Patroclus, in this speech, is accused of presuming to *put on* Agamemnon's *topless deputation*. Underlying the meaning that he puts on the great general's supreme office, is the sense that the actor is a *substitute* for Agamemnon: *deputation* is 'office' but also, in Shakespeare, used with the implication of substitution.[15] The word 'topless', with its suggestion, not only of 'immeasurably high' and 'supreme', but also of 'having no superior', suggests the sense of something inimitable.[16] Patroclus imitates this person by attempting to substitute his own body for that of Agamemnon. The significance of the speech lies in the emphasis that is placed on the *strain* involved in this contortionist's act. Patroclus twists and bends his body severely out of place in 'ridiculous and awkward action', because the accomplishment of this imitation rests solely on the operation of his thigh muscles straining to wrest the body into another's shape: his conception of the part, or *conceit*, 'Lies in his hamstring'. The purpose of this imitation, we are told, is the actor's delight in hearing the sound that is produced when his distorted body moves across the stage on muscle-strained legs, and he listens to the dialogue 'Twixt his stretch'd footing and the scaffoldage'.

Shakespeare's 'strutting player' is not a term used lightly as a vague reference to a swaggering actor. The attitude of the Arden editor of the play is representative: 'Whether the term means "flaunting, swaggering" or "affecting an air of dignity or importance" hardly matters'.[17] But the dramatist seems to think it matters a great deal. It has the precise and significant connotation of the actor's body being contorted into unnatural shape to imitate the corporeal presence of a real person, a process which the dramatist equates with the 'artificial strife' that lives in the artist's touches, and the 'strainèd touches' of rhetoric which poets produce in their unnatural struggle to re-present a human presence. They are all 'o'er-wrested seeming' because they pervert and distort nature in the process of imitating her.

Shakespeare's other use of the word 'imitation' in the sense of mimetic illusion, appears in Hamlet's advice to the players where he speaks of actors he has seen who 'strutted and bellowed', and 'imitated humanity so abominably' (III.ii.33, 35). The pun here, using the false etymology *ab homine*, meaning, 'away from man, inhuman, beastly', suggests more than Hamlet means. To imitate humanity is an inhuman act, the work of a beast, an idea that is expressed elsewhere as the aping of nature – 'Julio Romano' is 'so perfectly' nature's 'ape' (*The Winter's Tale*, V.ii.98–9) – and which is equated with the process by which the human subject of such imitation is 'mock'd' or set to nought: 'prepare / To see the life as lively mock'd as ever / Still sleep mock'd death' (V.iii.18–20). 'To mock' or 'to counterfeit' are the two terms used most frequently by Shakespeare to describe an act of imitation, and we find the association of imitation and bestiality early in the canon, in a play whose comic treatment of the dissolution and transformation of identity is modified by sinister undertones that are associated with agents which 'change the mind' and 'deform the body'. Dromio of Syracuse, like his master Antipholus, is bewildered that strangers are behaving as if they know him. He describes himself as a counterfeit, imitating his real self:

Syracuse Drom. I am transformed, master, am I not?
Syracuse Antiph. I think thou art in mind, and so am I.
Syracuse Drom. Nay, master, both in mind and in my shape.
Syracuse Antiph Thou hast thine own form.
Syracuse Drom   No, I am an ape.
                    (*The Comedy of Errors*, II.ii.195–8)

Dromio of Syracuse is insisting that imitation and counterfeiting involve a transformation of bodily shape. The 'aping' or imitating of his real self has turned him into a beast both in his mind and in his shape.

   This sense of imitation as a de-humanising process, a setting of humanity to nought, is what lies behind Shakespeare's insistence on the fictitiousness of his art. It is a dramatic illusion, not a mimetic one; we engage emotionally with a fiction, not with an imitation of life.

It has long been recognised that many, perhaps all, of Shakespeare's comedies have problematic endings, or, where endings are orthodox, are made ambiguous or problematic by the issues which have been explored in the play. More often than not,

and in varying degrees of subtlety, we are reminded of the distinction between life and Shakespeare's fiction. But as in all matters of
dramatic aesthetics, the playwright seems to complicate an already
complex idea. For there seem to be two sets of distinctions being
made in Shakespearean drama: art and life; and drama and life.
Shakespeare presents a dramatic illusion, not a mimetic illusion.
But he uses a convention of mimetic art to demonstrate how inadequate the imitation of life really is. Fiction is used to explore realities, not imitate them; realities can only be explored with such force
through fiction, a paradox which, as we will see, causes Hamlet so
much pain. When Shakespeare exploits conventional comedy
endings it is to reinforce this paradox. Just as mimetic art would
banish all that is 'brazen' in the world, so the happy ending would
resolve all conflict and unhappiness in the play. But it is often what
has gone before that exerts pressure on the ending and resists being
summarily sewn up in a golden world.

    Much Ado About Nothing brings a conventional comedy conclusion
to what has been, at times, a disturbing experience for the audience. Claudio, who had been so ready to believe in Hero's 'adultery' he could break her heart without a word of regret, utters no
apology or expression of love when she is finally restored to him
and he realises her innocence. In performance, the note of love
and harmony at Belmont which ends *The Merchant of Venice* can
rarely, if ever, wholly erase the effect of Shylock's tragedy, though a
whole act has gone by since we saw him take his final leave of the
play. The plot of *Twelfth Night* , we are told, cannot end until the
character who has stormed off the stage screaming 'I'll be
revenged on the pack of you' is found, and persuaded to free the
sea-captain who has Viola's clothes. In *Love's Labour's Lost* we find
the most explicit statement that the play we have been watching is a
fiction which life cannot be squeezed into. The resolution to the
love plot will take 'too long for a play'. Real time is repeatedly
evoked to alert us to the play's violation of the classical unities: the
suitors are sent away for a year, and only after twelve months will
the ladies answer their proposals (V.ii.832–60). In *Measure for
Measure*, in one of the most subtle, and disturbing, endings in the
canon, Isabella gives no answer to the Duke's offer of marriage,
and the audience is left to reflect on the nature of a love that has

allowed him to prolong her torture by allowing her to believe her brother has been executed. The continuous assault on the stability of our moral judgements that has been inflicted on us throughout the play means that a simple acceptance of a happy ending becomes an impossibility.

With *Pericles*, *Cymbeline* and *The Winter's Tale*, Shakespeare seems to have been concerned with presenting a more complete, less ambiguous, resolution, not by any attempt at 'life-likeness', but by one of fiction's most extreme forms, the fairy-tale. If we look at the realities which these plays are exploring we would have to say that in each of them the 'dark' elements are a good deal more disturbing than in most of the comedies which have problematic endings. *Pericles* begins with incest, and its virtuous heroine is put up for sale in a brothel; in *Cymbeline* a husband orders his wife to be murdered; and in *The Winter's Tale* a father orders his new-born child to be murdered, and imprisons his own wife. The 'romance' elements of these plays work towards, rather than against, an unproblematic ending. *The Tempest*, in this respect, is different. Its ending, for all the expressions of repentance and forgiveness, is ambiguous. Prospero's usurping brother, Antonio, obdurately refuses to repent of his past deeds, so the expected resolution never comes. Shakespeare's play, it seems, will never end: as we have seen, Prospero comes to the front of the stage as Prospero, not as the actor playing the part. Shakespeare's fiction, here, is shown to be completely cut off from any relationship with life outside it. The dramatic illusion stands by itself.

LOVE'S LABOUR'S LOST

In the final scene of *Love's Labour's Lost*, where we are told that we cannot be shown how the events we have been watching will end because 'That's too long for a play', much of the precious time that could have easily been utilised with forwarding the action and bringing it to a conclusion 'like an old play' has been taken up with a disproportionately long demonstration of what happens when spectators demand mimetic illusion from drama (V.ii.870, 866). The actors performing 'The Pageant of the Nine Worthies' freely acknowledge that they are impersonating historical and legendary personages. The spectators refuse to believe this fiction and complain that the illusion is not like life. The obvious, and straightforward, interpretation of this is that the courtiers are sending up the amateur actors, and that the theatre audience is encouraged to join in and laugh at the players. But it can be argued that the scene is doing something more than providing a comic interlude that will be punctured when news comes of the death of the French king. The scene merits careful examination, and needs to be 'staged' in our minds, if we are to explore its full implications for our understanding of the careful distinction the dramatist is here making between *mimetic* illusion and *dramatic* illusion.

Before the performance begins, Costard comes to the front of the stage, as it were, to have a quiet word with the audience. He says the players want to know 'Whether the three Worthies shall come in or no' (V.ii.486). The show has been billed as 'The Pageant of the Nine Worthies', and Berowne is the first of the spectators to raise the first of what will be many sceptical questionings about this drama's mimetic adequacy: 'What, are there but three?' Costard seems perfectly content that the nine parts will be played by only four actors, but is told he has got his sums wrong. The idea of an actor doubling or trebling will not affect the excellence of the pageant, he says. To Berowne's question, he replies: 'No, sir; but it is vara fine, / For every one pursents three'. When Berowne adds: 'And three times thrice is nine', Costard contradicts him (487–8).

Costard. Not so, sir; under correction, sir, I hope it is not so.
You cannot beg us, sir, I can assure you, sir; we know what we know:
I hope, sir, three times thrice, sir, –
Berowne.   Is not nine.
Costard. Under correction, sir, we know whereuntil it doth amount.
Berowne. By Jove, I always took three threes for nine.
Costard. O Lord, sir! it were pity you should get your living by reckoning, sir.
Berowne. How much is it?
Costard. O Lord, sir! The parties themselves, the actors, sir, will show whereuntil it doth amount: for mine own part, I am, as they say, but to parfect one man in one poor man, Pompion the Great, sir.

(V.ii.489–500)

Berowne is quibbling over Costard's arithmetic. The actor is becoming increasingly impatient with the difficult customer who will not only not let them get on with the show, but is also calling into question the actors' special 'knowledge' which allows them to transcend such mechanical reckoning, and renders them immune from such literal-minded measuring. Costard speaks in the didactic tones of an expert having to repeat his statement to an ignorant layman. He insists again and again that the players know how theatrical sums work – the implication being that Berowne could not possibly understand such matters – and pities the spectator for knowing only the orthodox method of 'reckoning'. Drama, Costard is suggesting, has its own rules, which the audience does not have to trouble its head about. If the spectators would allow the actors to 'show' 'whereuntil it doth amount' they will see that their anxious concern for mimetic exactitude is unwarranted. Costard speaks of a process in which such arithmetical quibbling and pedantic verisimilitude is an irrelevance, and within a single sentence repudiates the idea that drama must adhere to the rules which govern the real world *and* implicitly repudiates any suggestion that the actors are attempting to deceive their audience that they are the actual personages they represent. 'For my own part, I am, as they say, but to parfect one man in one poor man . . .' The cast list which Armado presents to the King reinforces this point: 'He presents Hector of Troy; the swain, Pompey the Great; the parish curate, Alexander; Armado's page, Hercules; the pedant, Judas Maccabaeus'. Berowne starts to protest again about the number of actors and parts failing to add up, this time with the King, and the audience is keeping the actors waiting again, so that we, the audience in the theatre, are beginning to wonder whether the stage audience is ever going to let the play begin. At last, Costard enters *for Pompey*, and it is as if a member of the audience is consulting the cast list, and interrupting the first line of a play by shouting out: 'You're not Henry V; you're Laurence Olivier!'

Costard. I Pompey am, –
Berown.   You lie, you are not he.
Costard. I Pompey am, –

                                                    (V.ii.541–2)

Costard manages to deliver his poem, the last line of which reminds his audience that he, Costard, is not really Pompey: 'If your ladyship would say, "Thanks, Pompey," I had done' (551).

It has been suggested that Berowne's 'You lie' is referring to 'Pompey' falling prostrate, having tripped over his cumbersome accoutrements, and that the point of the little scene lies in its ridiculing of the actor's failure to present the illusion that he has 'become' the person he is playing. It is true that the effect of Costard's 'I Pompey am' is comical, but our response here is qualified by an equally strong and progressively more powerful sense, as the pageant continues, of frustration at the intrusive heckling of the stage audience. Berowne and the other lords are demanding a mimetic illusion, not a dramatic one: if they were making these demands seriously, they would be asking the actors to treat them like credulous fools who can believe Costard *is* Pompey, Nathaniel *is* Alexander. The 'layering' of this scene is complex. If the spectators are sending up the whole notion of neoclassical verisimilitude by insisting that the actors of the Pageant adopt it, this does not prevent the spectators in the theatre audience from recognising the absurdity of their demands. The dramatist goes to some length in pointing out what it would mean if this stage audience were to be given what they are requesting. Boyet says Nathaniel cannot be Alexander: 'Your nose says, no, you are not; for it stands too right' (561). An actor playing a historical personage, then, must have exactly the same shaped nose as the man he is impersonating – in this case, a physical peculiarity commented upon by Plutarch, Robert Greene, and Puttenham – so that for Shakespeare's original audience the suggestion of art imitating that which is unique would have added emphasis.[18] Berowne then makes a joke about the famous hero's renowned sweet-fragranced skin and breath: 'Your nose smells "no", in this, most tender-smelling knight' (562). As well as being required to have the same distinctive nose, then, the actor must also possess a rare, if not unique (in which case, inimitable), body chemistry which causes a perfumed air to exude from the flesh. If he does not have it, the spectators will 'smell' him out, and realise he is a fake.

Shakespeare is here taking the mimesis concept of art to its logical conclusion to force us to recognise its fundamental flaws.

Firstly, it requires the imitation of a subject which, being unique, cannot, by definition, be perfectly imitated. Secondly, art cannot defy time: the imitated subject will always be lost to the present, the point being emphasised here by the actors playing people who existed in the distant past. Thirdly, and consequentially, if art offers a life-like illusion the spectators will spend all their time either complaining that it is not like life, like Berowne and the lords, or, enthusing that it is, like the Poet does in *Timon*. Either way, the spectator is prevented from engaging with the original subject.

Berowne and the lords demand mimetic illusion. They ridicule the actors for being nothing like the real people they imitate. It is Hal's attitude when he derides Falstaff for his total failure to achieve the perfect verisimilitude espoused by dramatic theorists like the Italian scholar, Ludovico Castelvetro, who had taken Aristotle's views on the Unities to an extreme, if logical conclusion. It is an attitude we find in Sidney who, employing a phrase which would have deep resonances for Shakespeare, wrote of Gorboduc:

> It is faulty in place and time . . . For where the stage should always represent but one place, and the uttermost time presupposed in it should be, both by Aristotle's precept and common reason, but one day, there is both many days, and many places, *inartificially imagined* . . . we must believe the stage to be a garden. By and by we hear news of shipwreck in the same place: and then we are to blame if we accept it not for a rock. Upon the back of that comes out a hideous monster with fire and smoke: and then the miserable beholders are bound to take it for a cave. While in the meantime two armies fly in, represented with four swords and bucklers: and then what hard heart will not receive it for a pitched field?[19] (my emphasis)

Shakespeare's answer to such humorously ironic attacks on dramatists who defy the Unities was to employ a similarly ironic approach and take the argument for adherence to neoclassical principles to its rational conclusion, in order to expose it as untenable. In *Love's Labour's Lost* he invites us to consider what it would mean if the subject of drama were to be, as Sidney might put it, *artificially* imagined. Watching the Pageant, the lords insist on a total life-likeness. But their demands could only be satisfied if Alexander III of Macedon, 356–323 B.C. was actually present before them, complete with nasal peculiarity, and perfuming the air they breathe, and marching on the actual soil of Persepolis or Babylon or Egypt. This being an impossibility, since art cannot deliver the physical presence of the subject imitated, nor move the past into the present, the drama must pretend it is delivering the original subject by using artifice. The actor must put on a false nose, soak his tunic with musk oil, and carry reserve supplies of the perfume concealed discreetly in his belt to be used when the performance wears on, and the fragrance, off. The stage must be filled with battlements, and ten thousand soldiers, and if it is supposed to be, say, Egypt, then a pyramid must stand in the background. Dr Johnson's reply to the neoclassicists' attacks on Shakespeare provides us with the best gloss on this scene:

The objection arising from the impossibility of passing the first hour at Alexandria, and the next at Rome, supposes, that when the play opens, the spectator really imagines himself at Alexandria, and believes that his walk to the theatre has been a voyage to Egypt, and that he lives in the days of Antony and Cleopatra.[20]

What is being emphasised in 'The Pageant of the Nine Worthies' is the irretrievability of an original, corporeal existence. When Armado steps forth as Hector it is, again, the individual *physical* characteristics of the long-dead hero that the spectators allude to when questioning the drama's mimetic adequacy:

Boyet. But is this Hector?
King. I think Hector was not so clean-timbered.
Longaville. His leg is too big for Hector's.
Dumain. More calf, certain.
Boyet. No, he is best indued in the small.
Berowne. This cannot be Hector.   (V.ii.630–5)

That Armado cannot be Hector is precisely where the significance of the entire scene lies. The actors have told the audience they are actors: they are not meant to 'be' the historical heroes they are playing; the lords ruin the show because they will not accept its fictitious status. What we are being invited to acknowledge is that there can never be a perfect imitation of that which is, or was, a living human presence. Art is not life, as the sudden entrance of Marcade explicitly demonstrates, reinforcing the point that has been made throughout the Pageant. When the French lord brings the Princess news of her father's death, Berowne dismisses the actors with the words, 'The scene begins to cloud' (714). The king utters his platitudinous, wholly inappropriate speech, *as if he were a character speaking at the end of a comedy*, urging the grief-stricken Princess to forget her sorrow, and continue the love story they have begun. But the Princess, unlike the King, knows the difference between art and life, which is why she refuses to go on with her part as a heroine in a traditional comedy ending. 'I understand you not' (744) is the voice of protest against those who confuse art with life; reality and fiction; true and false. It is the voice of Hermione, standing trial for her alleged coupling with Polixenes which took place only within the false imaginings of Leontes' mind: 'You speak a language that I understand not' (*The Winter's Tale*, III.ii.80). When the Princess and her ladies send off their wooers to discover what real life is, they are punishing the lords for making the mistake of believing that life can be imitated by art. Berowne grumbles because 'these ladies' courtesy / Might well have made our sport a comedy'. The King's *naïveté*, knowing no bounds, it seems, thinks the play can continue for another year, and reassures Berowne: 'Come, sir, it wants a twelvemonth and a day, / And then 'twill end.' Berowne, at least, has started to acknowledge that life is not a play: 'That's too long for a play', he tells the King (867–70).

Instead of betrothal and marriage, the play ends with a song about adultery, winter's hard labours and chesty ailments, and 'greasy Joan' endlessly stirring the pot to prevent the dinner burning (886–922). It is sung by the actors who have just been playing Pompey, Hector, Alexander, Hercules and Judas to a disruptive, jeering audience which has totally subverted their attempts to create a compelling fiction, by demanding that art be like life. As they sing of the cuckoo mocking cuckolds, of milk coming home frozen in the pail, of Dick who blows his nails, of Marian's nose red and raw from the cold, it as though they are rounding on the stage audience to take their revenge, and asking: 'Is this life-like enough for you?'

The dramatist has built into *Love's Labour's Lost* the means of its own destruction in order to remind its audience that his play is fiction, not life. It is not an example of what Philip Edwards has called Shakespeare's 'continuous battle, a quarter of a century long, against his own scepticism about the value of his art as a model of human experience'.[21] For Shakespeare, art which proclaims itself to be like life is to be distrusted. His battle was not against scepticism of the value of his own art, but against those who, making a nonsensical confusion of art and nature, real and unreal, imitate life, and only succeed in making it life-less; and who, like the King of Navarre, aspire to such absurd contradictions as to be 'Still and contemplative in living art' (I.i.14). The most significant objection to the King's Academy, voiced by Berowne, in an image often used by Shakespeare for mimetic artists, is that it will be sterile: 'Why should I joy in any abortive birth?' (I.i.104).

It is the King's Academy, itself an imitation of the academies at the European courts, with the sterile rhetoric their students must imitate, the enforced celibacy that will mean breeding takes place only in the head, that is the model of human experience that is held up to sceptical scrutiny in this play, not Shakespeare's own art. Life, in the shape of Marcade, breaks in upon the world of the Sonneteers because they thought art could masquerade as life, and then, when they broke their vows to become active wooers in love, lived life as if it were art. The verse they write to their beloveds is that of the Muse in Sonnet 21, 'Making a couplement of proud compare / With sun and moon, with earth and sea's rich gems' (5–6), and of all the rival poets who are accused, in the sequence, of imitating life with rhetorical dyes. Of Marcade's entrance in the final scene, Edwards writes: 'Death comes into the play from outside . . . News from a "real world" breaks in upon a world of fantasy'.[22] But a distinction needs to be made between the lapsed Academicians' world, the world of life lived as a play, and Shakespeare's play. If, as this critic says, *'Love's Labour's Lost* is the comedy which denies itself, and refuses to behave', it is to demonstrate, not the limitations of drama, or the 'confines of art', but the absurdity of all art which claims life-likeness. Nature is allowed to get her own back on the adherents of mimetic art in this fiction. 'Life' in the shape of nature's song about bleak reality sees off the lords' world of mimetic artifice. It is their false rhetoric, Navarre's confusion of the real and the unreal, their espousal of the fallacious dramatic theory of verisimilitude and neoclassical principles, the whole edifice of artifice the lords have constructed, that is banished from the play. None of this can be given a place in Shakespeare's fiction. They have been allowed into *Love's Labour's Lost* only so that they may be summarily dismissed. In the process, the theatre audience, like Navarre and the lords, is deprived of the traditional comedy happy ending, but it has been made quite clear that life is one thing; mimetic art, another. Shakespeare's fiction is altogether something else.

A MIDSUMMER NIGHT'S DREAM

When Puck comes to the front of the stage at the closing moments of *A Midsummer Night's Dream*, he dares us to call him a liar. He says '*If* we shadows have offended', think that all we have done on this stage is a dream. Then he challenges us, 'Else the Puck a liar call', knowing that since we have been happily enthralled for the past two hours, in the doings of a legendary hero, a mythological Queen of the Amazons, the King and Queen of the Fairies, and a bunch of mechanicals enacting scenes from Ovid's myths, all constantly reminding us that they are dramatic characters, we are going to feel rather foolish if we *do* call him a liar (V.i.409–22). But at a more profound level, we at the same time acknowledge that the play has been lying to us all along, and that we have colluded in the process. Only Peter Quince's amateur dramatics company has been concerned with literal truth, and their performance has demonstrated how spectacularly ill-suited this is to the operations of drama. Like the on-stage audience of 'Pyramus and Thisbe', we would not want to be told by the actor that he is playing the part of Wall; or that the Lion is no lion, but Snug the joiner. What is being brought home to the theatre audience by this play-within-a-play is not only that the imagination of the spectators completes the theatrical experience, but also what is required to create theatrical experience in the first place, and what happens when the audience is not expected to play its part. This does not mean we must imagine, for example, that a 'real' lion is 'really' roaring on the stage, or that an actor 'really' is a wall. Our part, as audience, is not to 'pretend' that a fiction is reality, but to believe in the fiction as fiction. In his presentation of the play-within-the-play in *A Midsummer Night's Dream*, the dramatist seems most concerned with emphasising what must come first – whether a playwright and his company of actors believe in the fiction as fiction. To give an actor the role of an animal or a static object is to reinforce the point that successful drama has nothing to do with 'passing off' an imitation as reality. To make the actor engage in extemporaneous dialogue with the audience to explain he is not really a lion demonstrates that successful drama cannot accommodate what late twentieth-century metadramatic criticism calls 'breaking' an illusion of reality.

The entire process of staging 'Pyramus and Thisbe' – the casting, rehearsal and performance scenes – is one of the most explicit explorations in Shakespearean drama of this question of mimetic illusion and its opposite, anti-illusionist symbolism, and it is important to examine not only the performance at the Duke's court, but also the preparation stages of the production. At the casting, when the mechanicals first discuss their parts, Bottom has no doubts about his ability to bring his audience to tears, so moving will his tragic lover be. Playing the part 'will ask some tears in the true performing of it. If I do it, let the audience look to their eyes: I will move storms, I will condole in some measure' (I.ii.21–3). It is Quince who introduces the issue that will cause this production to fail before it even gets started:

Bottom. Let me play the lion, too. I will roar, that I will do any man's heart good to hear me. I will roar, that I will make the Duke say: 'Let him roar again; let him roar again!'

Quince. And you should do it too terribly, you would fright the Duchess and the ladies, that they would shriek: and that were enough to hang us all.

All. That would hang us all, every mother's son. (I.ii.66–7)

As soon as Quince starts to voice his concerns about upsetting the ladies in the audience, all possibility of the company creating a dramatic illusion to compel belief is gone. To assuage the fears of their audience, Bottom says he

will aggravate my voice so, that I will roar you as gently as any sucking dove; I will roar and 'twere any nightingale. (I.ii.76–79)

What is being emphasised in this casting scene is not how bad these players are at acting as such, but what makes a dramatic production fail. And the point is reinforced as soon as the company starts to rehearse, instructed by Quince to 'do it as we will do it in action, before the Duke'. When Bottom starts to worry about frightening the ladies in the audience if their performances are too life-like he adopts a view that is the antithesis of the dramatic illusion he had predicted when he was first cast in the role: 'Write me a prologue, and let the prologue seem to say we will do no harm with our swords' (III.i.15–17). And once embarked on such anti-illusionist reassurances, he finds he cannot stop:

and that Pyramus is not killed indeed; and for the more better assurance, tell them that I, Pyramus, am not Pyramus, but Bottom the weaver. That will put them out of fear'. (III.i.17–21)

The anti-illusionist stance is infectious, and the whole company becomes preoccupied with the imagined responses of their prospective audience.

Snout. Will not the ladies be afeard of the lion?
Starveling. I fear it, I promise you.
Bottom. Masters, you ought to consider with yourself; to bring in (God shield us!) a lion among ladies is a most dreadful thing; for there is not a more fearful wild-fowl than your lion living; and we ought to look to't. (III.i.26–32)

Snout has the answer: 'Therefore another prologue must tell he is not a lion'. So far, this rehearsal of 'Pyramus and Thisbe' consists of composing a prologue in which the audience will be told that none of the parts they are about to see is to be believed. The actors are, in effect, relinquishing their roles before they've even started to rehearse the play: 'I, Pyramus, am not Pyramus, but Bottom the weaver'. Similarly, with Snout's part: when the prologue tells the audience the lion is not a lion, Bottom says it 'must name his name'. And he goes further:

and half his face must be seen through the lion's neck; and he himself must speak through, saying thus, or to the same defect: 'Ladies,' or 'Fair ladies. I would wish you,' or 'I would request you.' or 'I would entreat you, not to fear, not to tremble: my life for yours! If you think I come hither as a lion, it were pity of my life. No I am no such thing; I am a man, as other men are': and there, indeed, let him name his name, and tell them plainly he is Snug the joiner. (III.i.35–44)

Name, sex, occupation . . . Is this fiction or a testimony under oath for some kind of official document? What the theatre audience is at this point being invited to ask is whether this play rehearsal is ever going to get past the ever-lengthening prologue designed to obliterate all trace of dramatic illusion.

Immediately after this, the actors seem to show themselves to be adherents of Castelvetro's theory that only absolute verisimilitude will do. We are told that this play of theirs must be so realistic they will need to bring moonshine into the chamber, because as Quince very reasonably explains: 'For you know, Pyramus and Thisbe meet by moonlight'. Suddenly, we are made aware at this moment that, for Quince and his players, this is a story that is to be believed. It is the fiction, the myth, of an ancient poet's story-telling to which Quince is responding. His use of the present tense shows that his sense of these lovers is here-and-now and timeless, and it seems also to be suggesting that for him, the Pyramus and Thisbe of this present production are fully imagined characters. But what Quince fails to go on to recognise is that what has compelled his belief in the presence of moonlight in the story is not an actual moon he can see, but the power of the story-teller to create the illusion. Like Bottom, when he talks of moving his audience to tears, Quince reveals an instinctive sense of what effective and affective drama requires. The problem is, the 'Pyramus and Thisbe' actors keep forgetting what makes for good theatrical practice as soon as they start worrying that the audience will take them literally. In *A Midsummer Night's Dream*, it is the company of players in rehearsal who keep adopting the attitude of the stage audience in *Love's Labour's Lost* , the bad-mannered courtiers who seem intent on sabotaging 'The Pageant of the Nine Worthies' with their pedantic quibbling and impossible demands for absolute life-likeness on the stage. Berowne and the lords, however much they are allowed to encourage the theatre audience to laugh at Costard and his company, do not really get the last laugh. As we have seen, when Berowne questions the players' arithmetic, Costard refuses to start worrying, as Bottom and the others do, about literal-minded spectators. 'The Pageant of the Nine Worthies', Costard insists, is a dramatic illusion, not a mimetic one.

What is being shown with the 'Pyramus and Thisbe' production is of course the comical consequences of inept actors adopting an anti-illusionist attitude to drama, but it is perhaps saying even more about what happens to all drama when it is required to start thinking about its relation to mimesis. Each ridiculous suggestion for staging the play is shown to be prompted by the actors' assumption that their audience will believe that Bottom *is* Pyramus, and that Pyramus really does stab himself to death with a sword on the stage; that Snug is actually a lion, Snout really a wall. At one point, Snout and Bottom take the illusionist view of drama to such an extreme, they paradoxically (and, by now, logically) want to eliminate illusion altogether, and make the play more than life-like: they want to be able to dispense with the notion of drama being 'like' life, and *be* real life, and use a real moon for moonshine:

Snout. Doth the moon shine that night we play our play?
Bottom. A calendar, a calendar! Look in the almanac; find out moonshine, find out moonshine.
Quince. Yes, it doth shine that night.
Bottom. Why, then may you leave a casement of the great chamber window, where we play, open; and the moon may shine in at the casement. (III.i.48–54)

The rehearsal 'room' for the 'Pyramus and Thisbe' players is, of course, not a room at all. Before they start to rehearse they pointedly refer to their surroundings so that the audience is alerted to the ironic significance of all that we are about to see and hear. Quince, the actor-playwright, says:

Pat, pat; and here's a marvellous convenient place for our rehearsal. This green plot shall be our stage, this hawthorn-brake our tiring-house. . . (III.i.2–4)

Quince and company are rehearsing in a green plot, which they are pretending is a stage, which is supposed to represent a green plot, the trysting place of the two lovers in the play. None of the actors comments on this irony, but it is increasingly brought home to the theatre audience as the rehearsal is deferred so that urgent practicalities may be attended to. For the *Dream* audience, of course, there is a further layer of irony: within this fiction, real actors are playing actors on the actual stage before us. The fictional actors are pretending the stage is a green plot, pretending the green plot is a stage, which is meant to represent a green plot where the lovers in their fiction meet.

But the truly Shakespearean aspect of this scene is the way in which complex theoretical issues are explored through apparently simple comic devices emphasising the practical considerations of theatrical production. What we are given, in effect, is the material for a debate on the relative demerits of classical imitation and medieval signification. At one moment, the acting company is aspiring to imitate reality, to be so real, they want to commandeer the real moon to shine on the lovers in this play; and the next, they decide that instead of using a real wall, they will have one of the actors to 'signify wall'. The significance of the juxtaposition of these two theoretical positions is pointed to by Quince himself. After Bottom recommends keeping the window open to let the moon shine in, Quince suggests an alternative:

Ay; or else one must come in with a bush of thorns and a lantern, and say he comes to disfigure or to present the person of Moonshine. Then there is another thing: we must have a wall in the great chamber; for Pyramus and Thisbe, says the story, did talk through the chink of a wall. (III.i.55–60)

Snout thinks this a silly idea. Reinforcing Quince's reminder to the theatre audience that these actors in their rehearsal for staging the dramatic fiction of 'Pyramus and Thisbe' are imagining the physical location of the prospective performance (the Royal 'great chamber' of Theseus' palace), he objects: 'We can never bring in a wall'. Bottom has the answer: 'Some man or other must present Wall; and let him have some plaster, or some loam, or some rough-cast about him, to signify wall' (61–7). The discussion of how to present the play has moved away from any attempt at a dramatic illusion. The actors have unwittingly written themselves out of the script, a point that Quince seems dimly to understand when he talks of an actor not playing Moonshine, but presenting *the person* of Moonshine. It remains only for Snout to be given his part, 'Wall', the absence of the article denoting that this, too, is a person, and the confusion of theoretical perspectives on the nature of drama seems now complete. It is at this point that the rehearsal proper begins.

It is not enough to say, then, that the disastrous performance of 'Pyramus and Thisbe' results simply from Quince and his company aspiring to an illusionist or anti-illusionist drama. The critical deciding factor seems to lie in their perception of what the attitude of the audience will be. On the night of the performance they find themselves confronted with a sophisticated court audience who patronise them in more ways than one. Much fun is made by this audience of the company's description of the play as 'a tedious brief scene' of 'very tragical mirth', and the *Dream* audience laughs along with them, of course (V.i.56–7). It can also be seen as another example of the misguided lengths to which these actors will go in striving to please; a (futile) attempt to keep everyone happy. Philostrate primes the audience to mock what they are about to see by telling them he's seen the rehearsal, and they're so inept he wept merry tears at this tragedy. Theseus' response to this is that he is willing to be kind: 'Our sport will be to take what they mistake' (68–70, 90). This sport involves a running commentary of mockery and disparagement while the performance is in progress. That the actors are hearing every word the courtiers are saying about them is made clear at the point when Theseus undertakes to direct the performance: 'The wall, methinks, being sensible, should curse again'. Pyramus immediately turns to him to explain: 'No, in truth, sir, he should not. "Deceiving me" is Thisbe's cue: she is to enter now, and I am to spy her through the wall.' And he reassures him that the performance is going to plan ('if you would just let us get on with it!' is the unspoken line the *Dream* audience might be expected to provide for him): 'You shall see it will fall pat as I told you: yonder she comes' (180–5).

In the middle of the performance, at the end of the lovers' tryst, one of the spectators gives judgement on the play:

Hippolyta. This is the silliest stuff that ever I heard.
Theseus. The best in this kind are but shadows; and the worst are no
   worse, if imagination amend them.
Hippolyta. It must be your imagination then, and not theirs.

(V.i.207–10)

Within the sheer comic moment of this exchange lies the precise point at which all drama that sees itself as adhering or not adhering to mimesis falls apart. What has been demonstrated is that the players have got it wrong, and so has the audience. No amount of imagination on the part of the audience can remedy the defects of a performance that refuses drama's fictitious status, as Hippolyta's riposte implicitly suggests. The deeper irony of Theseus' next words lies in his reference to the capacity of acting companies to believe what they are doing.

Theseus. If we imagine no worse of them than they of themselves, they may pass for excellent men. Here come two noble beasts in, a man and a lion. (V.i.211–13)

Bottom and company, as we have seen, have been too busy worrying about what their audience will or will not 'imagine' for a fully realised fiction to even begin to take shape.

The Duke begins by insisting it is the spectators who remedy the actors' defects, and then implies that the audience's response depends on the actors' self-appraisal. This seems to lead us back to the question which the rehearsal scene of Act III had prompted: Which comes first: What the actors do with drama? Or what the audience is expecting them to do with it?

When the persons of Moon and Wall, Bottom who is not Pyramus, Flute who is not Thisbe, and Snug who is not Lion have left the stage, closely followed by their audience, Puck comes before the theatre audience to show us what it takes to create effective dramatic illusion. If a lion and a moon are summoned into our presence it is because the actor believes in his fiction as fiction, and compels us to do the same:

> Now the hungry lion roars,
> And the wolf behowls the moon;
> Whilst the heavy ploughman snores,
> All with weary task fordone. (V.i.357–60)

If we believe it is night-time now, it is not because the moonshine has been let into the theatre, and if we tremble at indefined fears, it is not because we are hearing a lion roar, listening to the sounds of screech-owls, or because we are seeing ghosts:

> Now the wasted brands do glow,
> Whilst the screech-owl, screeching loud,

> Puts the wretch that lies in woe
> In remembrance of a shroud.
> Now it is the time of night
> That the graves, all gaping wide,
> Every one lets forth his sprite
> In the church-way paths to glide. (V.i.361–8)

There is no question, then, of putting the *Dream* audience, like that of 'Pyramus and Thisbe, 'out of fear', or of reassuring us that the actors who are brought back on stage to end the play are not really fairies. Instead, we are asked to go on believing until the final moment before we are invited by the fiction to applaud . . . the fiction.

HAMLET

'Is it not monstrous', Hamlet asks, that it is the fictitiousness of drama which compels belief?

> O what a rogue and peasant slave am I!
> Is it not monstrous that this player here,
> *But in a fiction*, in a dream of passion,
> Could force his soul so to his whole conceit
> That from her working all his visage wann'd,
> Tears in his eyes, distraction in his aspect,
> A broken voice, and his whole function suiting
> With forms to his conceit? And all *for nothing!*
> For Hecuba!
> What's Hecuba to him, or he to her,
> That he should weep for her?
>   (II.ii.544–54, my emphasis)

There is no relation between the original subject, the sorrows of Hecuba, and the actor's impersonation Hamlet has just watched; the tears in the Player's eyes, the distraction in his aspect, the broken voice are 'All for nothing!': for Hecuba, who no longer exists and is irrevocably lost to us. What exists here and now is the actor's feigned passion in this fiction-within-a-fiction.

Why is the play concerned to make us so aware of an actor playing an actor, playing a character who is not among its *dramatis personae*, that we will not be allowed to get to know, has no theatrical status in this play? Our detachment from the Player, and from Hecuba, as a psychologically realised character places us in an unusually objective perspective from which to view the acting process. We see an actor get into his part, and then watch him act. We are being made aware of the technique that is being exploited in the performance, a sense that is reinforced by Polonius' running commentary as critic, and afterwards, when Hamlet analyses the Player's speech. And yet the speech has the power to engage the audience's attention even when we have been so deliberately distanced from the emotions the Player is re-presenting. In a good production we become irritated with Polonius' interruptions, and disappointed when, at the height of his passion, the Player is cut short. Hamlet draws our attention to the discrepancy between the passion and the rhetoric by contemplating, 'What would he do, / Had he the motive and the cue for passion / That I have?' (554–6) and in doing so, closes up the gap between the rhetoric and the emotion, making us realise how effective and affective drama works.

But is it not also monstrous, that this fiction, the play *Hamlet*, compels our belief? is the question the play's audience is being invited to consider. It is a remarkably confident expression of the dramatist's powers that an audience is being encouraged to challenge the integrity of the play it is watching. It is a confidence that comes from knowing that you can tell your audience they are being moved by a fiction in the certain knowledge that they will continue to be absorbed in it once you have told them it is not claiming to be real life. Shakespeare is showing us what Ovid insisted upon throughout the *Metamorphoses*: that it is how you tell the story, not whether it is true, that compels belief. In stressing the fictitious nature of the myths he told, Ovid was telling the reader that his art is not intended to be life-like. The poem is full of interjections drawing attention to the improbability of a situation, conflicting reports on what really happened, the far-fetched metamorphoses straining credulity. In Book XII, which opens with Priam mourning for his son, and which, significantly, in relation to *Hamlet*, precedes 'The Sorrows of Hecuba', Ovid gives the tale of strife between the Lapithae and half-human centaurs to Nestor to tell (XII.210–535). When Nestor reaches the episode of Caeneus' death, he says:

exitus in dubio est: alii sub inania corpus
Tartara detrusum silvarum mole ferebant;
abnuit Ampycides medioque ex aggere fulvis
vidit avem pennis liquidas exire sub auras,
quae mihi tum primum, tunc est conspecta supremum.
                                                    (XII.522–6)

His end is doubtful. Some said that his body was thrust down by the weight of woods to the Tartarean pit; but the son of Ampycus denied this. For from the middle of the pile he saw a bird with golden wings fly up into the limpid air. I saw it too, then for the first time and the last.

The metamorphosis of Caeneus into a bird, like that of so many mythological characters in the poem, is presented as an improbable fiction. After describing the death-into-life transformation, Nestor says: 'credita res auctore suo est' (532) 'This story was believed because of him who told it'. This, of course, is an allusion to the poet himself, to the poem we are reading. Just as Ovid makes his character draw our attention to the impossibility of determining the truth about what really happened to remind us that what is being presented is fiction, in order to make us realise how compellingly he has drawn us into the story, so Shakespeare makes his actor remind us that what we are watching is a play, in order to make us aware that we believe this fiction, not because it is like life, but 'because of him who told it'.

When, in *Twelfth Night*, Fabian says, 'If this were played upon a stage now, I could condemn it is an improbable fiction' (III.iv.128–9), it is not to remind us that life is as theatrical as a play, and/or, to break the illusion that we are watching real life. It is to tell us that this play is . . . a play. John Edmunds' essay, 'Shakespeare breaks the illusion', is an interesting example of a tendency, amongst commentators on 'self-reflexive' moments in Shakespearean drama, to assume that the plays are created from an essentially mimetic impulse, which leads to the further assumption that if the audience is 'lost' in the world of Illyria, it means that we are lost in this world as if it were real life:

What a nerve! This is being played upon a stage. To remind us at the very height of an elaborately contrived situation, when our belief in it is entire, when we are lost in the world of Illyria, to remind us that we are not watching real life but something played upon a stage! Why break the illusion? Does Shakespeare *want* us to condemn the gulling of Malvolio as an 'improbable fiction', to say, 'This is altogether too far-fetched', and reject it? That doesn't happen, and it's not the dramatist's purpose.[23] (Edmunds' emphasis)

Edmunds goes on to say that Fabian's comment 'is exactly what we should say in real life about a succession of events neat enough to serve as a stage plot', so it '*both* makes the play more like real life and reminds us that it is fiction' (Edmunds' emphasis).[24]

The familiar premise that the characters and events on stage are to be taken for real life provides the basis for the theory of 'illusion-shattering'. But if the events and characters we have been watching on the stage have intended to be a presentation of life, if we have meant to be 'lost in the world of Illyria' as if it were real life, why have we been presented with an obviously 'far-fetched' plot, a fairy tale set in an exotic location where the sea sits beside what might, or might not, be an English country manor house? As Peter Thomson, in his study of '*Twelfth Night* and playhouse practice', writes: 'The Elizabethan playwrights were not aiming to cajole the audience into mistaking the play for "real life"'.[25] The Arden editors of the play, commenting on the Malvolio-gulling scene, emphasise its status as fantasy. 'Malvolio is allowed to stalk off . . . nor do we worry about when or how Sir Toby's decision is carried out, for the whole incident is already manifest fantasy . . . There is hardly a moment's respite between one absurdity and the next.'[26] We do not need Fabian to tell us that this is an 'improbable fiction': there is no 'illusion' to be 'broken'. When Puck tells us at the end of *A Midsummer Night's Dream* to think that we have but dreamed all that we have just seen, it is the Ovidian technique of disclaiming access to the truth, only to make the confident assertion that we will believe whatever he tells us. In Book XI of the *Metamorphoses* Ovid describes the metamorphosis of Alcyone into a bird as a 'wonder' (XI.731). When she finds her husband's body, lifeless, in the sea, she embraces him with her new-found wings, and tries to kiss him with her beak: 'senserit hoc Ceyx, an vultum motibus undae/ tollere sit visus, populus dubitabat, at ille / senserat' (XI.739–41) 'Whether Ceyx felt this, or whether he but seemed to lift his face by the motion of the waves, men were in doubt. But he did feel it'. It is the characteristic Ovidian boast that the judgement and interpretation of truth is subject to uncertainty and instability, but what I say, in this fiction, will be believed. Here, and throughout the poem, Ovid demonstrates why mimetic art works *against* credulity. The eye-witnesses to the event, he says, were in doubt as to what really happened: whether Ceyx felt Alcyone's embrace. Ovid, however, assures us that he did feel it. And we believe him. If the moment had been prepared for by attempting a life-like imitation, we would be assured that the eye-witnesses certainly did know that Ceyx felt the embrace. As it is, we are reminded that this is fiction. Because we are lost in the world of Ceyx and Alcyone, we believe what the storyteller tells us.

This, I would argue, is the effect of those moments in Shakespearean drama when a play draws attention to its fictitious status. It is a boast. Self-reflexive devices in Shakespeare are *self-reflexive*. When we are reminded that we are sitting in a theatre and have been, in the words of one contemporary spectator at *Julius Caesar*, 'ravish'd' by events on the stage, it merely reinforces the power of the fiction to coerce our belief – *in the fiction*.[27] The illusion, far from being 'shattered', is given renewed force.[28] It is a boast; not an apology for being 'only' a play, a mere imitation of life. There is nothing 'life-like' about it. It is not supposed to be life. Mistress Quickly's response to the play put on by Falstaff and Hal might be interpreted as a comical, if affectionate, ridiculing of the theatre spectator. She watches an actor getting ready to play the character of a *real* king. Falstaff lowers himself on to the joint-stool that is to be his royal throne, puts a cushion on his head to be the crown, and clasps a stage-prop dagger for his golden sceptre. He calls for a cup of sack to make his 'eyes *look* red, that it *may be thought* I have wept, for I must speak in passion', and proceeds to rant in King Cambyses' vein. Mistress Quickly marvels that this play is just like a *play*: 'O Jesu, this is excellent sport, i'faith . . . O the Father, how he holds his countenance! . . . O Jesu, he doth it as like one of these harlotry players as ever I see!' (*I Henry IV*, II.iv.371–91, my emphasis).

The Hostess' response is neither the spectator's submission to mimetic illusion, where she would exclaim that the actor is just like the king – that is to say, like life – nor is it the position argued in much metadramatic criticism of Shakespeare, that 'life too is a play'. She is comparing this player to other players; this fiction to other fictions. Life is excluded from this world; the real king forgotten. Hal, who points out, like Berowne and the lords watching the 'Nine Worthies', what a poor imitation of life it all looks, scoffs that the stage props will be taken for nothing other than stage props: 'Thy state is taken for a joint-stool, thy golden sceptre for a leaden dagger, and thy precious rich crown for a pitiful bald crown'. But Quickly is delighting in the fiction; in the stool being manifestly not a chair of state, the cushion not a crown, the tears never shed, and eyes made red not from weeping, but from drinking. Her reaction might not be the response of Shakespeare's ideal spectator, but, then, neither is Hal's. The two responses are juxtaposed to show that they are both inadequate. Quickly's attitude towards drama involves the recognition that an awareness of its fictitious status is necessary, but Hal's demand for mimetic verisimilitude reminds us that if the actor does not have the power to compel belief in the fiction, the audience will be too conscious that the actor's 'crown' looks suspiciously like a cushion, and that his bloodshot eyes look as though they're swimming in sack, not tears. When Shakespeare's theatre audience is presented with examples of acting which highlight the fictitiousness of the performance, an affectionate indulgence colours our laughter: Falstaff may be a ham actor, but Hal seems to us more a killjoy of this 'sport', with his solemn appeal for verisimilitude, and his view of drama as an art which must hide deceit does little to win us over to his side. With Falstaff's performance there is no question of our mistaking the fiction for real life; the seeming, which in a more serious example we are shown must be distinguished from true grief: the distinction between fiction and real life which is preoccupying Hamlet when he first appears on stage. Gertrude rebukes Hamlet for continuing to mourn his father. Death, after all, she says, is commonplace. 'Why seems it so particular with thee?' Hamlet pounces on 'seems':

> Seems, madam? Nay, it is, I know not 'seems'.
> 'Tis not alone my inky cloak, good mother,
> Nor customary suits of solemn black,
> Nor windy suspiration of forc'd breath,
> No, nor the fruitful river in the eye,

> Nor the dejected haviour of the visage,
> Together with all forms, moods, shows of grief,
> *That can denote me truly*. These *indeed seem*,
> For they are actions that a man might play;
> But I have that within which passes show,
> These but the trappings and the suits of woe.
>
> (I.ii.75–86, my emphasis)

Hamlet's grief is something that cannot be *represented*. The point could hardly be made more explicit, and it constitutes the very first speech which the Prince utters. In a play whose plot centres on the difficulty of determining, exposing and acting upon the truth, the first time its protagonist comes on stage it is to tell us that truth cannot be represented. This is but the second scene of a play which, at this point, we are aware is about a war between Denmark and Norway, the restless ghost of a king, and a grieving son who clearly hates his new step-father. If this play is not going to deliver a true representation of human grief, what is it going to give us? An actor in the role of Hamlet has just walked on stage, conspicuous amongst the members of the court by his black garb and visibly grieving visage, and is then made to say that his inky cloak, dejected expression and all the moods of grief we have just been witnessing are outward show. These *indeed seem*; 'indeed' meaning in Shakespeare, 'in reality; in truth'. What we are being given, then, in reality, is *seeming*, not the fallaciousness and deceit of mimetic representation which would have us believe it is possible to imitate that which is unrepresentable.

What the speech (and entire play) is unequivocally insisting upon is that truth cannot be represented, and far from registering the playwright's unease with his own art, it is asserting his drama's dissociation from all art which pretends it can. In a general discussion of what she describes as 'Shakespeare's disillusionment with the stage', Anne Barton writes: 'It is the whole conception of the play, of something imitated, reproduced at second hand, which seems to disgust him'.[29] The concept of something imitated is what the plays and poems insist is offensive, and it is precisely this which Shakespearean drama abjures. This view demonstrates the process of logic which inheres in what seems to be a consensual understanding of what Shakespeare intends his drama to be; which is based on the prior assumption that the dramatist sees his art as an essentially mimetic exercise.[30] On this premise, it follows that any suggestion of moral distaste for the deceit and degradation involved in passing off an imitation as if it were real life, is directed towards his own art. For Shakespeare, Barton argues, 'The actor is a man who cheapens life by the act of dramatizing it; the shadows represented on the stage are either corrupt or totally without value, "signifying nothing"', and, equating this attitude with that of John Marston, she quotes from Marston's *Sophonisba*: 'Although a stage-like passion and weake heate / Full of empty wording might suit age, / Know Ile speake strongly truth'.[31] But the character here is purporting to speak the truth, is made to tell the audience that what it is being given is *not* a 'stagelike passion'. Hamlet is made to say the precise opposite: 'What you are being given *is* a staged passion. Truth cannot be represented. All that drama can offer *indeed* is outward show'; and what we are being invited to condemn is any drama which presumes to offer anything other than outward show. How could drama, or any art form, give us anything else? Shakespeare's drama does not pretend to represent truth; all it wants to do, and does, *in reality, in truth*, is seem, and it goes to inordinate lengths to ensure that this seeming is seen to be . . . seeming. We must not mistake it for the mimetic seeming which asks to be taken for reality, and cheapens life by the presumptuous act of imitating it. Such neoclassical verisimilitude, as the Poet of the Sonnets never tires of reiterating, is practised by 'others' who 'would give life and bring a tomb', because in seeking to imitate an inimitable, original presence, they destroy the very life they are purporting to re-present (Sonnet 83.12).

In his study of *Hamlet*, James L. Calderwood argues that 'instances of theatricalization in Denmark serve as Brechtian alienation devices to shatter our illusion of Danish reality and cut the cord of our imaginative life there', and, referring to Hamlet's 'Is it not monstrous . . . ?' soliloquy, writes:

It is not Hamlet we have been watching, the play tells us, but Burbage . . . And as for life in Denmark with its marvelous intensities of feeling, its flashes of eloquence, and its absorbing events? Merely a dream on stage, a fiction, a play. Alas, that it should come to this! Greasepaint and costumes, actors with memorized speeches and tears teased into their eyes. And all for nothing! For Hamlet? What is Hamlet to Burbage, or he to Hamlet, that he should weep for him?[32]

For Calderwood, the recognition that we have been watching, not Hamlet, but Burbage, brings with it a rueful realisation that the absorbing fiction is a mere play. William E. Gruber has argued that Shakespeare's audience had no difficulty in seeing how an actor 'can simultaneously be "in" and "out" of character'. He writes:

Renaissance commentators, when they describe their reactions to histrionic performance, frequently indicate an awareness simultaneously of the character and of the actor's degree of impersonation or metamorphosis. This awareness by no means distances them critically from the performance. Even when they describe empathic responses (what one would nowadays call 'identifications') to a character, Tudor and Stuart theatre-goers – unlike modern audiences – not only tolerate visible contradictions between actor and role, but apparently they consider them to be the affective basis of spectating. [33]

Gruber's insistence on what he calls the 'affective strategy' of the dissonances between actor and character is important, and I would argue that it applies to modern audiences too. When Burbage came on stage to the rapturous applause of his fans, and then began his speech, 'Now is the winter of our discontent . . .', the spectators clearly did not instantly switch from seeing the actor to seeing only Richard Gloucester. When Olivier four hundred years later came on stage to the rapturous (if rather more restrained) applause of his fans, and then began the same speech, did the audience instantly forget Olivier, and see only Richard?

William W. Worthen, commenting on Gruber's essay, writes: 'While the precise terms of this double vision may well be specific to a given theatre and its culture, I would argue that such perceptual "dissonances between actor and character" are essential to the act of theatrical seeing'.[34]

Calderwood's comments on *Hamlet* provide us with yet another example of criticism's assumption that Shakespeare wants his audience to take his fiction for real life. He goes on, 'The large question is, Why should Shakespeare want to *sabotage* the illusion of reality in his play?', then suggests that the answer lies with the Ghost. Adopting Coleridgean terms, he says: 'Our willingness to suspend our disbelief in the Ghost represents more largely our poetic faith in the reality . . . of the tragic affairs of Elsinore'. Hamlet's references to the Ghost in 'the cellarage', and the Ghost's repeated cries from below the stage, he says, 'literally undermine our poetic faith in the Ghost and return us abruptly from Elsinore to the Globe theater'. At a crucial point in the play, 'it seems, Shakespeare erases *the illusion of reality* in Denmark and presents us instead with the material inadequacies of the stage. All that we have seen and accepted up to this point seems suddenly fraudulent' (my emphasis).[35]

Calderwood bases his argument on the premise that the play operates on two planes which are set up in opposition to each other: the mimetic presence, or 'the illusion of reality in Denmark'; and the non-representational theatrical reality, which allows him to speak of the play's reminders of theatrical reality as 'sabotaging' devices which alert us to the fact that we are watching grease-painted actors and make us suddenly reject what before we had accepted. But is this really our experience as we sit watching *Hamlet?* The play is full of theatrical allusions, explicit commentary on drama and acting, contains a play performed by actors, and written by its protagonist. It is generally considered to be the most theatrically self-conscious play in the canon. How, then, can any-thing of what we have seen be described as 'fraudulent'? If this drama is supposed to be delivering an 'illusion of reality' which is repeatedly being undermined or 'sabotaged' when we are con-stantly reminded we are watching a play, where is the time for us to become absorbed in its characters and action? Would anyone argue that audiences have difficulty in getting involved in Hamlet's situation?

What is significant about Calderwood's analysis is that it richly conveys both the compelling power of the fiction, and the affective force of the reminders of theatrical reality. My argument is that the cogency of the fiction is not destroyed, but reinforced, by the strength of the insistence that it is fiction. The two constitute a potent mix, not a disturbing rupture.

When Hamlet views drama from the perspective of real life he is in no doubt that it cannot imitate the grief which a real, particular human being feels. Yet when, as a theoretician, he lectures the practitioners of the art on the purpose of their playing, he adopts the neoclassical principles of mimesis, and tells them it is 'to hold as 'twere the mirror up to nature' and to 'imitate humanity'. His advice on how to act, then, concentrates on techniques which will not alert the audience to the fact that they are 'indeed' seeming. If they saw the air too much with their hands, if they tear a passion to tatters, and 'o'erstep' the 'modesty of nature', the spectators are going to realise that this is not life, but a fiction.

It is a commonplace of *Hamlet* criticism that the Prince's advice to the Players is completely at odds with his creator's practice. Roy Battenhouse has pointed out that Hamlet's theory is tested in the play's orbit to such an extent that the protagonist not only violates his own rules, but forces us to recognise what intolerable drama it would be if he did not violate those rules.[36] Robert Weimann has made the important observation that, 'In *Hamlet*, more than any-where else in Shakespeare, the question of mimesis is central'. On Hamlet's advice to the players, he writes that at its centre is 'the tension (at least as strong as the attempt to achieve some balance) between poetic theory and theatrical practice, between drama as defined by the humanists . . . and theater as practised in the hands of travelling actors'. This seems to be a helpful way of viewing the distinction which Shakespearean drama explores between the two inadequate responses to drama as they are presented by Hal and Mistress Quickly and by the spectators and players of 'The Pageant of the Nine Worthies'. Weimann adds that what is challenged in *Hamlet* is 'the authority of the whole neoclassical theory of representation as a strategy of verisimilitude'. In accordance with this strategy, 'Hamlet would serve purely as a character or role, never as an actor, always as the product of characterization, never as a process of bringing out'.[37] Or, as Costard put it rather more succinctly, in a triumph of meaningful syntax: 'I Pompey am'. The actor playing the Prince of Denmark does not have to resort to so unsubtle a strategy, of course. He is not required to attempt a mimetic illusion, or to indulge in extra-theatrical addresses to his audience. In him, theatrical practice and dramatic theory combine to create a compelling fiction in which the question of mimesis becomes an irrelevance.

CHAPTER 6

'Thy registers and thee I both defy':
history challenged. 'Richard III', 'Henry VIII',
'Henry V' and 'Richard II'

INVENTED HISTORY AND HISTORY INVENTED

Shakespeare's explorations of the ways in which written poetry fails to deliver the immediacy and corporeal presence of primary experience involve an inextricably related questioning of its power to accommodate temporality and change. As we have seen in chapter 3, when Venus' rhetoric disembodies Adonis and turns living flesh and blood into a static literary device, the youth is no longer subject to time, process and change, and so becomes lost to the present: all that had given him life, warmth and sensuous presence and, therefore, the potential for self-renewal, is destroyed by the sterilising effects of poetry's rhetorical 'dyes'.

In Shakespeare's poem, Venus' poetry is shown to be emasculating because it is *derivative*, a parasitic echo of other poets' words, so that Adonis becomes a textual figurative device, itself borrowed from prior literary texts. No longer a unique, original, living human organism, the subject of such poetry becomes as remote and inaccessible as a long-dead character in the past whose only proof of existence depends upon the often belated narrative of historical record.

If written poetry, in seeking to re-present an 'original' presence, succeeds only in making its subject inaccessible and absent, what happens to events and characters that are written into history? Do historical records give us access to what was once a present event, a living person, an original moment in history? How truthful is history's transmission of knowledge? Is the past ever fully recoverable? These are the questions the young Prince Edward insists on

127

asking in a remarkable scene in *Richard III* where the dramatist creates an 'unhistorical' moment (that is to say, one that was nowhere upon historical record) in order to make a truly historical enquiry into history writing's claim to truth. Richard suggests that Edward should stay in the Tower of London until the Prince's coronation. For the audience, who has watched Clarence being murdered in the Tower by Richard's henchmen, and been alerted to Crookback's plan to kill off all who stand between him and the crown, the moment is charged with foreboding. But as soon as we are drawn into a sympathetic concern for the young boy's imminent fate, we find ourselves abruptly distanced from the events of these particular staged historical personages and, made to look back even further in time, to ancient history, are forced to confront the problematic status of history itself: how do we know that a certain event actually did take place? That the scene is able to produce this response whether it is a sixteenth-century audience or a twentieth-century one is, as we shall begin to see, a significant part of its very meaning.

Prince. I do not like the Tower, of any place.
    Did Julius Caesar build that place, my lord?
Buckingham. He did, my gracious lord, begin that place,
    Which since, succeeding ages have re-edified.
Prince. Is it upon record, or else reported
    Successively from age to age, he built it?
Buckingham. Upon record, my gracious lord.
Prince. But say, my lord, it were not register'd,
    Methinks the truth should live from age to age,
    As 'twere retail'd to all posterity,
    Even to the general all-ending day.   (III.i.68–78)

For the young Prince, historical truth must lie not in what is written down, *upon record*, but in what lives from age to age. To find out when – and whether – an event took place it is necessary to know when and in what circumstances the event was recorded. Did someone, in Julius Caesar's time, see the Tower being built, report that event, and was this eye-witness report then handed down generation after generation continuously over a millennium and a half until the present time? Or, if it is 'upon record', how old is the document? Was the event placed upon record then and there, or has it

simply been written down long after the time when it was supposed
to have taken place?

These are the kind of questions which, prompted by the combined influences of humanism, the new Protestantism and an
increased national consciousness, motivated the development of
English historical thought in the sixteenth century and led to new
ways of investigating the past.[1] The short dialogue between Prince
Edward and Buckingham in Shakespeare's play, written at the end
of the century which saw the invention of history in its recognis-
ably modern sense, constitutes a debate in miniature between the
old and new approaches to historical thinking, and a fundamental
issue involved in that debate was the concept of anachronism – a
recognition that events take place in and through time in a historical development that makes the past different from the present.[2]

The confidence with which Buckingham accepts what is written
upon record aligns him with the late medieval chronicle writers
who simply amassed vast quantities of random information from
their many and disparate, often conflicting, sources, without using
the concept of anachronism to localise each source temporally to
discover when and for what reason an event had been recorded. As
F. J. Levy states in *Tudor Historical Thought*, for the late medieval
chronicle writer, all history is present history: he shows no awareness of the essential differences between the present and the past.[3]
The Prince challenges this naïve trust in the belated narrative of
chronicle records by aligning himself with those who are develop-
ing new ways of understanding the past: he is showing the humanist impulse to scrutinise origins.[4] The kind of historical
consciousness revealed by the young Prince's curiosity about the
origins of an ancient building is one that is found in the methods of
humanist source criticism, expounded by Colet, popularised by
Erasmus, and drummed into the heads of sixteenth-century
English grammar school boys: a text had to be located in the specific time and place of its origins so that one could determine what
it had meant then and there. Erasmus' *Antibarbari* presents a debate
on medieval and Renaissance conceptions of history in which one
of the speakers expresses the new attitude to the past when he says
history is made by particular people in specific circumstances, at a
particular moment in time; and his *De duplici copia verborum ac rerum*

comentarii duo, written as a school textbook to encourage the humanist practice of *imitatio*, had an enormous influence on the development of historical consciousness in England because it instilled an awareness of anachronism by making the student recognise for himself that history is a dynamic process of temporality and change. It was certainly read by Shakespeare. In *De ratione studii ac legendi interpretandique auctores* students were instructed to write letters 'by' a person in the remote past, and even if the intention was to learn rhetoric and not history, the result was that the student could not write in an ahistorical vacuum: a sense of history was unavoidable. [5] But, as Thomas M. Greene has demonstrated, it was precisely this new awareness of anachronism which led to an acute anxiety about the impossibility of determining what a text had meant at the time it was written. In a chapter entitled 'Historical solitude' in his excellent study of imitation in Renaissance poetry, *The Light in Troy*, Greene quotes a letter from the architect and scholar Fra Giocondo to Lorenzo de' Medici which provides us with a helpful gloss on the Edward–Buckingham dialogue in Shakespeare's play:

The ancient appearance of the city of Rome, most excellent Lorenzo, is changed to such an extent . . . that we can scarcely understand what we read in the books of the ancients, and often those very scholars who profess themselves to be best informed concerning antiquity, prove to know less than others, since the authors whose writings have transmitted learning to us are so faulty and corrupt ('mendosi et corrupti') that if they themselves were to be reborn through some Varronian palingenesis, they would not recognize themselves. But even if these authors were not corrupt, *they would not sufficiently fill our need unless we could see the things which they saw.* (Greene's emphasis)

This text, says Greene, is characteristic of the humanist despair of repossessing 'the lost concrete specificity' of remote texts in the 'intimate relationship it postulates between the written work and the encompassing civilisation, in the hypothesis of rebirth, here played with only to be denied', and

most significantly, in the awareness revealed at the end of the passage of *inevitable hermeneutic anachronism*. The physical transmission of correct texts is not enough; the final enemy of historical knowledge is not simply the care-lessness of scribes and clerks but *history itself*. Not to have seen the place, not to possess the names, constitute fatal disqualifications for the belated interpreter.[6] (my emphasis)

What Greene describes as the characteristic concerns of the Renaissance anxiety about linguistic contingency that creates the unbridgeable gap between a present and a past culture has far-reaching implications for an examination of Shakespearean drama's treatments of history, and its attempt to accommodate temporality and change, to which the dialogue between Edward and Buckingham bears witness. It is what lies behind the doubts and anxieties in Fra Giocondo's letter, a consciousness of the inaccessibility of the past, that the dialogue is emphasising. Edward's argument for a living transmission of knowledge is asking for more than an extant contemporary text which first recorded the construction of the Tower. Even if the records were correct, they could not restore what historical time has rendered inaccessible.

It is significant that it is an ancient Roman building *re-edified* which the dramatist has chosen to serve as the mainspring for an enquiry into the origins and transmission of historical knowledge: the rebuilding of the Tower at different times in history is equated with the textual edifice of 're-recordings' of its re-edification. If it was begun in the remote past and succeeding ages have re-edified it, what of the surmised original contemporary record or oral report? Have succeeding ages altered that so it, too, is incapable of being fully recovered?

But say that none of this were registered, Edward says, in what seems to be a dismissal of historical record, and with what is almost certainly an implicit ironic allusion to Lydgate, Polydore Vergil, Lambarde, Stow, Grafton and G. Peele, all of whom set down the legend that Julius Caesar had built the Tower, history should 'live' from age to age.[7] Edward is asking of history what it cannot provide. If it were possible to find a contemporary text recording the building of the original Tower, or to establish that a contemporary eye-witness report had been handed down in a precise and accurate repetition successively from that day to this, how can we be sure these 'original transmitters' were telling – or writing – the truth?

This is the question we are being invited to ask as we sit listening to the dialogue between Edward and Buckingham. We hold two temporal perspectives in our minds: Edward cannot transport himself back in time to see what the Roman Britons saw; we cannot – *whether we live in the sixteenth or the twentieth century* – transport ourselves back in time to Edward's England to see what Edward saw. What we are left with is an awareness of temporality itself, and its effects on the transmission of historical knowledge. Instead of being asked to choose between two kinds of transmission – the textual and the oral – we are being made to question the veracity of both written record and oral report. What is the basis of our knowledge about events which took place in the past if we cannot determine the truth of what is happening in the present? Shakespeare's Sonnet 123 provides an illuminating insight into this epistemological dilemma:

> No, time, thou shalt not boast that I do change:
> Thy pyramids built up with newer might
> To me are nothing novel, nothing strange, –
> They are but dressings of a former sight.   4
> Our dates are brief, and therefore we admire
> What thou dost foist upon us that is old,
> And rather make them born to our desire
> Than think that we before have heard them told.   8
> Thy registers and thee I both defy,
> Not wondering at the present nor the past;
> For thy recórds and what we see doth lie,
> Made more or less by thy continual haste.   12
>   This I do vow and this shall ever be: –
>   I will be true despite thy scythe and thee.

Here, knowledge of both the past and the present is seen to be defective. Time and its registers (its historical records, chronicles) both lie. Time past and time present – what has happened and what we see happening now – are both equally deceptive. The point is emphasised by the way in which *pyramids* is made to work. The first quatrain asks us to hold two temporal perspectives in our minds. At the first line we are in the Poet's present, but also in the implied future. Immediately we are transported back in time to antiquity on the word *pyramids* which is residually sustained as we move onwards to the present again: Time's pyramids that *are built up with newer might* which are but *dressings of a former sight*, and we are back in the past again. Or are we? The cumulative effect as we are reading these first four lines is of making us experience a confusion of temporal viewpoints. The pyramids which we first apprehend as monuments of the remote past that were seen by people long ago, are not the buildings of Egyptian antiquity, but contemporary new buildings that we are seeing now in the present. But then the following line tells us that the buildings we see now are not new at all. By the end of line 3, just as we are revising our perception of the pyramids as newly built buildings by a belated realisation that the Poet has said newer and not new, the initial sense of antiquity is reinforced by line 4 where we are told that what we see now are but reworkings, re-erections, refashionings of things that were seen by people in earlier times. Ingram and Redpath gloss line 2 as 'Your vast buildings erected by modern techniques' and line 4 as 're-erections of things we've seen before', which does not allow for the sustained impact of *pyramids* which is still sufficiently strong in the reader's mind to make *a former sight* suggest buildings that were seen by people of former times. This serves to reinforce what the sonnet goes on to assert: that the present and the past are not to be trusted.[8]

Time's historical records deceive because what is past was once the present. If we make everything *born to our desire*, if we believe that everything is a product of our own invention, then people in former times must have done the same: *For thy records and what we see doth lie*. Our experience of the present is deceptive; their experience of their present was deceptive, so that any record or chronicle made by them would be a lie. If what is happening in the present seems to us more important than what happened in the past, the same must be true for people in earlier times: what was happening in their present seemed to them more important than what had happened in the past. Their present, as Cleopatra and so many of Shakespeare's characters are made to tell us, has become our past.[9] Moreover, our present will quickly become the past, and for the same reason, which is, time's *continual haste*.

Where, then, does truth reside? is the question we are asking by the time we reach the sonnet's couplet, and there given the answer: 'I will be true' the Poet says. The truth that I offer is not subject to the distortions wrought by Time's mutability, or to the uncertainty and unreliability of judgement found in his records, but shall live forever. When Shakespeare challenges history's claim to truth, it is not to make the simple distinction between fiction and history which his contemporaries put forward as an argument: that drama is a form of poetry and, as such, does not have to concern itself with what actually happened, as history does. Marston, in his address to the general Reader in *Sophonisba* (1606), wrote: 'I have not laboured to tie myself to relate anything as an historian, but to enlarge everything as a poet'. Dekker, in his address To the Reader in *The Whore of Babylon* (1607), said that the historian and the poet did 'not live under one law', and that he had written as a poet, not as a historian which is why he is justified in not attending to historical truth. Chapman, in the Dedication in *The Revenge of Bussy D'Ambois* (1613), scoffs at 'those poor envious souls who cavil at truth's want in their natural fictions', and that 'such authentical truth of either person or action is . . . not to be looked for in a poet, whose subject is not the truth but things like the truth'. Sidney denigrates the historian for 'authorizing himself (for the most part) upon other histories, whose greatest authorities are built upon the notable foundation of hearsay . . .' and because he 'must tell events whereof he can yield no cause; or if he do, it must be poetically', that is to say, in Sidney's usage, fictionally.[10] Sidney, then, defends the charge against poetry that it does not tell the truth, by making the same charge against history. Shakespeare starts off from the premise that history lies to lead him to a more complex consideration of the issue: what makes it impossible for history to tell us what actually happened? If it is established that the re-presentation of historical events is, by definition, an impossibility, requiring as it would a denial of history itself, then the mode of transmission which is based on the recognition that an original moment in history can never be fully restored to us is properly historical. A transparent fiction whose very workings are dependent upon temporality and change, operating within human history and through time, can thus be made to become part of history itself. History, as a record of events, on the other hand, can be charged with lying when it claims to tell the truth.

In Shakespeare, the Renaissance concept of anachronism can

be seen to have the effect of instilling an acute awareness that his present will become our past, and this is of fundamental importance to our understanding, not only of his treatments of history, but of the process by which he redefined drama itself. Triumph over the fact of continuous mutability must, by necessity, and paradoxically, lie in a resolute refusal to attempt a renaissance into the present of the past, an endeavour which becomes so obsessive a concern during the period. While Renaissance writers and historians are seeking to repossess the meaning of remote texts, to ascertain the physical geography of past cultures, to determine the truth of historical events, only to be confronted with the recognition of the impossibility of their task, Shakespeare writes plays about people in his remote and recent past to tell his audience that it is not possible to know the truth about them. While historians ponder such questions as, 'What was the precise configuration of Roman Italy?', and search records to ascertain what ancient coinage looked like, Shakespeare places a clock in a play about a Roman emperor who lived more than thirteen centuries before mechanical time-pieces were invented.[11]

Shakespeare's recognition of the relativity of human history means that for him, any attempt to conquer time, the very medium of process and change, is neither possible nor desirable, because such activity is a denial of history itself. Instead of trying to conquer the 'final enemy' of historical knowledge, which is 'history itself', the dramatist seeks to exploit the temporal and cultural gap between past and present, present and future, by means of a self-proclaimed fiction which openly acknowledges, indeed boasts, that it cannot repossess the past.

Of course, the alternative title for his late play, *King Henry VIII* , considered by the Oxford Shakespeare editors to be the title 'known to its first audiences', is *All Is True*, which would seem to be boasting the opposite.[12] But what the play itself repeatedly offers us is a demonstration of the relativity of judgement in the interpretation of characters and events, which casts a retrospectively ironic light on the Prologue's insistence on the truth of what the audience is about to see. We are first told that 'Such as give / Their money out of hope they may believe, / May here find truth too', and then, in the opening scenes, are shown how the narra-

tive of history gets written with second-hand knowledge and sub-
jective interpretation; indeed, throughout the rest of the play, the
audience is given many reports of what happened: we rarely see
events for ourselves.[13] At times, we are made to know, as we are
when watching Webster's plays, what it is to be the deceived spectators of the workings of the state, who are given only the official
version of events, only to be shown what really happens behind
the scenes. Our sense of the instability and uncertainty of interpretation emerges in that discrepancy. In the early part of the
play, we learn that Buckingham was not present at The Field of
the Cloth of Gold which Norfolk describes as a magnificent spectacle, but as soon as it becomes known that it was Wolsey who
guided the ceremonies, Buckingham declares the event 'fierce
vanities', and the Cardinal himself 'corrupt and treasonous'.
Moments later, Buckingham is arrested for high treason
(I.i.54,156), and in the scene which follows we see how treason is a
matter, not of what someone does, but of how an individual's
actions are interpreted. The Surveyor *narrates* Buckingham's trea-
sonable behaviour, and his narration is interrupted at one point
by Katherine's suggestion that his report may be based on
nothing more than a malicious slur on a noble person. The
Surveyor replies: 'On my soul, I'll speak but truth', and he goes
on with a direct quote as proof of Buckingham's guilt. Henry is
so quick to believe, he at once concludes: 'By day and night, /
He's traitor to th'height!' (I.ii.177, 213–14).

Wolsey, who is presented as a man who casually distorts the
truth, denies that he has been imposing unpopular taxes in Henry's
name, claiming that it is others who have been guilty of traducing
his actions: 'ignorant tongues, which neither know / My faculties
nor person, yet will be / The chronicles of my doing' (I.ii.72–4).
Judgement and interpretation of truth, he insists, are dependent on
subjectivity and relativity:

> What we oft do best,
> By sick interpreters (once weak ones) is
> Not ours or not allow'd; what worst, as oft
> Hitting a grosser quality, is cried up
> For our best act.   (I.ii.81–5)

Wolsey's actions, after delivering this speech, ironically reverse the process he has described, when he gives orders to the Surveyor to proclaim that he, not Henry, has rescinded the unpopular tax. The effect here, and elsewhere in the play, is unsettling. The audience is being invited to question its trust in what is represented as truth by a character whose operations of power are based on deceit and subterfuge: the 'trick of state' (II.i.44). Such moments in the play reinforce our sense that the alternative title *All Is True* can only be ironic.[14]

When we talk of the 'historical sources' for Shakespeare's plays, we need to define our use of the term 'historical'. Edward Hall, who printed Sir Thomas More's *The History of King Richard III* in its entirety in his large-scale chronicle which was to become the principal source for Shakespeare's *Richard III*, invented great chunks of dialogue for the personages of his 'historical' narrative to speak. One historian has pointed out that the introduction of invented speeches 'into what purports to be a historical narrative adds a fictitious element'.[15] Attention to factual veracity, objective judgement, recognition of the relativity of truth, a questioning of motive or of moral justice were deemed irrelevant to Hall's one, overriding concern. If the glorification and enduring fame of the House of Tudor required a distortion of the truth, the invention of dramatic, vivid speeches, an omission of certain facts, – then so be it.[16] This, we have to remind ourselves, is the chronicle which Shakespearean criticism describes as factual historical material. And it is 'history' which is itself based on a text which proliferates with explicit declarations that its material is based on conjecture and hearsay. If Thomas More, writing only a single generation away from the events he described in his *History of King Richard III*, and with the benefit of hearing accounts of what happened from contemporary witnesses, keeps pointing out that he has been given differing or conflicting reports of events, how do we ascertain the truth about the recent past, let alone something that happened over a thousand years ago?[17] Raphael Holinshed's *Chronicles of England, Scotlande and Irelande* included old legends and a rag-bag of disparate accounts of past events – the British *and* Roman histories, for example, which were in complete contradiction. Holinshed, along with Hall, provided Shakespeare with his principal sources for the history plays, and it really does need to be emphasised that when critics talk of the dramatist 'departing' from Hall, or 'inventing factual details not found in Holinshed', of making 'omissions' or 'additions' to 'historical facts', the true nature of Shakespeare's sources is being disguised. Fact and fiction, truth and error, and, more often than not, legend, hearsay, belated report, this is the stuff of sixteenth-century 'history' books, set down over and over again. Thus, Thomas More's *King Richard III* is printed in Holinshed, which had previously been reprinted in Hardyng, Grafton, Hall and Stow. Conjecture and innuendo had travelled far.[18] Despite the political bias in Hall's *Chronicle* being the subject of half a century's critical debate on Shakespeare's use of it in his history plays, we still find it being referred to as 'factual historical material'.[19] May McKisack (a historian and not a literary critic) makes a valuable contribution to our understanding of Shakespeare's history plays by demonstrating how Hall took great liberties with *his* sources, 'inventing at will the lengthy speeches which he puts into the mouths of his characters', so that introducing them into material that is presented as a historical narrative '*has tended to increase the confusion of readers unfamiliar with the sources on which Hall drew*' (my emphasis).[20]

   John Hayward's *The first Part of the life and raigne of King Henrie IIII*, published in 1599, is a notorious example of a historian tampering with dates. In the matter of benevolences, the forced loans or contributions exacted by English kings from their nobility and subjects, Hayward decided to transfer the event from the reign of Richard III to that of Richard II (which provided Bolingbroke with further justification for his actions). The question of benevolences was brought up in Hayward's trial as evidence that the author intended that his readers would understand that it was Elizabeth's reign and not Richard II's being described. One editor's gloss on the reference to benevolences at II.i.250 of *Richard II* cites Holinshed's mention of them in the reigns of Edward IV and Henry VII to conclude that 'Shakespeare was therefore guilty of anachronism'.[21]

   The Mirror for Magistrates was 'The History Lesson' conducted in public for the Elizabethan age, and what appears to us to be little more than a cosy, armchair chat about the recent history of its readers, recorded in poor verse, and with scant regard for the verification of sources, was an impressively serious tome to the Elizabethans. It was also easy to read. When the authors 'depart' from their chief source, Hall, it is not for the sake of historical accuracy: 'where we seme to swarve from hys reasons and causes of dyvers doynges, there we gather upon conjecture such thinges as seeme most probable, or at the least most convenient for the furderance of purpose'.[22] History had been invented over two hundred years before, with Petrarch, but the Elizabethans were clearly happy to have their 'history' invented.

THE TRIUMPH OVER CULTURAL HISTORICITY

Petrarch is credited with the 'discovery' of history because he was the first to express an awareness of anachronism, a recognition that events take place in and through time in a historical development that makes the past different from the present. Peter Burke, in *The Renaissance Sense of the Past*, has described the medieval attitude to the past as one of 'historical innocence'. At that time, the ruins of Rome, for example,

> were thought of as 'marvels', *mirabilia*. But they were taken as given. People seem not to have wondered how they got there, when they were built, or why the style of architecture was different from their own. The most they will do is to tell 'just so stories' or explanatory myths about the names of places.[23]

We need to examine Shakespeare's responses to this change in historical consciousness in relation to his history plays and to his theory of drama. Is there a distinction to be made between what he is attempting to do when he makes his players enact events of the past, and, say, Petrarch's desire to resurrect the dead authors of his remote past? Can we describe a Shakespeare history play as the dramatic equivalent of Erasmus' instructions to schoolboys to 'become' the historical personages whose texts they are attempting to imitate? Or is the dramatist's sense of anachronism serving a different purpose? When Petrarch writes his letters to the ancients in the present tense *whose* present tense is he using? His own medieval present, or their remote past? Is he trying to make an imaginative leap back in time, or is he pretending to move the past into the present? Where is the 'now' located, for example, in this letter to Virgil?

It is in this city that I have composed what you now are reading. . . . Constantly I wonder where it was that you rested upon the sloping sward, or that, reclining in moments of fatigue, you pressed with your elbow the grassy turf or upon the marge of a charming spring. Such thoughts as these bring you back before my eyes.[24]

The letter is registering a desire to restore what we might call the 'lost original' of Virgil's corporeal presence, so that he is *praesentem*, 'present'; 'in person'. Petrarch's original Latin is: 'Atque ea praesentem mihi te spectacula reddunt'. What it describes is an act of restoration (*reddunt*, 'restore'). Petrarch wonders where the ancient poet rested his weary body, wants to find the precise spot where he pressed his elbow on the grass, as though expecting to see the few blades of grass flattened where the flesh and bone left an impression. He claims the power to restore the living presence of the dead poet with all the particularity and concrete immediacy of Virgil's antique present. But the imagination which enables Petrarch to locate the presence in a specific place (in this case, Mantua), is also that which reminds him of the impossibility of transporting himself back fourteen centuries to Virgil's time, or, of projecting Virgil fourteen centuries forward to Petrarch's own time. *Where* is the temporal space in which past and present are able to coalesce? is the unspoken question which the letter is seeking to answer. In his opening line, Petrarch seems to be imaginatively placing Virgil *in Virgil's present*, and himself in his own medieval present *simultaneously*. In other words, the letter is attempting the impossible: 'What I am writing now in this city is what you are reading now in this city'. Petrarch knows that such an ideal is unattainable, yet is compelled to go on writing his epistles to the dead.

Here is Thomas Nashe, two centuries later, describing the effect on a London theatre audience of an extraordinary act of resuscitation:

How would it haue ioyed braue Talbot (the terror of the French) to thinke that after he had lyne two hundred yeares in his Tombe, hee should triumphe againe on the Stage, and haue his bones newe embalmed with the teares of ten thousand spectators at least (at seuerall times), who, in the

Tragedian that represents his person, imagine they behold him fresh bleeding . . . there is no immortalitie can be giuen a man on earth like vnto Playes.[25]

Where Petrarch must visit the actual sites frequented by Virgil, and must rely solely on his imaginative capacity to resurrect the flesh-and-blood presence of the ancient poet to 'behold' him in medieval Italy, the spectators of the play Nashe is referring to, believed to be Shakespeare's *Henry VI Part One*, are given the bodily presence of an actor to help them 'behold' Talbot 'fresh bleeding'. But this is precisely what makes Petrarch's resurrection of the dead different from Shakespeare's. The presence of audience and actor in Shakespeare's play cuts through the illusion that we are beholding the actual Lord Talbot bleeding. As Michael Goldman has reminded us: 'The play may rise in Shakespeare's imagination and come home to our own, but it takes place between two sets of bodies, ours, and the actors'.[26]

For Petrarch, the rebirth or reincarnation of Virgil into a living present requires him to superpose presence upon absence, past upon present, in a generative act of the imagination which is attempting to create the illusion that there is no temporal or cultural gap between past and present. When the 'Tragedian' represents the person of Talbot on Shakespeare's stage, the presence which is here being superposed upon absence is not purely an abstract activity of the mind, but the living presence of a human body and voice. 'The body of the actor', Goldman writes, 'works against the abstractness of his art', and the audience relates to figures on the stage 'as characters in a fiction, as real people moving and talking close to us, and *as actors, who are at once both real and ficti- tious, and neither*' (my emphasis).[27] Which is why we have to say that when Lord Talbot bleeds on Shakespeare's stage, it is neither a literal rebirth *nor* a staged re-enactment; that it is both real and fic- titious.

Nashe's much-quoted rave review must be placed within the context of the great humanist endeavour of renaissance or rebirth if its full significance is to be explored. 'The image that propelled the humanist renaissance', Greene writes, 'was the archaeological, necromantic metaphor of *disinterment*, a digging up that was also a resuscitation or a reincarnation or a rebirth'.[28] Nashe's use of the

metaphor in his description of Lord Talbot's disinterment is striking in its emphasis on the dynamic reciprocal process of actor and
audience. He is not insisting that what the audience is seeing is a
literal rebirth or reincarnation of Talbot, but his attempt to convey
the dynamic immediacy of the enactment of his triumph and
death seems to want to suggest that the theatrical performance is
something other than a metaphorical re-presentation of historical
personages and events. He seems to realise that the presence of
actor and audience means that the exhumation and resurrection of
Talbot's bones becomes, on Shakespeare's stage, something more
than a figure of speech: the bones get up and walk; the blood
makes the audience cry. The physical immediacy of the actor's
flesh 'fresh bleeding' sets in motion an organic process in the bodies
of the spectators: the bones are 'newe embalmed' with the tears
of ten thousand spectators at least. The audience is, literally,
moved to tears now by the performance of events which took
place two hundred years (in our case, six hundred years) before.
Thomas Heywood, in his *Apology for Actors*, probably written in
1607, echoes Nashe when he writes of the spectator 'wrapt in con-
templation . . . as if the performer were the man personated'.[29]

Most descriptions of theatrical performance in the period
emphasise drama's power to affect the spectator both physically
and emotionally. Even those who watched performances in order
to write virulent attacks on the theatre showed themselves to have
been physically affected – with rage – at the sight of other spectators being transported by what is taking place on the stage.[30]

When we talk of what happens in the theatre when an audience
is moved to tears by what is taking place on the stage, we can say
that what the spectators are responding to is real, and we must also
say that it is fictitious. A history play brings this complexity into
focus because the question of temporality is foregrounded. If an
actor playing a hero in history can make the audience weep or
bring it to its feet in a wave of patriotic fervour, what tense do we
use in describing the event? We can say that the play is staging
events from a remote past now, and that the audience is responding
to a staged re-enactment of past events. We can say that the actor
playing Talbot now, is impersonating a long dead character in
history. Or we can describe it all as a situation in which real people

are responding to real people who are giving a fictional representation of real people who existed in the past.

Is it a question, then, of an Erasmian exercise of the imagination in which the actor 'becomes' the historical character he is playing, and Talbot's world has been made to become our contemporary world? None of this explains the effect of the dramatic enactment of past events on Shakespeare's stage. If we say that the audience is being encouraged to believe that the actor 'is' the historical personage he represents, we are attributing to Shakespeare a method in which history itself is ignored because what would be aimed for then is a denial of temporality and change. What we find is the opposite: a deliberate accommodation of the passage of time, an insistence upon it. If we maintain that time is made to 'stand still', trapped in an ahistorical vacuum, on Shakespeare's stage, or that we enter the world of his plays leaving our 'present' outside the theatre, how do we explain the dramatist's frequent habit of reminding his audience of the great gap of time that has elapsed between its present and the past that is being created for them?

If, for the duration of a performance of *Julius Caesar*, we are supposed to 'be' in ancient Rome, or conversely, the ancient Romans are supposed to 'be' in our world, with no sense that historical time has intervened between us and them, why are we suddenly made to confront the historical fact that their present has become our past?

Casca.   How many ages hence
    Shall this our lofty scene be acted over,
    In states unborn, and accents yet unknown!
Brutus. How many times shall Caesar bleed in sport,
    That now on Pompey's basis lies along,
    No worthier than the dust!
Casca.   So oft as that shall be,
    So often shall the knot of us be call'd
    The men that gave their country liberty.
                    (*Julius Caesar*, III.i.111–18)

Shakespeare's supreme sense of anachronism here is matched only by the triumphant confidence in the immortality of his play, which is depicted as an event that will be repeated throughout future ages. When the conspirators prophesy their future reputations they see themselves, not being read about in books, but played by actors, their actions dramatised in scenes, not once, but over and over again, and the characteristic Shakespearean implication is that the play we are now watching replaces all previous versions of the events it enacts.

Thus, Henry V tells his troops that 'Crispin Crispian shall ne'er go by, / From this day to the ending of the world / But we in it shall be remembered . . .' (*Henry V*, IV.iii.57–9), and thereby prophesies the enduring fame of *Shakespeare's* depiction of the battle of Agincourt. Cleopatra talks of the squeaking actor who will boy her greatness, and the actor who will play Antony coming on stage drunk, to remind us that it is the play we have just seen, not the 'original' Alexandrian revels, that will be repeated in the future (*Antony and Cleopatra*, V.ii.215–20).

This effect is achieved, paradoxically, by the dramatist's insistence on our being made aware of the time-span which separates us from the characters and events that are being enacted on the stage. This is not, as some critics assert, a question of the actor 'becoming' a historical personage or their actions pretending to be the actual events of history. The assumption often inherent in this view is that Shakespearean drama is intent on overcoming the 'limitations' of staging history. Herbert Lindenberger, for example, argues that: 'The representation of "real" situations, despite the power it can exert, in one sense, is also a limiting factor on the effects which a dramatist can achieve'; that 'the true reality is one which the representation can at best point to but never fully embody', and concludes that in a 'fictive action . . . an actor, instead of being "only" an actor is much more likely to "become" the personage whom he claims to represent'. The assumption in much criticism is that the dramatist, recognising that his representation can 'never fully embody' the 'true reality', has had to resort to fiction. That way, the audience can be seduced into believing in the reality that is being enacted on stage, and is more likely to perceive the actor as 'being' the historical personage he is playing.[31] But why do we make this assumption? The evidence to be found within the plays themselves suggests that Shakespeare is not attempting to 'fully embody' the 'true reality', nor even to 'point to' it. Why does the Chorus in *Henry V* keep reminding us throughout the play that we are seeing actors on a stage, not the real kings and kingdoms of

England and France? Why does he tell us that we are sitting in the cock-pit watching not real horses in battle, hearing not real cannon-fire, not real cocks crowing at the dawn of battle?

The Chorus may say he wishes for a muse of fire to provide the real princes for us to see, the real English helmets that frightened the French at Agincourt, in the real 'vasty fields of France', and may ostensibly apologise for having to 'cram' all this within the 'girdles' of 'this wooden O', 'on this unworthy scaffold', but if the dramatist intended to deceive us into believing that we are privileged eye-witnesses to the battle of Agincourt, why does he distance us from the characters and events in this way? He makes an actor tell us that it is actors who are 'the ciphers of this great accompt' (Chorus I, 1–32). It is an actor who exhorts us to 'suppose' we have seen Henry embark for Harfleur (Chorus III, 1–35); who asks us to '*Now* entertain *conjecture* of a time / When creeping murmur and the poring dark / Fills the wide vessel of the universe' on the eve of Agincourt (Chorus IV, 1–53, my emphasis). For those of us who have read the previous versions of this history, the Chorus does 'humbly pray' forgiveness that the version we are now receiving is incapable of recapturing the true chronology and real time-scale of events: 'Of time, of numbers, and due course of things, / Which cannot in their huge and proper life / Be here presented' (Chorus V, 1–6).

To reinforce our sense of the inaccessibility of a long-dead character in history, and of the passage of time that has rendered him so, we are given yet another exhortation to use our 'imaginary forces':

> Now we bear the King
> Toward Calais: grant him there; there seen,
> Heave him away upon your winged thoughts
> Athwart the sea. Behold, the English beach
> Pales in the flood with men, with wives, and boys,
> Whose shouts and claps out-voice the deep-mouth'd sea,
> Which, like a mighty whiffler, 'fore the king,
> Seems to prepare his way: so let him land. . .
>
> (Chorus V, 6–13)

The original presence of the actual King at the original moment when he returned triumphant from France is irretrievably lost. The

play's emphasis on the absence and inaccessibility of both character and event is total: the actor who is impersonating Henry V is
not even on the stage!

What is on stage, however, is an actor playing the Chorus of
Shakespeare's play about Henry V, and in addition to his all-
important role of continuously alerting us to the fictitiousness of
what we are seeing, and to an awareness of the temporality and
change which makes all past events irrecoverable, he serves to
demonstrate what can happen to events and characters when
they are written into history. At the opening of Act II, the
Chorus tells us, 'Now all the youth of England are on fire . . .'
swept up in patriotic fervour to fight the French, '. . . and
honour's thought / Reigns solely in the breast of every man . . .'
(Chorus II, 1, 3–4) and, after another apology for the play's disregard of the unity of place, 'Unto Southampton do we shift our
scene' (42, my emphasis). Immediately, Corporal Nim and
Lieutenant Bardolph come on stage to show us that the war with
France is very far from being the sole thought of England's soldiers. Nim and Bardolph are preoccupied with a far more important fight: the quarrel between Nim and Ensign Pistol: the entire
scene is taken up with Nim and Pistol repeatedly unsheathing
and sheathing their swords in a ballet of an endlessly deferred
armed combat.

It can be argued that this scene is an example of the ways in
which Shakespeare gives psychological depth and realism to his
characters, and by such means he is reinforcing the effect of actuality. When we sit and laugh at the spectacle of two soldiers threatening to kill each other over a petty squabble while setting off to war
to fight their country's enemy, we are responding to the dramatist's
power to present characters and events we can believe in. But
which characters and events? The supposed 'original' ones of
history? Those given in the accounts of the Chorus? Or the ones
we are now watching on the stage?

When, at the opening of Act IV, the Chorus describes the silent
'battle' of the night between the two enemy camps on the eve of
Agincourt, such is the power of the poetry spoken by the actor, we
do 'behold' the scene:

> From camp to camp through the foul womb of night
> The hum of either army stilly sounds,
> That the fix'd sentinels almost receive
> The secret whispers of each other's watch:
> Fire answers fire, and through their paly flames
> Each battle sees the other's umber'd face;
> Steed threatens steed, in high and boastful neighs
> Piercing the night's dull ear; and from the tents
> The armourers, accomplishing the knights,
> With busy hammers closing rivets up,
> Give dreadful note of preparation. (Chorus IV, 4–14)

When the Chorus goes on to describe the King's tour of the camp, 'Walking from watch to watch, from tent to tent', to talk to his men as the hour of battle nears, there is no doubt that we are meant to 'see' 'A little touch of Harry in the night'. But which Harry? 'History's' Harry, or Shakespeare's? In fact, this eve-of-battle encounter between Henry and his soldiers is not to be found in Hall or Holinshed or *The Famous Victories of Henry V*, although the gesture of a disguised King meeting his subjects appears in other plays of the period (*Edward I*, *The True Chronicle History of King Leir*, and *The First Part of King Edward IV*, for example). But even if it were possible to establish that Shakespeare was using this theatrical 'tradition', he complicates it. The Chorus describes Henry as meeting his men, not in disguise, but as their King: 'Upon his royal face . . .' (Chorus IV, 35). We then see Henry, at the beginning of the next scene, ask to borrow Erpingham's cloak because 'I and my bosom must debate awhile, / And then I would no other company' (IV.i.31–2). When he does make his tour of the camp, the soldiers' responses to him flatly contradict the account the Chorus has just given us. We have been told that the King had bid his men good morrow 'with a modest smile / And calls them brothers, friends and countrymen'. We have 'seen' Henry bring comfort to every 'pining and pale' wretch, but now, when Henry comes on stage, we see no 'cheerful semblance and sweet majesty', but a despondent king who does nothing to seek out his men. Instead of cheering their King, the soldiers either curse him or do not even talk about him; they call into question the justice of this war, and one of them challenges him to a fight. One editor has pointed out the significant differences between the Folio and Quarto editions of this part of the play. The Quarto, he says, 'has clearly been adapted and debased to make it conform to the very expectations about Henry which previous plays would have aroused'. In the Folio, the soldiers speak first; in the Quarto, Henry approaches the soldiers first.[32]

Which 'version' is the audience invited to believe? The Chorus has asked us to 'Behold . . . A little touch of Harry in the night', then reminds us that the company only has four or five rapiers to represent a battle between two nations:

> And so our scene must to the battle fly;
> Where, O for pity! we shall much disgrace
> With four or five most vile and ragged foils,
> Right ill-dispos'd in brawl ridiculous,
> The name of Agincourt. Yet sit and see;
> Minding true things by what their mock'ries be.
> (Chorus IV ,48–53)

We are then shown the extent to which the Chorus' version of events is a mockery of 'true things', by seeing everything he has said being contradicted in the words and actions on the stage; only *then* are we given the substantiating evidence for our belief in the effect on the soldiers of 'A little touch of Harry in the night', and by this point, the play's repeated reminders that *this* Hal is not the historical Hal reinforces the piquant irony that if its audience has never heard of St Crispin's Day, it will now:

> This day is call'd the feast of Crispian:
> He that outlives this day, and comes safe home,
> Will stand a tip-toe when this day is nam'd,
> And rouse him at the name of Crispian.
> . . .
>   Then shall our names,
> Familiar in his mouth as household words,
> Harry the king, Bedford and Exeter,
> Warwick and Talbot, Salisbury and Gloucester,
> Be in their flowing cups *freshly remember'd*.
> This story shall the good man teach his son;
> And Crispin Crispian shall ne'er go by,
> *From this day to the ending of the world,*
> *But we in it shall be remembered.* (IV.iii.40–59, my emphasis)

The comfort Harry brings to his men is not given when the Chorus said it was, but at the moment of imminent defeat, when all hope is lost. This moment in the play, when Henry foresees the pride and glory of the men who will survive to become war veterans, has been anticipated with meticulous care in the play's structural choral device. It shows how Shakespeare's use of the Chorus in this play is more than a means by which to demonstrate the discrepancy between 'history' and the 'truth' it claims to present. Controversy over which account the audience is meant to believe – the Chorus's narrative, or the staged events – has raged since Samuel Johnson, and continues to do so today.[33]

There are three 'versions' of Henry V in Shakespeare's play. The Chorus gives one; the action which usually immediately follows it, is the second; and the action which follows the second is the dramatist's version. Thus, the Chorus asks us to imagine 'A little touch of Harry in the night', the action which follows shows us that this account is unreliable, and the third is the one we believe, *whether it is true or not.*

Shakespeare may turn to Hall or Holinshed or *The Famous Victories of Henry V* for the sources of his material, but the real 'source' of *Henry V* is to be found in *Henry V*. The dramatist has established the play's origins within the play itself, so that it can be returned to history and achieve an enduring fame. This Henry V is not *the* Henry V which historical time has made inaccessible to us. He cannot be resurrected in history books or on the stage. But if, as the play keeps insisting, the original presence of the King cannot be repossessed, which version of his story has the greater claim to permanence? The one which ignores the historical fact that the past is not the present? Or the version which confronts that fact, and attempts to accommodate the temporality and change which has rendered the past irretrievable, offering not the 'truth' of an event, but an interpretation of history?

The Richard II who gazes with sorrow at his reflected face, smashes the mirror on the ground, and leaves the stage an uncrowned king is not intended to be the actual Richard II who was deposed in 1399. The play of *Richard II* compels our belief in the reality of *Shakespeare's* Richard II. 'A woeful pageant have we here beheld', is the Abbot of Westminster's comment on the scene, reminding us, as the play has done all along, that to the protagonists themselves, the events are a staged spectacle. Then the Bishop of Carlisle adds, 'The woe's to come; the children yet unborn / Shall feel this day as sharp to them as thorn' (IV.i.322–3), and we are alerted to the recognition that their present will be a future generation's past – ours. It is the past of the audience whether in the sixteenth or the twentieth century. The effect, as with every instance in the play which draws attention to its theatricality, is to transform the historical subject matter into a piece of theatre, not in the simple sense that it is a pageant we are watching now, but that it is a pageant for those on stage. It is a critical commonplace that Richard is presented as someone who turns everything he says and does into a theatrical event, that he is poet, director and actor of his actions, dramatising the story of his life as he goes along, utterly absorbed in the stage effects he produces, and that he has been created as such to reinforce our sense of his weakness as a king. 'Richard's fall', writes R. D. Altick, 'is due to his preference for words over deeds'. Hardin Craig describes Richard as one who 'spent his life not living, but playing parts'. Walter Pater says 'He throws himself into the part of the deposed monarch (and) falls gracefully from the world's stage'.[34] Richard's misguided obsession with the spectacle and ceremony of kingship, his slavery to symbols which blinds him to the realities of the operation of power, is set up in opposition to Bolingbroke's political pragmatism and decisive action, slave to neither poetry nor symbol, which blinds him to the 'majesty' of kingship. Bolingbroke, the man of action, is also shown to be someone who stage-manages events; the execution of the King's favourites, for example, and, of course, the deposition scene itself. Richard rewrites the script, proving himself the more potent manipulator of the drama, destroying Bolingbroke's carefully planned stage directions by taking centre stage, but the 'ending' of Bolingbroke's play at least goes according to plan. When Bolingbroke turns the state into a theatre, assigning parts to Richard and Northumberland, it is not a question of the dramatist employing metaphor to convey the sense that all this is *like* a play;[35] all this *is* a play, and it is an *original* performance.

The anthropologist Richard Schechner, in writing about rituals and plays and their relationship to 'virtual' or 'original' events, provides an interesting insight into the way in which the treatment of history originates a new source for our knowledge of past events.

The event to be restored is either forgotten, never was, or is overlaid with other material, so much so that its historicity is irrelevant. What is recalled are earlier performances: history not being what happened but what is encoded and transmitted. Performance is not merely a selection from data arranged and interpreted: it is behaviour itself and carries with it a kernel of originality, making it the subject for further interpretation, *the source of further history*.[36] (my emphasis)

Schechner's essay suggests that performed events are not attempts at exact repetitions of 'original' events, are not concerned with re-enacting what actually happened. The play or ritual arranges and interprets the 'original', but is not a *re*-presentation of it because through performative action it presents itself as an 'original' event, and establishes its own origins, to become 'the source of further history'.

This takes us close to what Shakespearean drama does to history (indeed, to all the previous sources he used in his work). The 'original' which he arranges and interprets are his sources, which he knows, and repeatedly reminds us, do not constitute a true record – 'history not being what happened but what is encoded and transmitted' – and the play is the performative rein-terpretation which alters the 'original' and establishes itself as the new authority on the events which have been previously trans-mitted. Thus, the downfall of King Richard II becomes, on Shakespeare's stage, not a re-enactment of what actually hap-pened, nor a dramatisation of 'historical' sources, but an enact-ment that is altering and replacing earlier authorities. It is not a representation of what actually happened, but is a performance that is taking place now in a process which is historicising prior authorities on what happened.

When, in Act III, Richard returns to England and learns of the loss of his kingdom, he recalls the fates of earlier kings in a scene which has attained the status of a source for *our* knowledge of a his-torical event: 'For God's sake let us sit upon the ground / And tell sad stories of the death of kings' (III.ii.155–6). Richard, who is playing both an actor and a poet here, is also playing a dramatist, who is altering his source, *The Mirror for Magistrates*, whose authors

are depicted as sitting down to hear the sad stories of the ghosts of
dead kings.

> How some have been depos'd, some slain in war,
> Some haunted by the ghosts they have deposed,
> Some poisoned by their wives, some sleeping kill'd.
>
> (*Richard II*, III.ii.157–9)

Richard describes the life of each dead king as a theatrical event,
and is, of course, at the same time describing the dramatic performance which is his own life. This, in turn, reinforces our sense that
we are watching a played enactment that is not purporting to
restore to us any 'original' moment of the actual King Richard's
downfall. This is an original Shakespearean fiction:

> All murthered – for within the hollow crown
> That rounds the mortal temples of a king
> Keeps Death his court, and there the antic sits,
> Scoffing his state and grinning at his pomp,
> Allowing him a breath, *a little scene*,
> *To monarchize*, be fear'd, and kill with looks;
> Infusing him with self and vain conceit,
> As if this flesh which walls about our life
> Were brass impregnable; and, humour'd thus,
> Comes at the last, and with a little pin
> Bores thorough his castle wall, and farewell king!
>
> (160–70, my emphasis)

It is the characteristic Shakespearean technique of cancelling out
the authority of prior texts in order to establish a self-constructed
set of origins: the actual King Richard II has been replaced by
Shakespeare's Richard II, a fiction through which to explore the
realities of kingship and power. And the play which has achieved
this new authority through the mutable medium of language and
the transient spectacle of drama, has become an enduring source
of our understanding of a period in English history which saw the
gradual shift of emphasis from the medieval explanation of history
as divine Providence towards a secular view of history in which
religion was separated from politics.[37]

  In *Julius Caesar*, when the conspirators talk of future ages playing
their 'lofty scene', the dramatist includes a specific proclamation of

the play's triumph over linguistic and cultural mutability. *Because* the story of Julius Caesar has been told as a 'lofty scene', the events it is enacting will not only be repeated in 'ages hence', but will do so in states that have not even been created, and in languages 'yet unknown'.

CHAPTER 7

'Antony and Cleopatra' as 'A Defence of Drama'

DRAMA VERSUS POETRY AND HISTORY

' . . . a most triumphant lady, if report be square to her.'

Enobarbus' description of the time when Cleopatra 'purs'd up (Antony's) heart upon the river of Cydnus' is one of Shakespeare's closest and most sustained source borrowings. He follows every detail of Plutarch's narrative to create for us a Cleopatra that is nowhere to be found in his source.

Her barge in the river of Cydnus, the poope whereof was of gold, the sailes of purple, and the owres of silver, which kept stroke rowing after the sounde of the musicke of flutes . . .'[1]

> The barge she sat in, like a burnish'd throne
> Burn'd on the water: the poop was beaten gold;
> Purple the sails, and so perfumed that
> The winds were love-sick with them; the oars were silver,
> Which to the tune of flutes kept stroke, and made
> The water which they beat to follow faster,
> As amorous of their strokes . . .   (II.ii.191–7)

Shakespeare's Cleopatra is a biological magnet that draws all the elements of nature to her body. Where Plutarch writes, *Her barge*, Shakespeare has, *The barge she sat in*. In the former, the barge is static – it is not doing anything *to* the water. In the latter, it is Cleopatra's *body sitting*, not the barge, that we are aware of, so that there is a suggestion that it 'burn'd on the water' because this body was sitting in it. The motion of the barge in Plutarch is curiously static. The impression is of a clock-work device, a movement that must be made to keep time with the music. In Shakespeare, the water

154

delights in the amorous strokes of the oars. The winds make love to the boat's sails because they are pervaded by the perfumed air that comes from Cleopatra's body.

And now for the person of her selfe: she was layed under a pavillion of cloth of gold of tissue, apparelled and attired like the goddesse Venus, most commonly drawen in picture: and hard by her, on either hand of her, pretie faire boyes apparelled as painters doe set forthe god Cupide, with litle fannes in their hands, with the which they fanned wind upon her . . .[2]

> For her own person,
> It beggar'd all description: she did lie
> In her pavilion – cloth of gold, of tissue –
> O'er-picturing that Venus where we see
> The fancy outwork nature. On each side her,
> Stood pretty dimpled boys, like smiling Cupids,
> With divers-colour'd fans, whose wind did seem
> To glow the delicate cheeks which they did cool,
> And what they undid did.   (II.ii.197–205)

In the historian's narrative there is no mention of mimetic inadequacy, although he directly describes only the pavilion and the little fans in the boys' hands, not Cleopatra herself. All he does is refer us to the many images of Venus. If we want to find out what the subject of this narrative looks like, we will have to go elsewhere.

Shakespeare, too, directs us to artistic representations of Venus, only to tell us that this is *not* what Cleopatra looks like. 'Describe Adonis, and the counterfeit is poorly imitated after you', the Poet says in Sonnet 53. 'But you like none . . .' Cleopatra is like no one else. Describe Venus, and the counterfeit is poorly imitated after her. Cleopatra has only to exist to outwork nature. The blood in her cheeks glows when the air is blown on them, even as the fans are cooling it. What they *did* (cool, take away the glow); *Did* (restored the glow). Cleopatra has power over nature's elements. What nature makes cool, she can cause that same nature to make warm.

Shakespeare continues to closely follow Plutarch in order to show how completely he is replacing history's 'version' of Cleopatra, and why it is necessary to do so. In Plutarch's narrative, Cleopatra is not *there*:

. . .the barge, out of the which there came a wonderfull passing sweete savor of perfumes, that perfumed the wharfes side, pestered with innumerable multitudes of people. Some of them followed the barge all alongest the rivers side: others also ranne out of the citie to see her comming in. So that in thend, there ranne such multitudes of people one after an other to see her, that Antonius was left post alone in the market place, in his Imperiall seate to geve audience: and there went a rumor in the peoples mouthes, that the goddesse *Venus* was come to play with the god *Bacchus*.[3]

Where Plutarch's description makes Cleopatra's bodily presence absent, refuses her the right, even, to be herself, in Shakespeare, the organic process of her corporeal existence and its miraculous effects on nature is all that is described. Plutarch either turns her into a literary device: she is not Cleopatra, but 'the goddess Venus'; or, as we have seen, twice removes her from herself, by saying that she is 'like' an artistic representation of 'the goddess Venus'.

By the time Shakespeare reaches the episode of the multitudes flocking to see what in Plutarch seems to be the barge, our sense that Cleopatra is capable of charming the world into her sensuous presence is so powerful that we have only to be told, 'From the barge / A strange invisible perfume hits the sense / Of the adjacent wharfs' (II.ii.211–13), to believe that this air, which makes wind and water move, will cast its irresistible spell on people, too. Cleopatra can make humans move:

> The city cast
> Her people out upon her; and Antony,
> Enthron'd i' the market-place, did sit alone,
> Whistling to the air; which, but for vacancy,
> Had gone to gaze on Cleopatra too,
> And made a gap in nature.   (II.ii.213–18)

Shakespeare alludes to the maxim that 'nature abhors a vacuum' to make one of his most significant statements about the relationship between the artist and nature. One critic, commenting on this passage, writes: 'According to Enobarbus, she nearly confounds nature itself . . . And if Cleopatra cannot quite make a gap in nature, she can make a gap in time and achieve eternity.'[4] The implicit assumption here is that the ability to make a gap in nature is desirable but unattainable. But the point that is being made in the play is that Cleopatra does not confound nature; does not make 'a gap in nature', because she would not attempt to, nor would her creator want her to. To confound nature would be to go against herself. Cleopatra's power resides in her body which exists as a bio-logical organism in process, in time and change, and is dependent, therefore, on nature itself. There is no Cleopatra without the human body of the actor. Enobarbus' re-presentation of her phys-ical presence compels our belief in her astonishing powers, even though the subject of his poetry is not present before us, and the event it describes is past. It is an example of the ways in which the dramatist demonstrates the superlative heights which narrative poetry can attain. But it is a tease. It does not deliver the real thing. It intensifies our sense that what it describes is lost to us forever. What we will be given to 'replace' this narrative is Shakespeare's Cleopatra 'in the flesh', uttering her triumphant claim to immor-tality. When that moment comes, her body – and the breath that comes from it – will be all she has.[5]

> I saw her once
> Hop forty paces through the public street,
> And having lost her breath, she spoke, and panted,
> That she did make defect perfection,
> And, breathless, power breathe forth. (II.ii.228–32)

The editor of the Arden edition of the play glosses this last line, 'did breathe forth charm', but the dramatist says 'power', and the word possesses a particular significance.[6] Without breath, Cleopatra can not only speak, she can make . . . power *breathe* forth. She restores what is 'lost' and gives it greater strength in the process. She is the antithesis of Octavia who 'Shows a body, rather than a life, / A statue, than a breather' (III.iii.20–1).

Such power, of course, is the dramatist's power to breathe forth power, to 'cut breath', to present an art that lives and moves and breathes through the human bodies of the actors. We cannot prop-erly talk of Cleopatra as a 'figure' for the dramatist, because while being 'Cleopatra-as-Shakespeare', she is also Shakespeare's ideal work of art. In her Orphic power to move all of nature into her presence, she shows us what the dramatist does; but she is also the result of what he does, and this creation herself has power to create, as she will demonstrate in the final act of the play, when she tells Dolabella her dream.

That Enobarbus' description of Cleopatra is a verbal re-presentation of the real thing is explicitly signalled in the carefully structured 'preface' to it:

Maecenas. She's a most triumphant lady, *if report be square to her.*
Enobarbus. When she first met Mark Antony, she purs'd up his heart upon
          the river of Cydnus.
Agrippa. There she appear'd *indeed*; or my reporter devis'd well for her.
Enobarbus. I will *tell* you.
          The barge she sat in. . . (II.ii.184–91, my emphasis)

The Arden editor notes that a predecessor 'very reasonably, "suspects an omission, perhaps of 'triumphantly' or 'in triumph"'.[7] But the purpose and significance of the exchange is best served by leaving *indeed* as it is. We are *told* that Maecenas has been *told* that Cleopatra is a 'most triumphant lady'. Agrippa confidently asserts that she appear'd 'indeed' ('in reality'; 'in truth'), but the statement is undermined by the doubt introduced by 'Or my reporter devis'd ("invented") well for her'. Enobarbus has the advantage of having been an eye-witness to the event. The question the audience is made to ask is: Will his report be invented, too? She cannot appear 'indeed', because it is a past event, and because a verbal description of her cannot present her 'in reality'. Her physical presence at that original moment on Cydnus is lost to us.

Enobarbus is both poet and historian. The first cannot deliver the immediacy and sensuous presence of Cleopatra, however evocative the poetry is of that presence. The second cannot transport us back in time so that we can see for ourselves what he saw, however compellingly he tries to convince us that the past is (the) present. Mutability, time itself, has intervened and made the moment inaccessible. For Shakespeare's audience, the historical Cleopatra can never appear 'indeed'. The meeting at Cydnus between the two famous lovers is an event in history that history itself has made irretrievable. What spectators at the Globe in the seventeenth century, and spectators at the new Globe in the twentieth century, can see is Shakespeare's Cleopatra: there, she appears 'indeed'. In Plutarch's narrative, Cleopatra's physicality is nowhere described; in Enobarbus' report, little other than her physicality is described. What is missing in both – and this is where the very significance of the disparity between them lies – is her actual physical presence. Enobarbus' report, in effect, replaces Plutarch's historical record as the 'source' of our knowledge of an event which took place about a century before Plutarch himself recorded it. It is a 'source' that admits it cannot enable us to see what actually happened. In the words of the Second Gentleman in *The Winter's Tale*, we have 'lost a sight which was to be seen, cannot be spoken of'. History, however, does speak of what cannot now be seen and it claims to tell the truth. That is why we are not shown the meeting at Cydnus in Shakespeare's play. Instead, we are given Enobarbus' words as a 'source' which, in acknowledging its own inadequacy to restore what is 'lost', questions the authority of the prior text, the original source for this description. It cancels out the authority of Plutarch's 'historical' account to establish a new set of origins which exists only within the play, within the dramatist's fiction.

In her 'metatheatrical' reading of the play, Phyllis Rackin notes that the scene Enobarbus describes is 'not physically present', to support a different interpretation. She argues that the details which Shakespeare added to Plutarch, 'instead of making the speech more concrete or dramatic, emphasise that narrative is its necessary medium', and that Shakespeare transformed the 'limitation' of having to rely on poetry and the audience's imagination into an 'asset'. He 'used the technique his stage demanded to demonstrate the unique powers of the very medium that seemed to limit him' . But Enobarbus' speech is a narrative representation, and what it emphasises is not the limitations of drama, but the limitations of poetry. Rackin says the scene is 'evoked by and for the imagination', and, like most critics, assumes that Shakespeare equates poetry with drama. Such a view ascribes to Shakespeare an attitude towards drama that is negative, rather than positive, which sees it as a medium whose 'limitations' must be overcome. This is the underlying assumption of Rackin's statement that the details added to Plutarch 'say, in effect, that the scene, by its very nature, is impossible to stage'.[8] This suggests that the dramatist is telling us that he would have liked to have staged it, but that the 'limitations' of his art have prevented him from doing so. 'The subject cannot be represented, but only created, embodied in the uncategorical and alogical shifts *the poet works with words* '(my emphasis)[9] . But 'the subject' of poetry cannot be 'embodied' in words. This is the limitation of poetry. It dis-embodies its subject – which is what Shakespearean drama strives to show us.

Shakespeare's reworking of his source is drawing attention to the limitations of both history and poetry. He replaces Plutarch's history with Enobarbus' poetry in order to demonstrate how and why his drama does not attempt to close the gap between the present and the past, or to persuade us that his actors 'are' the historical personages whose names they bear. History may claim to tell the truth. Poetry may claim it never lies because it does not affirm, and gives a 'higher' truth. Shakespeare's drama claims only the status of fiction. All it can do, and wants to do, is lie.

Rackin's essay goes on to argue that the effect of the words which describe Cleopatra's barge performing the miracle of burning on water is, 'like Sidney's "golden world" of the poet's making, that Nature herself is outdone', and adds that the phrase 'O'erpicturing Venus' refers 'directly to the transcendent power of the artistic imagination, in terms which closely echo Sidney's as well as North's'.[10] It is true that this is the effect the words are calculated to have on us. It is why Enobarbus is given such magnificent poetry to speak. A 'golden world' is verbally created for our imaginations in a fine example of how Sidney instructed an ideal poetry to be, and we might just as well be reading these words, instead of sitting in a theatre watching an actor on the stage say them out loud for us. This is what Shakespeare used his 'medium' for in this scene. He can put superlative poetry into a play so that we can discover for ourselves how much more appealing the 'brazen world' of drama can be.

CLEOPATRA'S BRAZEN WORLD

Shakespeare's Cleopatra exists in the 'brazen world' of corruption and generation, of mutable process, where slime is fecund, and death breeds life. There is nothing of the prelapsarian perfection of a 'golden world' in Shakespeare's Egypt. It is a perpetual cycle of death and procreation, biological growth and decay, where nature's elements, left untamed, fructify the earth. The sun is 'the fire / That quickens Nilus' slime' (I.iii.68–9), and mud breeds serpents in a continuous state of parturition (II.vii.26–7). Famine or foison depends upon the rhythms of the Nile. Antony describes its flow as part of a sexual process, in which tumescence promises bountiful fertility:

> they take the flow o' the Nile
> By certain scales i' in the pyramid; they know,
> By the height, the lowness, or the mean, if dearth
> Or foison follow. The higher Nilus swells,
> The more it promises: as it ebbs, the seedsman
> Upon the slime and ooze scatters his grain,
> And shortly comes to harvest.   (II.vii.17–23)

To Cleopatra, the end of life is not corporeal death, but her body hoisted up as a victor's trophy to 'the shouting varletry / Of censuring Rome', a fate worse than her flesh putrefying in Nilus' slime:

> Rather a ditch in Egypt
> Be gentle grave unto me, rather on Nilus' mud
> Lay me stark-nak'd, and let the water-flies
> Blow me into abhorring.   (V.ii.57–60)

If her body is to be made into an object of disgust ('abhorring'), she would rather nature, not Rome, make it so. At least if flies deposit their eggs on her ('blow'), her flesh remains part of an organic process of generation, helping life breed life.

Cleopatra is so completely identified with Egypt's source of fertility, the tumescent Nile, ceaselessly overflowing, breeding life which has itself mysterious powers of renewal, that Roman conquest of her Queen is made to seem more than a metaphor for a triumph of martial values, rational logic and measure over the feminine principles of mutable process, fluidity and overflowing generative matter. What Cleopatra fears is not so much Roman rule, as the rules they will use to measure that which by its nature cannot be measured:

> Now, Iras, what think'st thou?
> Thou, an Egyptian puppet shall be shown
> In Rome as well as I: mechanic slaves

> With greasy aprons, rules, and hammers shall
> Uplift us to the view. In their thick breaths,
> Rank of gross diet, shall we be enclouded,
> And forc'd to drink their vapour.   (V.ii.206–12)

Cleopatra's body, like the Nile, an organic substance which 'O'er-flows the measure', is to be put into a straitjacket. The banks of the Nile are to be hammered into unnatural shape by Roman engineers. Nature, untamed, will be made to adhere, as it were, to the Roman calendar, and if fertility is to be made to conform to Octavius' rigid methods of controlling nature's cycle, Cleopatra will have none of this enforced contraception. The diet she would be fed is 'gross', flagrant, will outrage her senses, because the produce of a measured fertilisation of the earth, not the spontaneous, unchecked, action of the sun's heat impregnating moisture.

What Rome threatens, what Cleopatra fears, is sterility. What Cleopatra threatens, what Rome fears, is fecundity. Octavius Caesar is portrayed in this play as a man preternaturally incapable of a single, spontaneous, unpremeditated act, so terrified of losing control, he must 'possess' time, and never submit to it. As the gathering on Pompey's galley 'ripens' towards an 'Alexandrian feast', Octavius fears what all processes of fruition involve: a surrender to time. Antony urges the company to drink up 'Till that the conquering wine hath steep'd our sense / In soft and delicate Lethe'. Octavius cannot be 'a child o' the time', because to be that, he would have to allow time to conquer him. A bacchanalian lulling of the brain would render him oblivious to time, when his entire being is devoted to the pursuit of possessing it (II.vii.94–5; 105–6; 98–9).

This is why sex is a waste of time to Octavius; Antony 'wastes / The lamps of night in revel' (I.iv.4–5) is not simply the expression of understandable censurings of Antony's dereliction of duty, but an indication of its speaker's attitude towards time. Octavius lives by temperance in its precise, literal sense, wanting to regulate all that is subject to time, which means all that is subject to process and change.

OCTAVIUS'S ANTONY

Philo. . . .behold and see
Caesar. This is the news. . .

When Octavius Caesar first appears in *Antony and Cleopatra* it is to
announce; 'From Alexandria / This is the news . . .', and, proceed-
ing to characterise the absent Antony by interpreting an unnamed
correspondent's report written hundreds of miles away, days
(weeks? months?) before, demonstrates what happens when characters and events are turned into the written narrative of history.
Caesar reads from the letter that Antony

> fishes, drinks, and wastes
> The lamps of night in revel; is not more manlike
> Than Cleopatra; nor the queen of Ptolemy
> More womanly than he: hardly gave audience, or
> Vouchsaf'd to think he had partners. . .   (I.iv.4–8)

But we, the audience, know that this is 'yesterday's news'. We have
'been' in Alexandria as eye-witnesses to the events Caesar's spy has
described. We have seen for ourselves what was going on in Egypt
which is now a past event, and has already been superseded by
newer news of which this speaker (more accurately, and significantly, letter-reader) is unaware. In the second scene of the play
Antony responds to the news that Rome's enemies have seized Asia
with the words; 'These strong Egyptian fetters I must break, / Or
lose myself in dotage' (I.ii.113–14); and when news of his wife's
death immediately follows, he tells Enobarbus: 'I must with haste
from hence' (129), and in reply to Enobarbus' protest, repeats: 'I
must be gone' (133). In the longest speech thus far in the play,
Antony describes the imminent threats to Rome's power which
'require, / Our quick remove from hence' (193–4). In the one
hundred and six lines since the messenger brought news of the
occupation of Asia, a single-minded, steadfast purpose has gov-
erned the thoughts of the man who, Philo had told us at the
opening of the play, was a god-like triple pillar of the world emas-
culated at the hands of a lust-crazed whore: to serve his country,
even at the cost of leaving Cleopatra.

In the following scene we watch Antony taking leave of

Cleopatra, and at the moment we are imagining him travelling fast towards Rome, Octavius comes on stage to read a description of Antony languishing in Cleopatra's bed, dissipating his martial energy in nights of passion, oblivious of the pressing demands of affairs of state.

Caesar, who will be consistently identified throughout the play as one who controls time, seems ignorant of the 'great gap of time' (I.v.5) which has elapsed between the writing of the letter he is reading and its reception.[11] He can confidently assert, therefore, that now in Alexandria; 'You shall find there / A man who is the abstract of all faults / That all men follow' (I.iv.8–10), when we know that Antony is not only no longer 'there', is not now filling his 'vacancy with his voluptuousness' (26), but is speeding his way back to Rome, to an Italy which 'Shines o'er with civil swords' (I.iii.44–5), where his honour has called him.

Philo's 'Behold and see' has been turned into the written narrative of history. W. B. Worthen, in a stimulating essay on the play, argues that throughout the play, Octavius Caesar 'relies on narrative . . . to characterize his general', which enables him 'more easily to assimilate Antony's actions to an interpretive text', and the essay goes on to make the important point that 'Caesar's characterisation of Antony consistently privileges the absent "character" of history over the present "character" of performance'.[12]

Caesar's present knowledge of Antony is based on an eye-witness account which is out of date, and therefore no longer valid as a truthful reflection of Antony's character and actions now. But was it, anyway, true then? We, after all, have been eye-witnesses too, and have already been made to experience the relativity and uncertainty which inheres in the judgement and interpretation of events, even when they are happening before our eyes. The first four scenes of the play demonstrate what Sonnet 123 states: it is not only time's records which lie, but also 'what we see':

> Thy registers and thee I both defy,
> Not wondering at the present nor the past;
> For thy recórds and what we see doth lie,
> Made more or less by thy continual haste. (9–12)

The eye-witness who wrote his account of events in Alexandria for Caesar 'saw' what Philo, in the opening lines of the play, prepared the theatre audience to see: a once heroic warrior now a helpless, passive victim of female lust (I.i.2–10).

Antony and Cleopatra now come on stage, and Philo tells Demetrius, but more importantly, the audience, to

> Take but good note, and you shall see in him
> The triple pillar of the world transform'd
> Into a strumpet's fool: behold and see. (I.i.11–13)

Holding in our minds the recollected image of a martial hero and the present state of enfeebling desire which Philo has described, what we actually see is two middle-aged lovers acting like two young lovers, delighting in an innocent, flirtatious game. But Philo's interpretation of their characters and actions has ensured that our judgement of their behaviour is distorted.

What Shakespeare leaves out in the final comment on the scene by Demetrius and Philo is any suggestion that the two Romans are aware that the Egyptian 'strumpet' has shown herself to be on their side. Cleopatra, throughout the scene, has been preoccupied with Antony's responsibilities to Rome, but Demetrius and Philo have seen only Antony's behaviour: the Antony of the 'common liar's' report and of the 'news' report Caesar is reading in the opening of scene iv.

But what of the Antony who has been subject to time, process and change since the writing of the report sent to Caesar? Critics have examined the play's emphasis on the unreliability of judgement, its treatment of flux and change, the distinctions it draws between Egypt and Rome, and the question of Antony's shifting identity.[13] But why are identity and time being presented as indissolubly bound together? Why is there this concern to draw a contrast between the fluid, fructifying world of Egypt where time and identity dissolve and overflow, and the Roman world of temperance and measurement where time is adhered to with obsessive rigidity and must be 'possessed', and identity remains trapped in a permanent stasis? The displacement of identity, as evidenced in Antony, the rapidly changing scenes, the proliferation of messengers delivering news that is too late, all combine to make the audi-

ence experience the dizzying sense of temporal and spatial dislocation of a world in constant motion and metamorphosis. The
implied question the play asks, is: How can the narrative of history
give us access to temporality and change?

In the play's three short opening scenes, we are given two
Antonys: the two identities which Philo had described at the beginning of the play. He has changed, through time, from being the
'plated Mars' on the battlefield, to the 'strumpet's fool', and back
again to the brave general thinking only of war. When Antony
comes to tell Cleopatra he is leaving, her initial protests are quickly
replaced by the words:

> Your honour calls you hence,
> Therefore be deaf to my unpitied folly,
> And all the gods go with you! Upon your sword
> Sit laurel victory, and smooth success
> Be strew'd before your feet!   (I.iii.97–101)

Antony takes his leave of Cleopatra, and *immediately*, Octavius
Caesar comes on stage to read the report from Rome. The effect is
pantomime-like: we know so much more than Caesar does, so that
when he tells us that Antony is filling 'his vacancy with his voluptuousness' in Alexandria, we want to shout:, 'Oh No He's Not!!',
and almost expect Antony to walk on to the stage while Caesar is
still reading the letter.

Caesar's reliance on written report and belated oral report
reflects the crucial and determining factor in his character: he does
not allow for the temporality and change which affect identity and
action. Shakespeare has developed the obsessive concern with the
written word found in the character of Plutarch's Octavius Caesar
into a fundamental part of the play's exploration of the inadequacies of the narrative and textual transmission of knowledge. In his
Life of Augustus Caesar, translated by Thomas North, Plutarch
wrote:

He never spake unto the Senate nor people, nor to his souldiers, but he
had first written and premeditated that he would say unto them, although
he had speech at commaundement, to propound or aunswer to anything
in the field. And because he would not deceive his memory, or lose time in
superfluous speech: he determined ever to write all that he would say: and

he was the first inventer of it. If he had to conferre with any man, or with his wife in any matters of importance: he would put that downe in his writing tables, because he would speake neither more nor lesse.

What strikes the reader here is a fastidious desire to prevent any loss of time and yet the very act of writing down what 'he would say unto them' obviously takes considerably longer than an oral communication. Indeed, the impression which Plutarch seems to want to convey in his descriptions of Augustus, is of a person whose every action is laborious, taking an inordinate length of time:

And he tooke pleasure to pronounce his words with a sweete voyce and good grace, having continually about him for this purpose a fine man to frame his voice. . . . He made many bookes and verses of diverse sorts: but all is dead with time. . . . He delighted to reade good authors, but he gathered nothing other then the sentences teaching good maners: & having written them out word by word, he gave out a copy of them to his familiars: and sent them about to the governours of provinces, and to the magistrates of ROME and of other cities.[14]

The premeditative character of Plutarch's Octavius Caesar is shown to be bound up with a neurotic determination to fit speech and action into carefully measured and allotted time spans. When Shakespeare introduces his Octavius in *Antony and Cleopatra*, he emphasises a logical corollary of the belief that all communication of thought must be written down and not spoken: a naïve trust in the validity and integrity of what is read. Octavius is brought on to the stage reading a letter and the effect of this is to suggest that the textual transmission of knowledge has an in-built propensity to distort the truth: atemporality. *Antony and Cleopatra* shows a highly developed historical sense, repeatedly reminding the audience of the temporality and change which makes the 'truth' of all past events irrecoverable.

When Octavius Caesar comes on stage in *Antony and Cleopatra* to alert the audience to the distortions to the judgement and interpretation of truth that are wrought by time, the meaning is heightened, and indeed brought fully home, because we know that the characters in this play are historical personages centuries-long dead. If Octavius Caesar, living at the same time as Antony, does not know the truth about events that are taking place in his present, how can it ever be possible for us to know what really happened in Roman times, when many centuries separate us from them? This recognition of the temporal and cultural gap between past and present is experienced by every audience in whatever time and whatever place the play is being performed. The effect, as with Prince Edward's sceptical questionings about the origins of the Tower of London in *Richard III*, examined in the previous chapter, is the same whether it is the original audience or today's, and is another example of the ways in which Shakespeare builds into his plays a means of accommodating time and mutability even as he explores and demonstrates the very workings of their distorting effects on 'truth'.

But if Octavius is shown to be lacking in this awareness of temporal change and development so that we are made to acknowledge their effect, can we say that our interpretation of Antony's character and actions is the true one? We are already, at this early moment in the play, made to experience the destabilising effects of Shakespeare's complex manipulations of the disruption of the unities of time and place with which he explores the problem of identity and its two crucial elements: the synchronic (identity at a particular moment), and diachronic (continuity of identity over time). We are discovering for ourselves how impossible it is to identify the 'present', and it is a confusion that is signalled throughout the play every time somebody on stage frantically asks: 'Where is Antony?' The question will bounce back and forth within and between Alexandria and Rome, Rome and Messina, with ever-increasing frequency and urgency to convey a compelling sense of Antony being at once everywhere and nowhere, of his being simultaneously absent and present. This oscillation is made to compound our sense of uncertainty to the point where we are not only asking, Where is Antony? but, Which Antony? In the first few scenes of the play, in what takes minutes, we are shown how time and space disrupt identity and the perception of it.

When Enobarbus announces, in scene ii, the second entrance of Antony, Antony *does not appear*:

Enobarbus. Hush, here comes Antony.
  Enter Cleopatra

Charmian.   Not he, the queen.
Cleopatra. Saw you my lord?
Charmian.   No, lady.
Cleopatra.   Was he not here?
Charmian. No, madam.
Cleopatra. He was dispos'd to mirth; but on the sudden
    A Roman thought hath struck him. Enobarbus!
Enobarbus. Madam.
Cleopatra. Seek him, and bring him hither. Where's Alexas?
Alexas. Here at your service. My lord approaches.
Cleopatra. We will not look upon him: go with us. *(Exeunt)*
    Enter Antony, *with a Messenger.* (I.ii.76–84)

Our first two encounters with Antony and Cleopatra have been
carefully constructed to produce a sense of dislocation in Antony's
identity. When he proclaims his love for Cleopatra he is unequivocally 'in' Alexandria, and refuses to shift his identity 'to' Rome,
even when Cleopatra is repeatedly reminding him that he should
be 'in' Rome, that is to say, thinking of his duty as a Roman leader
and soldier. He tells her that Rome means nothing to him, in the
significant metaphor that suggests the submergence and dissolution of his identity, 'Let Rome in Tiber melt', and his new identity
belongs to Alexandria, 'Here is my space'. After they leave the
stage in pursuit of 'sport', having given the impression of two
inseparable lovers, the next we see and hear of Antony and
Cleopatra is their separation. Enobarbus' 'misrecognition' of
Antony can be taken to be his natural assumption that if Cleopatra
is approaching Antony must be with her. But Cleopatra is alone
and looking for her inseparable lover. They were, she says, supposed to be having fun, 'Antony was dispos'd to mirth', but he has
'left' Alexandria, and is now 'in' Rome: 'A Roman thought hath
struck him'. She asks Enobarbus to seek him out, but as soon as she
realises Antony is coming, she chooses to avoid seeing him, and
leaves. Antony then enters with a messenger from Rome and, as we
have seen, is completely absorbed in Roman thoughts, determined
to leave Alexandria. At this moment, then, Antony, though physically present in Alexandria, is 'in' Rome. Immediately after Antony
tells Enobarbus they are leaving and goes off to prepare his departure, Cleopatra comes on stage and asks: 'Where is he?' Antony
enters and tells her that though his duty calls him home to Rome,

'my full heart / Remains in use with you', and 'I go from hence / Thy soldier, servant, making peace or war / As thou affects' (I.iii.1, 43–4; 69–71).

Where, at this moment in the play, is Antony? And which Antony is speaking? He seems to be both 'in' Alexandria, and 'in' Rome. In the letter, he is trapped in a spurious present. But can we be sure that our knowledge of Antony's present identity and whereabouts is any more accurate than Caesar's? As Octavius reads the letter, it is not true now that Antony is in Alexandria. Or is it? For if we can say that Caesar's construction of Antony's identity, privileging as it does knowledge based on belated report, is no longer valid, because what Antony was doing then is not what he is doing now, we must also acknowledge that in one sense, and this the one the play ultimately demonstrates to be the most important, Antony is still in Alexandria. Antony himself has alerted us to the epistemological problematic inherent in the idea of a central, continuous self.

> Let us go. Come;
> Our separation so abides and flies,
> That thou, residing here, goes yet with me;
> And I, hence fleeting, here remain with thee.
> (I.iii.101–4)

It is a statement of ideal desire in which the vast geographical space between Alexandria and Rome is spanned by a self which can at once go and come, and thereby accommodate the temporal and spatial distance that would otherwise separate the two lovers. The complex and tortuous syntax of the lines suggests that the desire remains as yet an ideal, but though it will not be achieved until the final act when its realisation is expressed in Cleopatra's contrastingly bare 'Husband, I come' (V.ii.286), the moment of its utterance, here in the first act, exerts a powerful effect on the audience's imagination to believe in the possibility of its realisation.

Caesar can, then, paradoxically, address the absent character of his general by means of a report that is out of date because of the space it has had to travel through, since one part of Antony is still in Alexandria, and one part of Cleopatra is with him *en route* to Rome: 'thou, residing here, goes yet with me; / And I, hence fleeting, here remain with thee'. Caesar's apostrophising plea, 'Antony / Leave thy lascivious wassails' (I.iv.55–6), speaks of what is both true and untrue. Though there is one part of Antony's self travelling West at this particular moment, the other part has remained in the East. In his statement simultaneously desiring to go and stay, Antony expresses a longing to centre himself in a 'space' where he is not required to choose between two mutually exclusive identities: Cleopatra's lover, or Rome's soldier. But the statement suggests that Antony knows that any attempt to make his two identities coalesce must address the problem of the 'time of space' and the 'space within time'. In travelling West, Antony's displacement is irretrievably linked to temporality: once he starts off, it will be impossible to repossess this present moment in Alexandria with Cleopatra, because time cannot go backwards. He is trying to establish a central, continuous self that can exist in a continuous present. It is not that he wishes to make time 'stand still' in a spatial vacuum: he wants to travel through space and time to Rome. He wants a cohesion of the synchronic and diachronic elements of identity, so that what he is now he can continue to be over time, not by 'conquering' time or in a 'denial' of it, but by accommodating time.

Our sense of Antony 'being in two places at once' is emphasised again in the first scene of Act II when Varrius arrives at Pompey's house to deliver his 'most certain' news:

> Mark Antony is every hour in Rome
> Expected: since he went from Egypt, 'tis
> A space for farther travel.   (II.i.29–31)

By a subtle, syntactical touch in the line break, we are momentarily imagining Antony in Rome before the word 'Expected' reveals that he is still travelling from Egypt. But this is immediately followed by the puzzling statement that Antony left Egypt so long ago he could have travelled further than Rome by now. This sets up further uncertainty about Antony's present whereabouts all the more forcibly since a moment ago we had been led to believe that he was certainly in Rome. We are reminded, too, of the inextricable relations of time and space in the wording of the message, which reinforce our sense of Antony travelling through time as well as space.

The sense of the passage of time in the word 'since' is combined with the phrase *a space for farther travel* to give space a temporal dimension which suggests the 'time of space' and the 'space within time'.

It is the sense of the temporal dimension of space and the spatial dimension of time that Cleopatra recognises when she wonders how she might 'sleep out this great gap of time / My Antony is away' (I.v.5–6). Time, space and the sense of movement through them are all present when she evokes the absent Antony:

> O Charmian!
> Where think'st thou he is now? Stands he, or sits he?
> Or does he walk? or is he on his horse?
> O happy horse to bear the weight of Antony!
> Do bravely, horse, for wot'st thou whom thou mov'st,
> The demi-Atlas of this earth, the arm
> And burgonet of men. He's speaking now,
> Or murmuring, 'Where's my serpent of old Nile?'
>
> (I.v.18–25)

It is the effect of Orpheus' song whose power resides in its evocation of concrete things. Antony, riding his horse westwards, towards Rome, becomes more fully present to us 'here' in Alexandria, though he is 'really' *there*. Cleopatra can evoke Antony's presence by means of a power that is not dependent on knowledge of what Antony is actually doing or where he really is. Cleopatra does not know. He is the demi-Atlas of the world: Cleopatra says so. And yet she has explicitly declared her account to be based on surmise and conjecture: there is no suggestion of any claim to 'truth'. She invents it all, and in this fiction, Antony achieves the ideal he had expressed on leaving her: he is with her in Alexandria, and she is with him on the way to Rome.

It is the second time the audience has been given a description of the absent Antony's present actions, and there are important differences between Cleopatra's and that of Caesar which, significantly, appears in the scene immediately preceding this one. (Philo's recollections of 'plated Mars' and Caesar's reminiscences of Antony's stoical endurance of hardships in war (I.iv.56–70) are characterisations of the absent Antony's past actions.) Caesar's interpretation, as we have seen, is based on written report, belated and no longer an accurate assessment of his captain's present actions, but there are two things about it which should give it a greater claim to truth than Cleopatra's. Firstly, we have seen for ourselves Antony neglecting his duty to Rome because he wants only to spend his time with Cleopatra; and secondly, there is the confidence of the speaker in the unequivocal truth of his description. Caesar's claim to knowledge of the truth is invalidated, of course, because it is out of date, but we know that it once possessed some approximation to the truth.

What, though, is the basis of our belief in Cleopatra's interpretation of Antony? We have not seen Antony travelling towards Rome (and, given his propensity to 'change' identity, revealed in the first scenes, he may be returning to Egypt for all we know). Moreover, we are given no assurances from this transmitter of knowledge that what she is telling us is the truth, nor even that she herself believes it is the truth. In Octavius' description of Antony, the question of accuracy is paramount in our minds. In Cleopatra's, the question does not even arise. What Antony is actually doing is irrelevant, because Cleopatra's language is an Orphic utterance in that it does not depend on an act of mimesis: she is not concerned with re-presenting Antony in a skilled imitation of him. She has only to imagine the absent Antony and tell us what he is doing now, and we believe her, *whether it is true or not*.

The problematic status of Antony's identity, the uncertainty of judgement and interpretation of his actions which have been foregrounded from the very start of the play, are instantly dissolved by Cleopatra's fictitious creation. When, much later in the play, after the defeat at Actium, Antony speaks of his body as a rack which 'dislimns, and makes it indistinct / As water is in water' (IV.xiv.10–11), we will recognise this as the identity that must be dissolved before a new Antony can be created. We are being prepared for that moment, here, in the first act of the play, when we are made to experience Cleopatra's power to originate her subject.

If we look again at the Orpheus myth, and to what Gerald L. Bruns has described as the primordial poet's power to 'bring the world into being for the first time' and 'maintain it there as the ground of all signification', we can begin to find a way of understanding how Cleopatra's language is made to work on us. Orpheus made all nature move into his presence. His song has power over the world of natural things but is itself part of nature. The ideal identity of word and thing which his song creates is achieved because the subject of his poetry exists in an organic process of time and change, its growth and development not arrested in a stopped momentum by the sterilising effects of written poetry's rhetorical excesses.

We have seen, in chapter 3, the ways in which *Venus and Adonis* demonstrates what happens when a poet's subject is steeped in rhetorical dyes: all that has life, warmth and movement, and is an immediate physical presence becomes trapped in a sterile stasis and dies, irretrievably lost to the present. Cleopatra's poetic activity creates an exact reversal of the process which Venus produces when she touches Adonis' cheek and with her painted rhetoric turns warm, organic flesh and blood into a passive, cold whiteness: 'As apt as new-fall'n snow . . .' (354). Or when the goddess takes the young boy's palm and turns biological movement of sweat coming through the pores of his flesh into a life-less metaphor: 'With this she seizeth on his sweating palm, / The precedent of pith and livelihood, / And . . . calls it balm' (25–7).

Cleopatra, in direct contrast, has the power to create presence where there is absence, and in language that we would not readily describe as 'poetic'. 'Stands he, or sits he? / Or does he walk? or is he on his horse?' So far, not one simile or metaphor or example of any kind of figurative rhetoric. None in the next line, 'O happy horse to bear the weight of Antony!', where a plain utterance is heightened and intensified by the simple, physical act of it being spoken as an exclamation. It is language at its most prosaic describing the most commonplace of human actions. But what it conveys, and conveys most powerfully, is the sense of a human body: the man's solid weight of flesh and bone is what we are aware of. Cleopatra has made this Antony move into her presence by imagining his body, with a three-line utterance of spare, literal and distinctly anti-literary words. Cleopatra's description of Antony is the equivalent of the line which the Poet of the Sonnets insists is the highest form of poetry: 'You alone are you' (Sonnet 84. 2).

It is by this insistence on the uniqueness and individuality of her subject, the 'You alone are you' poetry, that Cleopatra is able to summon her particular Antony into an immediate presence by a few lines of utterly bare words. Instead of describing him in second-hand rhetoric, in which he would have been 'grossly dyed', as the Friend is in the verse of the rival poets, Cleopatra uses language that is completely untainted by the literary devices of other poets; language that is not promiscuously bestowed on many subjects, but on one, and one alone. By doing this, she is able to establish a self-constructed set of origins in her poetry. Because her true plain words have succeeded in summoning the bodily presence of Antony, she can now use a figurative device that is not an imitative construct, but born of an originating poetry which is capable of reinstating the body in all its sensuous and organic power: 'O happy horse to bear the weight of Antony!' is not poetry as mimesis. This is not Sidney's 'speaking picture', an act of 'representing, counterfeiting, figuring forth . . .',[15] because she is not describing her subject as an onlooker. Cleopatra is 'in' the picture. In imagining herself to be in the enviable position of the horse between Antony's legs, she becomes an active participant in her creation, as both the user of language, and the nature that is bringing it into being. These are the workings of myth which, Elizabeth Sewell's study of Orpheus stresses, are as much physical as mental. It involves 'the correlation of perception (the active process of body and mind) with concept. The active participation of the user of language is part of nature itself.'[16] It is an Orphic language, an activity which Albert Hofstadter describes as 'genuinely creative, for in it man's world and self are originated and maintained, not found already finished'.[17]

The world that is 'found already finished' is the skilled imitation of nature that has been made with 'found' images, the rhetorical devices that have been promiscuously used by previous poets on any and every subject indiscriminately. Orphic speech does not represent the world of natural things. It summons the world into presence. This is why it is possible for Cleopatra to make Antony the giant who holds up half the world: 'The demi-Atlas of this earth'

(I.v.23). It is not an exaggeration of the truth, is not hyperbole. The Antony Cleopatra has created is a fiction. We are not being asked to take it as the 'truth'. This Antony is not metaphorically the 'Demi-Atlas', he *is* the Demi-Atlas of this earth, his physicality firmly upheld by the effect of Cleopatra's compelling plain words. Her language is fertile because she is part of nature itself, something which Enobarbus recognises and knows is the reason 'Age cannot wither her'. All of nature makes love to Cleopatra. In his description of her first meeting with Antony, it is she who is making the barge move. Nature, he tells us, surpassed art: 'she did lie / In her pavilion . . . /O'er-picturing that Venus where we see / The fancy outwork nature'. Cleopatra's flesh-and-blood presence surpasses the art which has surpassed nature. Her achievement, then, lies in her power to surpass nature while remaining within nature. This sense of something doubly real is the antithesis of Ovid's *imagine falsi*, the image of a corporeal presence which is false. In the picture of Venus, the body of the goddess is not present, she has been de-corporealised by the artist's skill. *Antony and Cleopatra* shows us why such insubstantial illusions must be avoided, and representations of past events which claim to tell the truth are to be distrusted.

Time is explicitly or allusively identified with biological process and generation in *Antony and Cleopatra*, and it is the indissoluble link between organic process and time that powers the play. It is what makes the contrast between Rome and Egypt absolute and irreconcilable. It is why, throughout the play, there is a structural, thematic and figurative insistence on the fluidity, the constantly shifting, dissolving, dislimning, descandying of all existence; and it is why the question of Antony's metamorphic identity is kept before us from beginning to end.

   If there is one line which discloses the peculiarly Shakespearean impulse behind the play's exploration of mutability and generation, it is the image of time giving birth to news, given to a minor character to say before the battle for the mastery of the world at Actium: 'With news the time's in labour, and throws forth, / Each minute, some' (III.vii.80–1). Time, here, is seen not as an abstraction, but as a biological organism capable of giving birth. What it 'breeds' is 'news', events which happen in and through time, which change in time. People cannot keep pace with what time 'breeds': 'each minute' produces multiple births. There is an implicit allusion here to the fourth scene in the play when Octavius reads the out-of-date 'news' from Alexandria, and shows us how quickly 'history' gets overtaken by time, not allowing for change which always makes the present different from the past. There is also a reminder, here, of the reason there is such a proliferation of Messengers in this play: despite the number and frequency of reports bringing news of what is happening, no one possesses accurate present knowledge of characters or actions at any time in the play. News is obsolete before it even arrives. Octavius sends 'Too slow a messenger' to claim his final victory: time breeds Cleopatra's death, and the conqueror's defeat. Caesar is too late to make 'her life in Rome . . . eternal in our triumph' (V.ii.320; V.i.65–6).

The image of time giving birth to news also alludes to the explicitly physical and erotic reception Cleopatra gives to news: 'Ram thou thy fruitful tidings in mine ears, / That long time have been barren' (II.v.24–5). If time gives birth to news, news itself can cure sterility and perform the function of a generative phallus. A woman who identifies herself with Isis, the Moon, the Mother of the world, knows that time breeds.

Several passages in Plutarch's essay 'Of Isis and Osiris' seem to have provided Shakespeare with richly suggestive material for his development of Cleopatra as the allusive centre of the play's concern with time and generation.[18]

and this is the beginning of the Spring season: and thus they put the power of *Osiris* in the Moone. They say also, that *Isis* (which is no other thing but generation) lieth with him; and so they name the Moone, Mother of the world; saying, that she is a double nature, male and female: female, in that she doth conceive and is replenished by the Sunne: and male, in this regard, that she sendeth forth and sprinkleth in the aire, the seeds and principles of generation.[19]

Plutarch records that Osiris is the Nile, but also 'all vertue and power that produceth moisture and water, taking it to be the materiall cause of generation, and the nature generative of seed'. The Moon has a generative light 'multiplying that sweet and comfortable moisture which is so meet for the generation of living creatures, of trees and plants'. Typhon is the sea, but also the fiery sun

which turns the earth into desert, who destroys the union of insem-
inating moisture (Osiris) and fertile matter (Isis).[20]

Shakespeare develops these apparent ambiguities and contra-
dictory aspects of the myth as a means of creating the complex
ambiguities of Antony's identity. The simplistic equation to be
drawn from the myth is: Cleopatra is Egypt, the Nile, fertile
Mother of the earth. Octavius is Rome, Typhon whose fire
destroys the union between Isis and Osiris. But what seems to have
interested Shakespeare is the repeated identifications of Osiris
with the Nile, and the double role of Typhon as the sea and the
sterilising sun. Plutarch writes that Typhon is the sea 'into which
Nilus falling loseth himselfe . . .' Typhon, in his other role as
drought, conquers Nilus: 'then Typhon, that is to say, drouth, is
said to winne the better, and to burne up all; and so having gotten
the mastery cleane of Nilus, who by reason of his weaknesse and
feeblenesse, is driven in, and forced to retire a contrary way, he
chafeth him, poore and low into the sea'.[21] Antony's decision to
fight the battle for the world at sea is thought by his soldiers to be a
disastrous strategy, and they are proved right. At sea, he 'loses'
himself. Scarus describes his general's fleeing from the fight to
follow Cleopatra: 'I never saw an action of such shame; /
Experience, manhood, honour, ne'er before / Did violate so itself'
(III.x.22–4). Antony himself talks of the land as being 'asham'd to
bear me . . . I am so lated in the world that I / Have lost my way for
ever'. He sees his loss of identity as absolute: 'I have fled myself'
(III.xi.1–4; 7). Antony's shame at his violation of martial duty can
also be seen, in the context of the Osiris–Typhon opposition in
Egyptian mythology, as a bitter realisation that he has forsaken the
place where his generative potency can be fulfilled. Shakespeare
seems to have found particular significance in the idea of
Osiris/Nilus being saved from losing himself in the sea if he is 'protected' by the fructifying earth. Plutarch writes:

By *Osiris*, the Aegyptians meane *Nilus*, which lieth and keepeth company
with Isis, that is to say, the earth: that *Typhon* is the sea, into which *Nilus*
falling loseth himselfe, and is dispatched heere and there, unlesse it be that
portion therof, which the earth receiveth and whereby it is made fertill . . .
The *Nilus* therfore, arising on the left hand, and lost in the sea on the right
hand, is said truly to have his birth and generation in the left side. . .[22]

Enobarbus warns his general: 'Your ships are not well mann'd'; that by sea 'you therein throw away / The absolute soldiership you have by land . . .' (III.vii.34; 41–2).

Antony sees his downfall in terms of a dissolution of his body, rather than in abstract concepts of martial failure: 'The rack dislimns, and makes it indistinct / As water is in water', is echoed, two lines later, in 'here I am Antony, / Yet cannot hold this visible shape . . .' (IV.xiv.10–11, 13–14). Then he tells Mardian 'O, thy vile lady! / She has robb'd me of my sword!' (22–3). This last line is a metaphor for his martial valour, and would seem to confirm that Antony's sense of his own manhood is dependent upon his bravery and prowess on the battlefield. It refers us back to Cleopatra's speech describing the night she drunk Antony to his bed, 'Then put my tires and mantles on him, whilst / I wore his sword Philippan' (II.v.22–3). But perhaps references to Antony's 'sword' have too readily been interpreted as synonymous with his Roman martial strength, itself a symbol of his 'manliness' and sexual potency. When Cleopatra 'robs' him of his sword, it must mean, therefore, an act of sexual emasculation. This is the view which the Romans in the play hold, including, of course, Antony, when he is calling Cleopatra a 'witch', a 'triple-turn'd whore' and 'false soul of Egypt!' (IV.xii.47, 13, 25). But immediately after Antony exclaims 'She has robb'd me of my sword', Mardian brings news of Cleopatra's death, and the very first thing Antony does is to take off his military 'tires and mantles':

> Off, pluck off,
> The seven-fold shield of Ajax cannot keep
> The battery from my heart. O, cleave, my sides!
> Heart, once be stronger than thy continent,
> Crack thy frail case! Apace, Eros, apace!
> No more a soldier: bruised pieces, go,
> You have been nobly borne.   (IV.xiv.37–43)

Antony's sense of shame and dishonour, it turns out, reaches its nadir, becomes insupportable to him, when he compares his own 'baseness' with what he believes is Cleopatra's bravery:

> Since Cleopatra died,
> I have liv'd in such dishonour that the gods

> Detest my baseness. I, that with my sword
> Quarter'd the world, and o'er green Neptune's back
> With ships made cities, condemn myself, to lack
> The courage of a woman, less noble mind
> Than she which by her death our Caesar tells
> 'I am conqueror of myself'.   (IV.xiv.55–62)

His Roman sword with which he 'quarter'd the world', which the Roman code of honour equates with the virility of its wielder, is now seen by him as a thing of weakness. Antony lacks the courage of a woman; yet his martial world holds that courage is 'manly', his sword the symbol of that courage. Caesar had scoffed that Antony 'is not more manlike / Than Cleopatra; nor the queen of Ptolemy / More womanly than he . . .' (I.iv.5–7) but this, as Antony has known all along, but has had such difficulty in accepting, is where his creative fulfilment lies. In our first encounter with the lovers, Antony and Cleopatra give expression to the hermaphroditic union found in the Isis–Osiris myth:

Cleopatra.   Antony
> Will be himself.
Antony.   But stirr'd by Cleopatra. (I.i.42–3)

Antony knows that he can be fully himself only when 'stirr'd' by the fertile, parturient powers of matter; when, like Osiris, his 'power' is put 'in the Moone' who 'sendeth forth and sprinkleth in the aire, the seeds and principles of generation'. The shared line, two halves as a whole, registers this sense of hermaphroditic wholeness right at the beginning of the play. Plutarch records that though Nilus first loses himself in the sea, he then expels and drives back the sea, transforming the physical geography of Egypt:

The island of Pharos, once far from Egypt lying in the sea, is now a very part of Egypt, because the sea which was betweene, gave place unto the river that continually *made new earth* with the mudde that it brought.[23] (my emphasis)

In the opening scene of the play Antony had told the woman he identifies with the worm bred in the mud of the Nile: 'Then must thou needs find out new heaven, new earth'. It is not only time which moves in this play, but place, too. Cleopatra, in her actions,

and in the words which describe her when Antony and Enobarbus
speak of her, is the Isis which Plutarch records:

for her whole power consisteth and is emploied in matter which receiveth
all formes, and becommeth all maner of things, to wit, light, darknesse,
day, night, fire, water, life, death, beginning and end.[24]

'Fie wrangling queen! / Whom every thing becomes', Antony
exclaims just after he has insisted that he will be himself, only if
made complete by Cleopatra. Enobarbus says that 'vilest things /
Become themselves in her, that the holy priests / Bless her, when
she is riggish'. But Cleopatra speaks of Antony in such terms, when
she says 'Be'st thou sad, or merry, / The violence of either thee
becomes, / So does it no man else' (I.i.48–9; II.ii.238–40;
I.v.59–61). When Antony and Cleopatra take to the sea they
cannot exist as a creative whole, 'the mutual pair' which Antony
spoke of when he renounced political power, and told Cleopatra,
'Here is my space' (I.i.37, 34). They have left behind the Nile and
the Earth, and therefore, their mutually fulfilling generative
powers. At sea, Antony is 'robbed' of his sword. The reason
Shakespeare gives for Antony's decision to fight at sea is not
Plutarch's. L. T. Fitz has pointed out, it is not on Cleopatra's insti-
gation, but in response to Caesar's dare (III.vii.27–40).[25] In the
story of Isis and Osiris, Osiris is murdered by his brother Typhon.
His body is dismembered and his phallus is eaten by fish.[26] His wife-
sister, Isis, re-collects the fragmented parts of his body and assem-
bles them into a whole again. But she makes him a new phallus; the
original being irrecoverable. This new phallus is capable of perpetual generation. It is immortal.

But generally throughout wheresoever the image of Osiris is exhibited in
the forme of a man, they purtray him with the naturall member of generation stiffe and straight, prefiguring thereby the generative and nutritive
vertue.[27]

Isis 're-members' her husband's body, but there is no restoration of
the member that had been his power to procreate. The phallus is
not a 'restored' phallus, but a newly created source of sexual
potency. It is an original creation, one which can originate a new
and immortal line of succession.

After Antony's death, Cleopatra talks of a god-like Antony with cosmic powers to shake the universe and hold the world in the curve of his arm. As critics have often noted, this is not the Antony we have seen, nor the Antony whose martial exploits have been recounted for us by Caesar and other Romans in the play. Who, then, is this new Antony? If it is the hyperbolic assertions of a lover who endows the beloved with transcendent virtues he did not actually possess, why do we, along with the lover, believe this dream? Cleopatra herself tells us that what she is about to tell us is a dream. The importance of the dialogue which introduces her speech on Antony cannot be over emphasised.

Dolabella. Most noble empress, you have *heard* of me?
Cleopatra. I cannot tell.
Dolabella.   Assuredly you *know* me.
Cleopatra. No matter, sir, what I have *heard or known:*
    You laugh when boys or women tell their dreams,
    Is't not your trick?
Dolabella.   I understand not, madam.
Cleopatra. I dreamt there was an Emperor Antony.
    O such another sleep, that I might see
    But such another man! (V.ii.71–8, my emphasis)

Cleopatra's 'No matter, sir, what I have heard or known' is often taken to be an inattentive answer by one who is distracted, preoccupied with her own thoughts. But Cleopatra has fully understood the question, and it has prompted her to consider an issue that is infinitely larger than the questioner's purpose. Cleopatra seizes on two words of Dolabella's to deliver one of the most significant lines of the play. Asked if she has heard of Dolabella, she replies 'I cannot tell'. To her statement of sceptical disavowal of knowledge, Dolabella's 'Assuredly you *know* me' provides the antithetical statement of certainty of knowledge. The shared line contains two diametrically opposed epistemological standpoints. Dolabella does not recognise that Cleopatra is here considering the fundamental epistemological dilemma: 'What do we know? How does one justify the basis of one's knowledge?' She is repudiating the truth of all knowledge reported or seen and experienced: both Philo's 'Behold and see', and Octavius' 'This is the news'; but also Enobarbus' beggar'd description, which subsumes these two. It is the statement, quoted several times in this study of Shakespeare's theory of drama, made by the Poet in Sonnet 123 when, apostrophising time, he says: 'Thy registers and thee I both defy, / Not wondering at the present nor the past, / For thy recórds and what we see doth lie'.

Cleopatra mocks those who believe what they have 'heard or known' for mocking those who 'tell their dreams'. Dolabella's answer, 'I understand not . . .', confirms what Cleopatra has just accused him of. He does not understand what she is talking about, being one not given to questioning the stability of the interpretation of truth. If he will not understand, she will show him what she means, and try to teach an unwilling pupil why what he has 'heard or known' does not matter.

Antony is dead now, 'And there is nothing left remarkable / Beneath the visiting moon', Cleopatra had said (IV.xv.67–8). She does not want to try to resurrect him. Instead, she invents a new Antony, not a re-collection of what was 'heard or known' about him, not an attempted corporeal restoration of him, but a new, original creation. A pure fiction. It has the power revealed early in the play when Cleopatra transformed Antony-on-a-horse into a demi-god holding up half the world: the Orphic singing that brings everything into being for the first time. For this is a new Antony she is creating. It is the body Cleopatra sings of, and it is a body which moves and speaks:

Cleopatra. His *face* was as the heavens, and therein stuck
     A sun and moon, which kept their course, and lighted
     The little O, the earth.
Dolabella.   Most sovereign creature, –
Cleopatra. His *legs* bestrid the ocean, his rear'd *arm*
     Crested the world: his *voice* was propertied
     As all the tuned spheres, and that to friends:
     But when he meant to quail, and shake the orb,
     He was as rattling thunder. For his bounty,
     There was no winter in't: an autumn 'twas
     That grew the more by reaping: his *delights*
     Were dolphin-like, they show'd his *back* above
     The element they lived in: in his livery
     Walk'd crowns and crownets: realms and islands were
     As plates dropp'd from his pocket.
                         (V.ii.79–92, my emphasis)

Antony's cosmic properties are grounded in the concrete, physical parts of his body. The first simile moves the concrete into the abstract, 'His face was as the heavens', but only so that we are returned to the concrete with a renewed and striking force: 'and therein stuck' is a stark and startlingly literal abrupt intervention of the simile. *Stuck* hangs suspended at the end of the run-on line in a hiatus, which, in its spoken delivery, seems not brief, but long (it is physically impossible for the tongue to move instantly from the position underneath the teeth required for 'u-c-k', to the gums behind the lower teeth, as the jaw simultaneously drops, for the delivery of 'A'). By the time we reach the second line, it is in Antony's face, and not some vague impression of celestial skies, that 'A sun and moon' are placed. The effect is of a human face encompassing in itself the heavenly universe, and of such immense size that the earth which it lights, is a little O. The movement of these three lines takes us from a comparison of Antony's face to the vast, infinite dimensions of the heavens, to this same face so large it is itself of infinite proportions, and the earth is merely a 'little O' in comparison. Notice how the face is first compared to the heavens, and at the end of the three lines, the earth is compared to the face. It is the Shakespearean technique of making the human body the only valid means of comparison.

The Poet of the Sonnets emphatically refuses to compare his Friend or his Mistress with anything else. In 21, he declares he is not like 'that Muse':

> Who heaven itself for ornament doth use
> And every fair with his fair doth rehearse,
> Making a couplement of proud compare
> With sun and moon, with earth and sea's rich gems,
> With April's first-born flowers, and all things rare
> That heaven's air in this huge rondure hems.   (3–8)

The greatest praise he can give to his love, is to say 'My mistress' eyes are *nothing like* the sun', and proceed to compare everything else to her: 'Coral is far more red than her lips' red; / If snow be white, why then her breasts are dun'. Ingram and Redpath's general note on Sonnet 130 is valuable: 'It is a satirical repudiation of false comparisons current in contemporary poetry ("couplements of proud [but false] compare"). The poet is affirming by implication the physical reality of the woman.'[28]

The Poet vehemently protests that his mistress's cheeks are not like roses, either in appearance or smell. Our post-Swiftian understanding of the word 'reek' has led to a misinterpretation of Shakespeare's use of the word in this sonnet, where it means 'emanated':

> I have seen roses damask'd, red and white,
> But no such roses see I in her cheeks;
> And in some perfumes is there more delight
> Than in the breath that from my mistress reeks:
> I love to hear her speak, yet well I know
> That music hath a far more pleasing sound;
> I grant I never saw a goddess go, –
> My mistress when she walks treads on the ground.
> And yet by heaven I think my love as rare
> As any she belied with false compare.   (5–14)

Though this sonnet would appear to have little in common with Cleopatra's speech on Antony, the subject in both is treated in exactly the same way. The Mistress cannot be compared with anything other than herself. Antony cannot be compared with anything other than himself. To compare Antony with the heavens is to show that they are 'but figures of delight [representations of the Platonic idea of Delight] / Drawn after you, you pattern of all those' (Sonnet 98.11–12). 'His face was as the heavens' works in precisely the same way as the descriptions of the Friend as the pattern of the universe, the original of this world, the source of nature's beauty and its powers of renewal and fecundity: 'Speak of the spring and foison of the year, / The one doth shadow of your beauty show, / The other as your bounty doth appear; / And you in every blessèd shape we know' (Sonnet 53.9–12).

It is not that Antony, in this speech, is made god-like. He is not presented to us as a man who behaves 'like' a god, or who *is* a god. He is Antony. It is *his* face, *his* legs, *his* arm, *his* voice, *his* back, and no one else's. In Sonnet 130, the Poet says he does not need to turn his love into a goddess, to believe she is 'rare'. It is her uniqueness and individuality which makes her extraordinary and precious (rare denoting *individuality* as well as *precious* in the period). He tells us that he has never seen a goddess 'go', but he has seen his mistress, and she 'treads on the ground'. In 'some' perfumes, he says, there are perfumes that smell sweeter than his mistress's breath, implying that her breath is more delightful than *many* perfumes. He loves to hear her voice, even though music has 'a far more pleasing sound'. And he ends with a 'couplement' of *true* 'compare': *others* may be compared to his love, but she cannot be compared with others, for if she is, she shows them to be untrue – any comparison would be a false one.

In Cleopatra's speech, Antony's body encompasses the universe. Some fourteen or so years before, in the poem in which the life-destroying effects of gross painting and false compare of contemporary poetry were mercilessly exposed by an insistence on the incomparable flesh-and-blood existence of the human body, metaphoric displacement was repeatedly cancelled out by means of a language which reinstates the body. 'She kiss'd his brow, his cheek, his chin' (*Venus and Adonis*, 59). When Adonis, who is presented throughout the poem as an 'embryonic' poet struggling to resist the painted rhetoric and false compare of Venus, revives the 'dead' goddess, resuscitation is by means of getting her blood circulating though the vessels of her body again: 'He wrings *her nose*, he strikes *her* on the *cheeks*, / He bends *her fingers*, holds *her pulses* hard, / He chafes *her lips*' (475–7). In this way, 'his *breath breatheth life* in her again' (474, my emphasis).

Adonis is shown here as a figure for the dramatist, trying to breathe new life into 'dead' poetry, with breath that will make its subjects live. The only way that it can be done is through reinstating the body as an organic being. By emphasising, as it were, the nose, the cheeks, the pulses, the lips, the fleshly existence of the body, the subject can be made to do anything. Antony's legs can bestride the ocean, his arm can crest the world, his voice can be the music of the spheres, and he can drop realms and islands as effortlessly as though they were coins in his pocket.

If we believe it, it is not because Antony has been made to 'outdo' nature, by being removed from the quotidian world and delivered to us in a 'golden' one. Or that we have been encouraged to make an imaginative leap back in time to perceive the superhuman exploits of a famous Roman general. This story of Antony, to paraphrase Ovid, is 'believed because of she who told it'.

Cleopatra. Think you there was, or might be such a man
      As this I dreamt of?
Dolabella.   Gentle madam, no.
Cleopatra. You lie up to the hearing of the gods.
      But if there be, or ever were one such,
      It's past the size of dreaming: nature wants stuff
      To vie strange forms with fancy, yet to imagine
      An Antony were nature's piece, 'gainst fancy,
      Condemning shadows quite.   (V.ii.93–100)

Cleopatra reminds us again that this Antony is a fiction. Yet when
Dolabella replies 'No' when she asks him if he thinks there was or
might be 'such a man as this I dreamt of', she says: 'You lie . . .'.
Dolabella's answer is based on the discrepancy between the
Antony he has known, and the Antony of this dream. The Antony
that Dolabella has known is dead now, and Cleopatra refuses to
turn that Antony into a recollected image which would provide
only an abstract, dis-embodied representation of the original. She
has invented a new Antony, an original creation which will replace
what is now lost to the present.

    This is what *Antony and Cleopatra* does to Antony and Cleopatra.
The real Marcus Antonius, Roman triumvir and general, who
lived from c. 82–30 BC, is dead now. *No matter what you have heard or
known* about him. Shakespeare refuses to turn him into an artificial
representation of himself, but invents a new Antony. It is an
Antony who has been conspicuously presented to us as a corporeal
being, bungling his suicide in a mess of flesh and blood, the solid
weight of his body having to be clumsily heaved up several feet of a
towering 'monument' that is most emphatically not the mighty
monument which housed Cleopatra's tomb. It is a body whose
dead weight we see being borne off by the actors playing Cleopatra
and her women, and who are staggering from what Cleopatra has
just told us is a superhuman effort of strength. 'Here's sport indeed!
How heavy weighs my lord! / Our strength is all gone into heavi-
ness, / That makes the weight. Had I great Juno's power, / The
strong-wing'd Mercury should fetch thee up . . .' (IV.xv.32–5). If
this were a 'golden world' being delivered to us, Cleopatra would
have the power of Juno, or would be a metaphoric Juno, and
Antony's corpse would be left safely where it is, not breathing, so

that it would be so 'life-like' we could be deceived into thinking it is dead (!)

This is why the play's denial of mimetic status is a triumphant boast. It is not that its creator cannot re-present Cleopatra sailing in her barge on Cydnus. He has proved he can. He prefers to invent a new Cleopatra. That so much criticism of the play is concerned with exploring the discrepancies between the play's two main presentations of Antony is a measure of the dramatist's success in replacing previous versions of Antony. We try to reconcile the Antony we have seen on the stage with the Antony of Cleopatra's dream, instead of trying to reconcile Shakespeare's Antony with anyone else's. Shakespeare's Antony, which Cleopatra is made to create, can only be compared with Shakespeare's Antony, as it were.

Cleopatra's impassioned protest that Dolabella lies when he says 'No', is also directed at those in the audience who are trying to reconcile the Antony of previous literary and historiographical accounts with the Antony they have just seen on the stage. Just as the dreamt Antony is not meant to 'be' the Antony Dolabella has known, so Shakespeare's Antony is not meant to 'be' the actual historical personage we have heard of, or had knowledge of. Cleopatra's question, 'Think you there was or might be such a man / As this I dreamt of?', is asking for the same response as Puck demands from his audience at the end of *A Midsummer Night's Dream*. She is daring us to call her a liar.

After Cleopatra's vehement insistence that Dolabella lies, her next line, which starts with a conditional, *But if there be*, is a logical progression from that line, not a contradiction of it. Cleopatra is saying, '*If* such an Antony were to exist, he would be mightier than our thinking, greater than anything we could mentally perceive in the abstract activity of ordinary "dreaming"'. The human mind is not big enough to conceive of such an Antony, because this Antony is *past the size of dreaming*. She then tells us why. Nature requires *stuff* to compete with *fancy*. *Stuff* here denotes both 'matter, substance', and 'to fill out or complete': 'Nature needs matter, to be filled out, if it is to rival the insubstantial images of the mind and, by implication, of artifice, in the creation of new forms'. The art versus nature dichotomy is here claimed to be untenable. To create new life, nature needs matter, and so does art. There is an allusion here, to the opening of Ovid's *Metamorphoses*, a work which, as we have seen, is preoccupied with distinctions between that which has corporeal substance, and that which is a bodiless shadow: 'My mind is bent to tell of forms changed into new bodies'.

'Yet to *imagine* / An Antony', Cleopatra continues, 'were nature's piece, 'gainst fancy . . .'. *Imagine* comes at the end of the line as the dramatist's direction to hold it there, and so give the word an emphatic force to suggest that this activity is quite unlike the operations of *fancy*: 'to create a new Antony, would be to provide nature with what it needs to vie with art. Furthermore, such a creation could not only rival the artifice or "fancy" of mimetic art, it would completely negate it. All other so-called "strange" ("new") forms would be shown to be mere substanceless shadows.' 'Nature's piece 'gainst fancy, / Condemning shadows quite' reverses the positions of attack and defence in the struggle between nature and art. 'Nature's piece' begins by having to struggle against art, but ends by making art having to struggle against *it*. It is a triumphant reversal of the artist's strife against nature praised so fulsomely by the Poet, and ironically mocked by his creator in *Timon of Athens*. *Nature's piece* is the substance; *fancy*, the shadows of that substance. Art's forms are *strange*, not in the sense of being 'new', but in that they belong to another, not their own: the substance which is 'nature's piece'. The two meanings for *strange* – 'new' and 'belonging to someone else, not one's own' – have been assigned to their rightful places. The first describes an art that has the power to create new, substantial life; the 'eternity' which 'Julio Romano' lacked. The second is that art which steals from life, copying the original and thereby de-materialising it. In the words of Sonnet 53, millions of strange shadows tend on 'nature's piece':

> What is your substance, whereof are you made,
> That millions of strange shadows on you tend?
> Since every one hath, every one, one shade,
> And you, but one, can every shadow lend:
> Describe Adonis, and the counterfeit
> Is poorly imitated after you.   (Sonnet 53.1–6)

The precise Ovidian sense of *imaginis umbra*, we have noted in this sonnet throughout this study, is making its presence felt in Cleopatra's exposition of her dream. The substance is, like the dreamt Antony, 'condemning shadows quite'. It is 'but one', and yet millions of shadows tend on it. The shadows are bodiless imitations of corporeal matter, and because both bodiless and imitations, are Ovidian, insubstantial shadows; likenesses which are insubstantial.

In *Antony and Cleopatra*, the actor is not subjected to the embarrassment of having to pretend to be effortlessly heaved up ten feet or more by three women in an o'er-wrested seeming. It is why we do not see Cleopatra in her barge sailing up the Cydnus to meet Mark Antony in *Antony and Cleopatra*. For Shakespeare to stage such a scene would be to repudiate all that his art had worked to accomplish. Which has not, however, prevented producers from putting Cleopatra inside a barge 'sailing' on to the stage, a production gimmick whose only merit is that it certainly makes the playwright's point for him.[29] We would be looking at the substanceless artifice, the artificial strife against nature, and not the body on which his art is made. Instead, all we are given is Cleopatra's body, standing on a bare stage: 'I am again for Cydnus' announces the dramatist's triumph over all insubstantial versions of Cleopatra that have gone before, including that of Enobarbus in this play. The body that stands before us is 'nature's piece, 'gainst fancy, / Condemning shadows quite'.

Notes

I INTRODUCTION

1 For an account of the major critical movement treating the plays as literary poems, see S. Viswanathan, *The Shakespeare Play as Poem: A Critical Tradition in Perspective* (Cambridge: Cambridge University Press, 1980).

David P. Young, in the epilogue to his book-length study of *A Midsummer Night's Dream,* has commented that this play demonstrated that Shakespeare was 'quite able to express conventional attitudes at the same time that he was exploring their opposites and transcending them', and that 'If his art set him off from the conventional, it is only natural that he should have been aware of it and that this awareness might to a large extent govern his outlook'. The valuable suggestion remained stated, however, rather than its possible implications explored. *Something of Great Constancy: The Art of 'A Midsummer Night's Dream'* (New Haven and London: Yale University Press, 1966), 180.

2 Ekbert Faas' informative study of Shakespeare's 'craft and creativity' is entitled *Shakespeare's Poetics* (Cambridge: Cambridge University Press, 1986), ix; for the subsequent quotations see, respectively, Alvin B. Kernan, *The Playwright As Magician: Shakespeare's Image of the Poet in the English Public Theater* (New Haven and London: Yale University Press, 1979), 158; Philip Edwards, *Shakespeare and the Confines of Art* (London: Methuen, 1968), 10; Anne Barton, *Shakespeare and the Idea of the Play* (Westport Conn: Greenwood Press, 1977; first published 1962), 165, 192.

3 For a review essay on work published between 1962 and 1979 on 'dramatic reflexivity' see Michael Shapiro, 'Role-playing, reflexivity, and metadrama in recent Shakespearean criticism', *Renaissance Drama,* n.s. 12 (1981), 145–61.

4 For example, Harriet Hawkins examines 'Shakespeare's own fascination with dramatic illusion itself' to argue that 'Prospero's art is frequently analogous to, and occasionally identical with, the art of

191

his creator'. *Likenesses of Truth in Elizabethan and Restoration Drama* (Oxford: Clarendon Press, 1972), 27, 38; while David P. Young emphasises an unproblematic presentation of contrasts: 'Where the mechanicals fail at dramatic illusion, unity and appropriateness, *A Midsummer Night's Dream* succeeds'. Young, *Something of Great Constancy*, 105.

2 SHAKESPEARE AND SIDNEY

1 'Most of Shakespeare's "ideas" . . . are unsystemized and belong to the common thought of his age.' E. C. Pettet, 'Shakespeare's conception of poetry', *Essays and Studies*, n.s. 3 (1950), 46. Although Pettet argues that 'the representation of Shakespeare as a writer totally uninterested in matters theoretical' is questionable (p.29), he goes on to assert that 'Everything in his poetry goes to suggest that it was created . . . by a largely spontaneous and often sub-conscious, process of self-generation . . .'(p.37).
2 H. J. Oliver (ed.), *Timon of Athens,* Arden edition, 3rd edn (London: Methuen, 1977; first published 1962), 6.
3 Faas, *Shakespeare's Poetics*, 75, 76.
4 For Jonson's quotation see *Works*, ed. C. H. Herford, and Percy and Evelyn M. Simpson, 11 vols. (Oxford: Clarendon Press, 1954; first published 1925), I, 133 [Conversations with Drummond].
5 I hyphenate the word 'no-thing' here, and elsewhere, to bring out the resonance it possesses in Elizabethan pronunciation which helps to alert us to its precise meaning of no matter, no material substance, no real thing. It is a necessary irritation because the present study is examining the precise significances of the language the dramatist uses in relation to mimetic representation of real things, particularly corporeal matter.
6 Sir Philip Sidney, *A Defence of Poetry*, ed. J. A. Van Dorsten (Oxford: Oxford University Press, 1966; repr. 1982), 24. All subsequent quotations will be from this edition, and cited 'Sidney'.
7 Sidney, 52.
8 Gerald L. Bruns, *Modern Poetry and the Idea of Language: A Critical and Historical Study* (New Haven and London: Yale University Press, 1974), 1–5.
9 *Ibid.*, 5, 1. *Selected Letters of Gustave Flaubert*, trans. Francis Steegmuller (New York, 1953), 127–8, quoted in Bruns, *ibid.*, 1.
10 Bruns, *Modern Poetry and the Idea of Language*, 1.
11 Albert Hofstadter, *Truth and Art* (New York and London: Columbia University Press, 1965), 38; quoted in Bruns, *Modern Poetry and the Idea of Language*, 206.

12 Elizabeth Sewell, *The Orphic Voice: Poetry and Natural History* (London: Routledge and Kegan Paul, 1960), 59.

13 I draw attention here and elsewhere to the actor's body as Shakespeare's 'instrument' of drama to support the argument that one element of his theory of drama is the primacy of the human body of the actor, but Shakespeare 'performance criticism' is not the concern here.

14 All quotations from Ovid are from the Loeb Classical Library: *Metamorphoses*, trans. Frank H. Justus Miller, rev. G. P. Goold, 2 vols. (Cambridge, Mass.: H. U. P., Vol I, 3rd edn repr. 1984; Vol II, 2nd edn repr. 1984).

15 Bruns, *Modern Poetry and the Idea of Language*, 207.

16 Sidney, 23. A. D. Nuttall, *A New Mimesis: Shakespeare and the Representation of Reality* (London and New York: Methuen, 1983), 190.

17 Walter J. Ong, *The Presence of the Word: Some Prolegomena for Cultural and Religious History* (New Haven and London: Yale University Press, 1967), 111–12, 41.

18 Bruns, *Modern Poetry and the Idea of Language*, 260.

19 Derrida's coinages, *itérabilité* and *dérivé*, seem particularly appropriate terms to describe the processes which Orphic speech is intended to avoid: the drift from an original speaker and signified. Jacques Derrida, *Marges de la philosophie* (Paris: Minuit, 1972), 378, 376.

20 The four plays which Jonson suppressed were: *Hot Anger Soon Cold*, *Robert II, King of Scots*, *Page of Plymouth*, and *Richard Crookback*. The contents of the volume are described in Gerald Eades Bentley, *The Profession of Dramatist in Shakespeare's Time* (Princeton NJ: Princeton University Press, 1971; repr. 1986), 290–1. Bentley comments: 'Never before had plays from the commercial theatres been collected in a single volume, much less published under the aspiring title "Workes"', and that it 'constituted a direct claim to status and permanence unprecedented in the English theatre world and quite foreign to the practices of the attached professional dramatists' (p. 290).

21 *Gargantua and Pantagruel*, trans. Sir Thomas Urquhart and Peter le Motteux 3 vols. (New York: E. P. Dutton & Co., 1934), III, 85.

22 'Jonson and the loathèd stage', in *A Celebration of Ben Jonson*, ed. William Blisset *et al.* (Toronto and Buffalo: Toronto University Press, 1973), 31; repr. in Jonas A. Barish, *The Antitheatrical Prejudice* (Berkeley and Los Angeles: University of California Press, 1981), ch. V. Barish examines in some detail Jonson's desire to make the play move 'formally into the domain of literature', 'Loathèd stage', 34.

23 Much as I would have wished to explore this question, there has been space only to touch on it in the hope of prompting further enquiry.

3 SHAKESPEARE AND OVID

1 See, for example, F. T. Prince, Introduction to *The Poems*, Arden edition (London: Methuen, 1960; repr. 1982), xxvi; and Geoffrey Bullough (ed.), *Narrative and Dramatic Sources of Shakespeare*, 8 vols. (London and New York: Routledge and Kegan Paul, 1957; repr. 1977), I. 161.

2 The Oxford Shakespeare editors suggest that Shakespeare 'probably' wrote it at this time, 'perhaps seeing a need for an alternative career'. *The Complete Works*, ed. Stanley Wells and Gary Taylor (Oxford: Clarendon Press, 1986), 253.

3 Prince, *The Poems*, xxvi. Marlowe's fragment *Hero and Leander* was entered in the Stationers' Register in 1593, the same year *Venus and Adonis* was published, although *Hero* was not published until June 1598. We do not know which influenced which. See M. C. Bradbrook, *Shakespeare and Elizabethan Poetry* (Harmondsworth: Penguin 1964; first published 1951), 57, 226.

4 Prince, *The Poems* xxvi.

5 Richard Wilbur, 'The Narrative Poems: Introduction', in *William Shakespeare: The Complete Works*, ed. Alfred Harbage (New York: Viking Press, rev. edn, 1969; repr. 1977), 1403; F. E. Halliday, *The Poetry of Shakespeare's Plays* (London: Duckworth, 1954; repr. 1964), 62; Robert Ellrodt, 'Shakespeare the non-dramatic poet', in *The Cambridge Companion to Shakespeare Studies*, ed. Stanley Wells (Cambridge: Cambridge University Press, 1986), 45.

6 Richard Lanham, 'The Ovidian Shakespeare: *Venus and Adonis* and *Lucrece*', in *Motives of Eloquence: Literary Rhetoric in the Renaissance* (New Haven and London: Yale University Press, 1976), 82. I am indebted to Professor Lanham's book for helping me clarify my own ideas on Shakespeare's responses to rhetorical poetics, which do not always coincide with his.

7 Traditional editorial glosses on the meaning of Sonnet 111 (following Shelley's, that Shakespeare is complaining of the ignominy of writing for the public stage) have encouraged the plausibility of this view:

> Oh, for my sake do you with Fortune chide,
> The guilty goddess of my harmful deeds,
> That did not better for my life provide
> Than public means which public manners breeds.
> Thence comes it that my name receives a brand,
> And almost thence my nature is subdu'd
> To what it works in, like the dyer's hand.   (1–7)

8 See, for example, Nancy Lindheim, 'The Shakespearean *Venus and Adonis*', *Shakespeare Quarterly*, 37 (Summer 1986), 190–203.

9 E. K. Chambers quotes Sidney Lee's theory that there is 'reason to believe that the first draft lay in the author's desk through four or five summers and underwent some retouching before it emerged from the press in its final shape', in order to counter it with his own suggestion that it 'need mean no more than that it was his first published work'. *William Shakespeare: A Study of Facts and Problems*, 2 vols. (Oxford: Clarendon Press, 1930), I, 545.

10 *Henry VI, Parts One, Two and Three; Richard III; The Taming of The Shrew; The Comedy of Errors; The Two Gentlemen of Verona.* Dating of the early plays is, of course, problematic. For the purpose of this present study I wish merely to support the supposition that Shakespeare is already an · experienced playwright at the time of his writing *Venus and Adonis*.

11 The poem explicitly draws on three stories from Ovid's *Metamorphoses*: Venus and Adonis (*Met.* X.519–59; 705–39); Salmacis and Hermaphroditus (*Met.* IV.285–388); and Narcissus and Echo (*Met.*III. 339–510). The epigraph is taken from Ovid's *Amores* I.xv.35–6.

12 'As the soule of *Euphorbus* was thought to liue in *Pythagoras*: so the sweete wittie soule of *Ouid* liues in mellifluous & hony-tongued *Shakespeare*, witnes his *Venus and Adonis*, his *Lucrece*, his sugred Sonnets among his priuate friends, &c.' Francis Meres, *Palladis Tamia: Wits Treasury* (London, 1598), 281–2.

13 For example, Charles Martindale states that the 'extreme literariness' of Ovid's work was seen as a virtue 'to Shakespeare and the Elizabethans'. *Ovid Renewed: Ovidian Influences on Literature and Art from the Middle Ages to the Twentieth Century*, ed. Charles Martindale (Cambridge: Cambridge University Press, 1988) 14.

Since the writing of this book, Jonathan Bate has published his excellent study of Shakespeare's creative responses to Ovid which explores the relationship with the kind of complexity I am advocating here to address concerns different from my own. The overarching thesis of Bate's book is that it is the psycho-pathological concerns of Ovid which exert the greatest influence on Shakespeare, with which I agree, but I am suggesting that the artistic concerns of Ovid's works represent an equally pervasive presence in Shakespeare. *Shakespeare and Ovid* (Oxford: Clarendon Press, 1993).

14 Karl Galinsky, *Ovid's 'Metamorphoses': An Introduction to the Basic Aspects* (Oxford: Basil Blackwell, 1975), 3. The translation, emphasising Ovid's syntax, is my own.

15 *Ibid.*, 2.

16 *Ibid.*, 4. Calypso repeatedly asks Odysseus to tell her the story of the fall of Troy: each time he told her the same story, but he told it *aliter*:

'ille referre aliter saepe solebat idem' (II.123–42). Galinsky writes: 'As Odysseus in the *Art of Love,* Ovid in the *Metamorphoses* would look upon a traditional myth in terms of the challenge to *referre idem aliter*'.

17　Galinsky, *Ovid's 'Metamorphoses',* 15.

18　Martindale, *Ovid Renewed,* 16, 17.

19　Commentators have drawn attention to the discrepancies between the prose argument and the poem. To discuss this as an example of Shakespeare's techniques for *referre idem aliter* would have to be the subject of another study, but it is worth noting in passing how in *The Rape of Lucrece* we find Shakespeare saying, in effect: 'This is the version you are used to, now read my version'.

20　I am assuming *Richard III* had been produced on the stage by the time *Venus and Adonis* was entered in the Stationers' Register on 18 April 1593, following the Oxford editors' view that its first performance was 'probably in late 1592 or early 1593, outside London'. *Complete Works* (Modern Spelling Edition) ed. Wells and Taylor, 207. Anthony Hammond, however, suggests late 1591 in the Arden edition (London: Methuen, 1981), 62.

21　Marlowe's *Tamburlaine I* and *II* were published in 1590, and Kyd's *Spanish Tragedy* in 1592.

22　See Hammond (ed.), *King Richard III,* 14–21, 62–5.

23　See Madeleine Doran, 'Some Renaissance "Ovids"', in *Literature and Society,* ed. Bernice Slote (Lincoln, Neb.: University of Nebraska Press, 1964), 44–62; on English translations of Ovid as a major literary subgenre in the Renaissance, see Lee T. Pearcy, *The Mediated Muse: English Translations of Ovid 1560–1700* (Hamden, Conn.: Archon, 1984); chapters on Marlowe and Sandys.

24　The traditional view of the artistic motivations behind the poem can be found in Prince, *The Poems,* xxvi-xxvii. It has long been recognised that Shakespeare makes explicit use of Ovid's stories of Narcissus and Hermaphroditus in *Venus and Adonis.* See, for example, Bullough, *Narrative and Dramatic Sources of Shakespeare,* I, 161–3.

25　For one of the alternative interpretations of the myth found in the positive Renaissance reading of Ovid, see Bate's interesting discussion, *Shakespeare and Ovid,* 61–3.

26　Galinsky writes: 'Ovid presents Phaethon's quest not only as an external search for parentage, but as a psychological quest for identity' (*Ovid's 'Metamorphoses',* 49).

27　*Ovid's Metamorphoses. The Arthur Golding Translation,* ed. John Frederick Nims (New York and London: Macmillan, 1965), I, 952–3. Miller (trans.), *Metamorphoses,* 55; Galinsky, *Ovid's 'Metamorphoses',* 50; Mary M. Innes, (trans.), *The Metamorphoses of Ovid* (Harmondsworth: Penguin, 1955) 53.

28 Miller, (trans.), *Metamorphoses*, 155; Galinsky, *Ovid's 'Metamorphoses'*, 57. Golding reads: 'He thinkes the shadow that he sees, to be a lively boddie' III.523.

29 See Galinsky, *Ovid's 'Metamorphoses'*, 52–3.

30 My translation here is based on that of A. D. Nuttall, but 'she answers nothing but', which tries to convey Ovid's sense of what Echo omits in her repetition, is my own clumsy construction. Nuttall, 'Ovid's Narcissus and Shakespeare's *Richard II*: the reflected self', in *Ovid Renewed*, ed. Martindale, 141. Golding's translation is: 'And sayth: I first will die ere thou shall take of me thy pleasure. / She aunswerde nothing else thereto, but Take of me thy pleasure' III.487–8.

31 An increasingly disgruntled Adonis chastises Venus for falling again 'Into your idle over-handled theme' (770).

32 Nuttall, 'Ovid's Narcissus', 142.

33 *Ibid.*, 145.

34 Prince, *The Poems*, 5.

35 'Now when the rosy fingered morning faire / Weary of aged Tithones saffron bed, / Had spred her purple robe through deawy aire.' Spenser, *F.Q.*, I.ii.7; 'Rose-cheek'd Adonis', Marlowe, *Hero and Leander*, I.93.

36 Prince's gloss on stain cites Pooler quoting Lyly: 'My Daphne's beauty staines all faces' (*Works*, ed. Bond, III, 142); and Sidney's 'sun-stayning excellencie' (*The Countess of Pembrokes Arcadia*, ed. A. Feuillerat (Cambridge, 1912), 7). Prince, *The Poems*, 4.

37 Discussing Spenser's Garden of Adonis in *The Faerie Queene*, James Nohrnberg notes the well-known physical allegories of Adonis which characterise him as a 'genital field', and the traditional mons veneris 'with its uncut foliage and enclosing grove (which) stands for the female pudenda'. Nohrnberg, *The Analogy of 'The Faerie Queene'* (Princeton, NJ: Princeton University Press, 1976), 526.

38 As Shakespeare wrote elsewhere: 'My mistress' eyes are nothing like the sun' (Sonnet 130).

39 I follow the 1609 Q order of the Sonnets. Quotations are from Ingram and Redpath's edition because their commentary has been helpful in my discussions. W.G. Ingram and Theodore Redpath, *Shakespeare's Sonnets* (London: Hodder and Stoughton, 1964; repr. 1982).

40 Ingram and Redpath, *Shakespeare's Sonnets*, 122.

41 See *Ibid.*, 122.

42 *Ibid.*

43 *Ibid.*, 188–9.

44 See especially Sonnets 78, 79, 83, 85, 101.

45 The gloss on *modern* is that of Ingram and Redpath, *Shakespeare's Sonnets*, 190.

46 *Ibid.*, 192.

47 Quoted in Prince, *The Poems*, 19.

48 Bate suggests that the alternative Renaissance interpretation of the Hermaphrodite myth as an ideal image of union between a man and woman is reflected in Shakespeare's poem in Adonis' '*potential*' to participate in such a union: 'violent death takes the place of the unfulfilled Salmacian / Hermaphroditic potential'. Bate, *Shakespeare and Ovid*, 64.

49 The gloss on *compeers* is that of Ingram and Redpath, *Shakespeare's Sonnets*, 197.

50 Prince's gloss reads: 'Venus is recurring to commonplace arguments for enjoying beauty, her "idle over-handled theme". Her last metaphor had been used in *Hero and Leander*, I.232–6.' Prince, *The Poems*, 44.

51 Falstaff and Hal will exceed the limits of Erasmian *copia* with a comparative hyperbole contest in a hilarious send-up of the rhetoricians' ideal text:

> *Prince.* I'll be no longer guilty of this sin. This sanguine coward, this bed-presser, this horse-back-breaker, this huge hill of flesh, –
> *Falstaff.* 'Sblood, you starveling, you eel-skin, you dried neat's-tongue, you bull's-pizzle, you stock-fish – O for breath to utter what is like thee! – you tailor's-yard, you sheath, you bow-case, you vile standing tuck!
> *Prince.* Well, breathe awhile, and then to it again, and when thou hast tired thyself in base comparisons, hear me speak but this.
>
> (1*HIV*, II.iv.237–47).

52 Robert Ellrodt provides an interesting example of criticism's failure to respond to the presence of Shakespearean irony in matters theoretical: 'One would like to think the poet mocked the Elizabethan partiality to *copia* when he compared the "tedious" lament of Venus to "copious stories" that "End without audience and are never done". Vain wish, since wordiness grew worse in Lucrece!' Ellrodt, (Shakespeare the non-dramatic poet), 45–6.

53 Sonnet 86.7; *Ven.* 770; Sonnet 82.10; *Ven.* 790.

54 Quoted in Ingram and Redpath, *Shakespeare's Sonnets*, 90.

55 C.T. Onions, *A Shakespeare Glossary*, 2nd edn (Oxford: Clarendon Press, 1980), 15.

56 Ingram and Redpath, *Shakespeare's Sonnets*, 138.

57 Bradbrook notes that 'Though a goddess, Venus has no supernatural powers . . . She is not responsible for his metamorphosis into a hyacinth: it seems to be spontaneous. Shakespeare abandoned the supernatural: his gods are identified with Nature, physically one with it, enmeshed in its toils even more firmly than Marlowe's.' She goes on

to say that Venus's 'inappropriate conceits' are an attempt to convey her grief by 'fantastic elaborations. Yet the horror of the blank glazed stare of the corpse is physically realised.' *Shakespeare and Elizabethan Poetry*, 62–3.

4. 'IN SCORN OF NATURE ART GAVE LIFELESS LIFE': EXPOSING ART'S STERILITY

1 Sidney, 25.
2 Plutarch, *The Philosophie, Commonlie Called, The Morals written by the learned Philosopher Plutarch of Chaeronea*, trans. Philemon Holland (London: Arnold Hatfield, 1603), 22.
3 For an informative study on 'lifelikeness' in the period, see Lucy Gent, *Picture and Poetry 1560–1620: Relations between Literature and the Visual Arts in the English Renaissance* (Leamington Spa: James Hall, 1981), *passim.*
4 George Hakewill, *The Vanitie of the eie*, 1st edn (Oxford: Joseph Barnes, 1608), 86.
5 Numerous allusions to Pliny's stories of paintings deceiving the spectator are to be found in texts of the period, especially Zeuxis' grapes which deceived birds into believing they could be eaten, echoed in Lucrece's tearing at 'Sinon' in the painting of Troy. Pliny, *The Historie of the World, Commonly Called the Natvrall Historie of C. Plinivs Secvndvs*, trans. Philemon Holland (London: Adam Islip, 1601).
6 Sidney, 23–4.
7 Onions, *A Shakespeare Glossary*, 13.
8 Henry Peacham (the Elder), *The Garden of Eloquence* (London: H. Jackson, 1577), sig. Oii^r.
9 Onions, *A Shakespeare Glossary*, 42.
10 John Lyly, *Works*, ed. R. W. Bond, 3 vols. (Oxford: Oxford University Press, 1904), II, 89.
11 'The passage indicates that the whole statue, in form and colouring was a speaking likeness.' J. H. P. Pafford (ed.), *The Winter's Tale*, Arden edition (London: Methuen, 1963; repr. 1982), 150.
12 Jean H. Hagstrum, *The Sister Arts: The Tradition of Literary Pictorialism and English Poetry from Dryden to Gray* (Chicago and London: University of Chicago Press, 1958; 2nd edn 1965), 87–8.
13 Sidney, 23–4.
14 Sidney, 52–3, 23. Puttenham writes: '. . . all artes grew first by observation of natures proceedings and custome'. George Puttenham, *The Arte of English Poesie*, ed. G. D. Willcock and Alice Walker (Cambridge:

Cambridge University Press, 1936), 128. All subsequent quotations will be from this edition and cited 'Puttenham'.

15 'Neither let it be deemed too saucy a comparison to balance the highest point of man's wit with the efficacy of nature; but rather give right honour to the heavenly Maker of that maker, who having made man to His own likeness, set him beyond and over all the works of that second nature: which in nothing he showeth so much as in poetry, when with the force of a divine breath he bringeth things forth surpassing her doings – with no small arguments to the credulous of that first accursed fall of Adam, since our erected wit maketh us know what perfection is, and yet our infected will keepeth us from reaching unto it.' Sidney, 24–5.

16 Puttenham, 303.

17 *Ibid.*, 154.

18 *Ibid.*, 262.

19 When he is talking about the horticultural practice of grafting, King Polixenes is in favour of 'marrying' gentle to wild; but the idea of nobility being married to peasant stock is another matter, as he is about to show when he discovers his son wants to marry a lowly 'shepherdess'.

20 Pafford (ed.), *The Winter's Tale*, 94.

21 Onions, *A Shakespeare Glossary*, 13.

22 In *Physics*, Aristotle says that art 'partly completes what nature cannot bring to a finish'. *The Basic Works*, ed. Richard McKeon (New York: Random House, 1941), 250 (*Physics* 199 a 16–17).

23 See E. A. J. Honigmann, 'Secondary sources of *The Winter's Tale*', *Philological Quarterly*, 34 (1955), 27–8.

24 Frank Kermode (ed.), *The Tempest*, Arden edition, 6th edn. (London: Methuen, 1958; repr. 1980), 103.

25 This interpretation seems to be universally accepted. I have not come across a contradiction of it.

26 Stanley Wells and Gary Taylor, with John Jowett and William Montgomery (eds.), *William Shakespeare. The Complete Works: A Textual Companion* (Oxford: Clarendon Press, 1987), 612, 615.

27 See, for example, Enid Welsford, *The Court Masque: A Study in the Relationship between Poetry and the Revels* (New York: Russell and Russell, 1962), 343ff; Allardyce Nicholl, *Stuart Masques and the Renaissance Stage* (London: Harrap and Co., 1937), 19ff.

28 See Nicholl, *Stuart Masques*, 21.

29 See chapter 2, 16–17.

30 Sidney, 23.

5. O'ER-WRESTED SEEMING : DRAMATIC ILLUSION AND THE REPUDIATION OF MIMESIS

1 'We choose to be deceived' is from S. T. Coleridge, 'Lecture on *The Tempest*' (1818–19), in *Coleridge's Shakespearean Criticism*, ed. T. M. Raysor, 2 vols. (London: Constable, 1930), I, 129; 'The True Theory of Stage Illusion' is from *Collected Letters of Samuel Taylor Coleridge*, ed. Earl Leslie Griggs, 6 vols. (Oxford: Oxford University Press, 1956–71), IV, 642; 'to produce a sort of temporary half-faith. . .' and 'negative belief' are from *Shakespearean Criticism*, ed. Raysor, I, 200, 202; 'willing suspension of disbelief' is from *Biographia Literaria* (ch. 14), ed. John Shawcross, 2 vols. (Oxford: Oxford University Press, 1907), II, 6.

2 Samuel Johnson, 'Preface to Shakespeare', in *Selected Writings*, ed. Patrick Cruttwell (Harmondsworth: Penguin English Library, 1968; repr. 1982), 274; hereafter referred to as 'Johnson'.

3 Johnson, 274–5.

4 Keir Elam, *The Semiotics of Theatre and Drama* (London and New York: Methuen, 1980), 102.

5 *Ibid.*, 108, 102.

6 Johnson, 275.

7 Elam, *The Semiotics of Theatre and Drama*, 103, 107.

8 *Ibid.*, 108.

9 Robert Weimann, *Shakespeare and the Popular Tradition in the Theater: Studies in the Social Dimension of Dramatic Form and Function*, ed. Robert Schwartz (Baltimore and London: Johns Hopkins University Press, 1978), 190. A. D. Nuttall, *A New Mimesis*, 192.

10 L. C. Knights, 'How many children had Lady Macbeth? An essay on the theory and practice of Shakespearean criticism' (Cambridge: Minority Press, 1933); repr. in L. C. Knights, *Explorations: Essays in Criticism Mainly on the Literature of the Seventeenth Century* (London: Chatto and Windus, 1946; Harmondsworth: Peregrine Books, 1964), 17.

11 Faas, *Shakespeare's Poetics*, 36–7

12 Howard Felperin, *Shakespearean Representation: Mimesis and Modernity in Elizabethan Tragedy* (Princeton, NJ: Princeton University Press, 1977), 60, 66 (there is a typographical error in the passage quoted from p. 66 which I have corrected: 'to' and 'rival' are transposed).

13 G. G. Smith (ed.), *Elizabethan Critical Essays*, 2 vols. (London: Oxford University Press, 1976; first published 1904), I, 369.

14 Kenneth Palmer (ed.), *Troilus and Cressida* (London: Methuen, 1982), 133.

15 *Ibid.*

16 'Immeasurably high' in Onions, *A Shakespeare Glossary*, 229; 'Supreme, having no superior' in Palmer (ed.), *Troilus and Cressida*, 133.

17 Palmer (ed.), *Troilus and Cressida*, 133.

18 For the quotations on Alexander, see the gloss on this passage in Richard David (ed.), *Love's Labour's Lost*, 5th edn (London: Methuen, 1951; repr. 1980), 164–5.

19 Sidney, 65. For Castelvetro's theory, see *Castelvetro on the Art of Poetry*, trans. Andrew Bongiorno, Medieval and Renaissance Texts and Studies, vol. 29 (Binghampton, NY, 1984). For a discussion of Castelvetro's theory, see Faas, *Shakespeare's Poetics*, 56–60.

20 Johnson, 275.

21 Edwards, *Shakespeare and the Confines of Art*, 10.

22 *Ibid.*, 44.

23 John Edmunds, 'Shakespeare breaks the illusion', *Critical Inquiry*, 23 (1981), 3.

24 *Ibid.*, 3–4.

25 Peter Thomson, *Shakespeare's Theatre* (London, Routledge and Kegan Paul, 1983), 87.

26 J. M. Lothian and T. W. Craik (eds.), *Twelfth Night*, Arden edition (London: Methuen, 1975; repr. 1987), lxxiii.

27 Leonard Digges (Commendatory verses to Shakespeare's Poems, 1640) quoted in E. K. Chambers, *William Shakespeare: A Study of Facts and Problems*, II, 233.

28 Among innumerable discussions of 'illusion-shattering' in Shakespeare are: Doris Fenton, *The Extra-Dramatic Moment in Elizabethan Plays before 1616* (Philadelphia: University of Pennsylvania Press, 1930); Maynard Mack, 'Engagement and detachment in Shakespeare's plays', in *Essays on Shakespeare and the Elizabethan Drama in Honor of Hardin Craig*, ed. Richard Hosley (Columbia: University of Missouri Press, 1962), 275–96.

29 Barton, *Shakespeare and the Idea of the Play*, 171.

30 Robert Egan's comment is representative: 'Mimesis, then, the ability to reflect reality in an effective image that codifies and communicates the artist's vision: this is what Shakespeare defines as the utmost power of drama in *Hamlet*'. *Drama Within Drama: Shakespeare's Sense of his Art in 'King Lear', 'The Winter's Tale', and 'The Tempest'* (New York and London: Columbia University Press, 1975), 11.

31 Barton, *Shakespeare and the Idea of the Play*, 171–2.

32 James L. Calderwood, *To Be and Not To Be: Negation and Metadrama in 'Hamlet'* (New York and London: Columbia University Press, 1983), 167; 168.

33 Gruber, 'The actor in the script: affective strategies in Shakespeare's *Antony and Cleopatra*', *Comparative Drama*, 19 (Spring 1985), 33.

34 William B. Worthen, 'The weight of Antony: staging "character" in *Antony and Cleopatra*', *Studies in English Literature, 1500–1900* 26 (Spring 1986), 307.

35 Calderwood, *To Be and Not To Be*, 168–9.

36 Roy Battenhouse, 'The significance of Hamlet's advice to the Players', in *The Drama of the Renaissance: Essays for Leicester Bradner*, ed. Elmer M. Blistein (Providence, RI: Brown University Press, 1970), 26.

37 Robert Weimann, 'Mimesis in *Hamlet*', in *Shakespeare and the Question of Theory*, ed. Patricia Parker and Geoffrey Hartman (New York and London: Methuen, 1985), 279, 280, 282–3.

6. 'THY REGISTERS AND THEE I BOTH DEFY': HISTORY CHALLENGED

1 For much background information for this chapter I am indebted to F. J. Levy, *Tudor Historical Thought* (San Marino, Calif.: The Huntington Library, 1967).

2 The most illuminating work on the subject of anachronism in the Renaissance which I have come across, and to which the present study is greatly indebted, is Thomas M. Greene, *The Light in Troy: Imitation and Discovery in Renaissance Poetry* (New Haven and London: Yale University Press, 1982).

3 Levy, *Tudor Historical Thought*, 21.

4 It was this impulse which had motivated, for example, the textual and historical criticism of ancient documents carried out by the fifteenth-century Italian scholar, Lorenzo Valla, whose proof that the supposed fourth-century Donation of Constantine was a fake, led to the appearance of the first correct application of the technique of anachronism to historical research in England: the examination of King Arthur's supposed seal in Westminster Abbey by John Rastell, brother-in-law to Thomas More. His *Pastyme of People* (1529) shows that the spirit of humanist source criticism existed in England at that time.

5 Erasmus started to write the *Antibarbari* in 1488 (if not earlier) and it was first printed in 1520; see *Antibarbari*, trans. Margaret M. Phillips, in Erasmus, *Collected Works*, ed. Craig R. Thompson (Toronto, Buffalo and London: Toronto University Press, 1978), XXIII, 24ff; *De duplici copia verborum ac rerum comentarii duo* was written in the 1490s, and first published in 1512; *De ratione studii ac legendi interpretandique auctores*, begun in 1496, was first printed in 1534; *Copia*, trans. Betty I. Knott, and *De Ratione studii*, trans. Brian McGregor can be found in vol. XXIV of Erasmus, *Collected Works*, ed. Thompson. On the influence

of Erasmus on Shakespeare, see Emrys Jones, *The Origins of Shakespeare* (Oxford: Clarendon Press, 1977) ; and Paul Dean's informative essay, 'Tudor humanism and the Roman past: a Background to Shakespeare', *Renaissance Quarterly*, 41 (Spring 1988), 84–111.

6 Greene, *The Light in Troy*, 9, 8, 9.

7 See May McKisack, *Medieval History in the Tudor Age* (Oxford: Clarendon Press, 1971), 76.

8 For the meaning of 'but dressings of a former sight' as 'trimmings, refashionings' see Onions, *A Shakespeare Glossary*, 64. The glosses given for lines 2 and 4 are in Ingram and Redpath, *Shakespeare's Sonnets*, 282.

9 'The quick comedians/ Extemporally will stage us, and present / Our Alexandrian revels: Antony / Shall be brought drunken forth, and I shall see / Some squeaking Cleopatra boy my greatness / I' the posture of a whore.' (*Ant.* V.ii.215–20); see Henry V's speech in *Henry V* IV.iii.40–67; the conspirators in *Julius Caesar*, III.i.110–18; also, see Cressida, Troilus and Pandarus predict their reputations in *Troilus and Cressida*, III.ii.171–208; Othello's request for his story to be told to listeners not present at the events themselves (*Oth.* V.ii.339–57), and Hamlet's exhortation to Horatio 'To tell my story' (*Ham.* V.ii.354) as further examples.

10 Sidney, 30, 36.

11 On the search for material evidence in the study of history, such as the geography of ancient Italy, see Levy, *Tudor Historical Thought*, 38–9, 146ff.

12 *The Complete Works*, ed. Wells and Taylor, 1343. On the question of authorship, this brief discussion of the play assumes that the passages examined are by Shakespeare.

13 See Pierre Sahel, 'The strangeness of a dramatic style: rumour in *Henry VIII*', *Shakespeare Survey*, 38 (1985), 131–43.

14 Paul Dean examines the play's emphasis on 'the second-hand nature of our acquaintance with historical events' in 'Dramatic mode and historical vision in *Henry VIII*', *Shakespeare Quarterly*, 37 (Summer 1986) 175–89.

15 See McKisack, *Medieval History in the Tudor Age*, 109.

16 Edward Hall's *The Union of The Two Noble and Illustre Famelies of Lancastre & Yorke . . .*, a principal source for Shakespeare's *Richard III*, was printed in 1548; see *Hall's Chronicle*, ed. Sir Henry Ellis (1809).

17 For example, when More is about to give his account of the murders of the Princes in the Tower, he says he will tell the story 'not after every way that I have heard, but after that way that I have so heard by such men and by such means, as me thinketh it were hard but it should be true.' *The Complete Works of St. Thomas More*, ed. Richard S. Sylvester, 16 vols. (New Haven and London: Yale University Press,

1963), II, 8, 9, 83. For discussions on More's use of conjecture see Judith H. Anderson, *Biographical Truth: The Representation of Historical Persons in Tudor-Stuart Writing* (New Haven and London: Yale University Press, 1984), 75ff.

18 Raphael Holinshed, *The Chronicles of England, Scotlande and Irelande*, published in 1577; Shakespeare used *The First and Second Volumes of Chronicles*, published in 1587. Another example of the multi-derivative nature of history writing during this period is Francis Bacon's *Historie of the Raigne of King Henry the Seventh*, published in 1622. Bacon relied almost entirely on Polydore Vergil's history and Tudor chronicles, and used his materials selectively and sometimes dishonestly. See Wilhelm Busch, *England under the Tudors*, Vol.1: *King Henry VII*, trans. Alice M. Todd (London: A. D. Innes, 1895), 416–23.

19 Antony Hammond (ed.), *King Richard III*, 73, to give just one example.

20 McKisack, *Medieval History in the Tudor Age*, 110.

21 Peter Ure (ed.), *King Richard II*, Arden edition (London: Methuen, 1961; repr. 1982), 65.

22 *The Mirror for Magistrates*, ed. Lily B. Campbell (Cambridge: Cambridge University Press, 1938), 267.

23 Peter Burke, *The Renaissance Sense of the Past* (London: Edward Arnold, 1969), 2. An excellent discussion of Petrarch's sense of the past is to be found in Thomas M. Greene, *The Light in Troy*, chs 5 and 6, but see also chs 1, 2 and 3.

24 *Petrarch's Letters to Classical Authors*, ed. and trans. Mario Emilio Consenza, (Chicago: University of Chicago Press, 1910), 138–9, quoted in Greene, *The Light in Troy*, 90 and slightly altered by Greene.

25 Thomas Nashe, *Pierce Penilesse his Supplication to the Diuell*, in *Works*, ed. R. B. McKerrow, reprinted from the original edn with corrections and complementary notes by F. P. Wilson (Oxford: Basil Blackwell, 1966), I, 212. R. L. Smallwood cites Nashe to support his argument that Shakespeare's principal enterprise in his history plays was to turn 'the overwhelmingly informative then-narrative . . . into the liveliness of now-theatricality'. 'Shakespeare's use of history', in *The Cambridge Companion to Shakespeare Studies*, ed. Stanley Wells (Cambridge: Cambridge University Press, 1986), 146.

26 Michael Goldman, *Shakespeare and the Energies of Drama* (Princeton, NJ: Princeton University Press, 1972), 4.

27 *Ibid.*, 6.

28 Greene, *The Light in Troy*, 92.

29 Thomas Heywood, *Apology for Actors* (London, 1612), B4[v].

30 Stephen Gosson, *Playes confuted in Fiue Actions* (1582), G5[r].

31 Herbert Lindenberger, *Historical Drama: The Relation of Literature and Reality* (Chicago: University of Chicago Press, 1975), 24.

32 See Gary Taylor (ed.), *King Henry V*, Oxford Shakespeare edition. (Oxford: Oxford University Press, 1984), 41–4.

33 For a brief survey of opinions on the character of Henry, see J. H. Walter (ed.), *King Henry V*, Arden edition (London: Methuen, 1954), xii–xiv.

34 R. D. Altick, 'Symphonic imagery in *Richard II*', *PMLA*, 62 (1947), 351; Hardin Craig, *An Interpretation of Shakespeare* (New York: Doubleday, 1948), 128; Walter Pater, 'Shakespeare's English kings', in *Appreciations* (London, 1889; 4th edn 1944), 206.

35 Leonard F. Dean, '*Richard II*: the state and the image of the theatre', in Leonard F. Dean (ed.), *Shakespeare: Modern Essays in Criticism* (New York: Oxford University Press, 1957), 188–205.

36 Richard Schechner, 'Collective reflexivity: restoration of behaviour', in *A Crack in the Mirror: Reflexive Perspectives in Anthropology*, ed. Jay Ruby (Philadelphia: University of Pennsylvania Press, 1982), 43. I am indebted to William Worthen for this quotation which appears in his essay, 'The weight of Antony', 304.

37 A history which took as its starting-point not a moral system, but political reality was put forward by Machiavelli in his influential treatise on statecraft, *The Prince* (written in 1513–14 and translated into English in 1640, although his works were being widely read in academic circles before 1580). See J. G. A. Pocock, *The Machiavellian Moment* (Princeton, NJ: Princeton University Press, 1975).

7 *ANTONY AND CLEOPATRA* AS 'A DEFENCE OF DRAMA'

1 *Plutarch's Lives of the Noble Grecians and Romanes*, trans. Sir Thomas North, 8 vols. (Oxford: Basil Blackwell, 1928), VI, 326–7. All quotations are from this edition, referred to as Plutarch, *Lives*.

2 Plutarch, *Lives*, VI, 327.

3 *Ibid.*

4 Janet Adelman, *The Common Liar: An Essay on 'Antony and Cleopatra'*, (New Haven and London: Yale University Press, 1973), 151.

5 This is examined in the last section of this chapter.

6 M. R. Ridley (ed.), *Antony and Cleopatra*, Arden edition, 9th edn (London: Methuen, 1954; repr. 1977), 61.

7 *Ibid.*, 58.

8 Phyllis Rackin, 'Shakespeare's boy Cleopatra, the decorum of nature and the golden world of poetry', *PMLA*, 87 (1972), 204.

9 *Ibid.*

10 *Ibid.*, 204–5.

11 Antony tells the soothsayer, 'The very dice obey him' (II.iii.32); 'Be a child o' the time' Antony urges. Octavius replies: 'Possess it'

(II.vii.98–9); 'Is it not strange . . . / That from Tarentum, and Brundusium / [Octavius] could so quickly cut the Ionian sea, / And take in Toryne?' When the news is confirmed, Antony exclaims: 'Can he be there in person? 'Tis impossible; / Strange, that his power should be' (III.vii.20–3; 56–7).

12 Worthen, 'The weight of Antony', 299.

13 Few studies of the play have not included some examination of these aspects of the play, but see particularly, Adelman, *The Common Liar*, *passim*; and William D. Wolf, '"New heaven, new earth": the escape from mutability in *Antony and Cleopatra*', *Shakespeare Quarterly*, 33 (1982), 328–35.

14 Plutarch, *Lives*, VIII, 134.

15 Sidney, 25.

16 Sewell, *The Orphic Voice*, 24.

17 Hofstadter, *Truth and Art*, 38.

18 Two critics who have examined the influence on Shakespeare's play of the Isis myth as it is found in Plutarch, Apuleius' *The Golden Asse* and Spenser's *The Faerie Queene* are Michael Lloyd, 'Cleopatra as Isis', *Shakespeare Survey*, 12 (1959), 88–94; and Harold Fisch, '*Antony and Cleopatra*: the limits of mythology', *Shakespeare Survey*, 23 (1970), 59–67. See also Barbara J. Bono, 'Fiction as myth: of Isis and Osiris, or the myth of Egypt', in *Literary Transvaluation: From Vergilian Epic to Shakespearean Tragicomedy* (Berkeley and Los Angeles: University of California Press, 1984), 191–213.

19 *The Philosophie, Commonlie Called, The Morals written by the learned Philosopher Plutarch of Chaeronea*, trans. Philemon Holland (London: Arnold Hatfield, 1603), 1304–5. All quotations are from this edition, referred to as *Moralia*.

20 Plutarch, *Moralia*, 1300, 1304.

21 *Ibid.*, 1300, 1303.

22 *Ibid.*, 1300.

23 *Ibid.*, 1303.

24 *Ibid.*, 1318.

25 One of the depressingly prevalent examples of sexist bias in criticism of the play, exposed by Fitz in a much-needed corrective to almost all commentators on Cleopatra, is the charge that she instigates the plan to fight at sea. L. T. Fitz, 'Egyptian queens and male reviewers: sexist attitudes in *Antony and Cleopatra* criticism', *Shakespeare Quarterly*, 28 (1977), 297–316. On Caesar's dare, see 311–12.

26 Bono writes: 'Isis's restoration of the sexual potency of Osiris is a metaphor for creative movement back to original unity.' 'Fiction as myth', 203.

27 Plutarch, *Moralia*, 1308.

28 Ingram and Redpath, *Shakespeare's Sonnets*, 298.
29 For productions which have staged the absent barge scene, see Margaret Lamb, *'Antony and Cleopatra' on the English Stage* (Rutherford: Fairleigh Dickinson University Press, 1980), 79–91.

Bibliography

Adelman, Janet. *The Common Liar: An Essay on 'Antony and Cleopatra'*. New Haven and London: Yale University Press, 1973.

Altick, R. D. 'Symphonic imagery in *Richard II*'. *PMLA*, 62 (1947) 339–65.

Anderson, Judith H. *Biographical Truth: The Representation of Historical Persons in Tudor-Stuart Writing*. New Haven and London: Yale University Press, 1984.

Aristotle. *The Basic Works*. Edited and with an introduction by Richard McKeon. New York: Random House, 1941.

Barish, Jonas A. 'Jonson and the loathèd stage'. *A Celebration of Ben Jonson*. Edited by William Blisset *et al*. Toronto and Buffalo: Toronto University Press, 1973. Reprinted in *The Antitheatrical Prejudice*. Berkeley and Los Angeles: University of California Press, 1981.

Barton, Anne. *Shakespeare and the Idea of the Play* . Westport, Conn.: Greenwood Press, 1977. (First published 1962.)

Bate, Jonathan. *Shakespeare and Ovid*. Oxford: Clarendon Press, 1993.

Battenhouse, Roy W. 'The significance of Hamlet's advice to the Players'. *The Drama of the Renaissance: Essays for Leicester Bradner*. Edited by Elmer M. Blistein. Providence, RI: Brown University Press, 1970. 3–26.

Bentley, Gerald Eades. *The Profession of Dramatist in Shakespeare's Time*, 1971. Princeton, NJ: Princeton University Press, 1986.

Bono, Barbara J. *Literary Transvaluation: From Vergilian Epic to Shakespearean Tragedy*. Berkeley and Los Angeles: University of California Press, 1984.

Bradbrook, M[uriel] C. *Shakespeare and Elizabethan Poetry*. Harmondsworth: Penguin, 1964. (First published 1951.)

Bruns, Gerald L. *Modern Poetry and the Idea of Language: A Critical and Historical Study*. New Haven and London: Yale University Press, 1974.

Bullough, Geoffrey. Ed. *Narrative and Dramatic Sources of Shakespeare*. 8 vols. London and New York: Routledge and Kegan Paul, 1977. (First published 1957.)

Burke, Peter. *The Renaissance Sense of the Past*. London: Edward Arnold, 1969.

Busch, Wilhelm. *England under the Tudors: King Henry VII*. Translated by Alice M. Todd. London: A. D. Innes, 1895.

Calderwood, James L. *To Be and Not To Be: Negation and Metadrama in 'Hamlet'*. New York and London: Columbia University Press, 1983.

Castelvetro, Lodovico. *On the Art of Poetry*. Translated by Andrew Bongiorno. Medieval and Renaissance Texts and Studies 29. Binghampton, NY, 1984.

Chambers, E. K. *William Shakespeare: A Study of Facts and Problems*. 2 vols. Oxford: Clarendon Press, 1930.

Chapman, George. *The Revenge of Bussy D'Ambois*. London, 1613.

Coleridge, S. T. *Coleridge's Shakespearean Criticism*. 2 vols. Edited by T. M. Raysor. London: Constable, 1930.

—*Collected Letters of Samuel Taylor Coleridge*. 6 vols. Edited by Earl Leslie Griggs. Oxford: Oxford University Press, 1956–71.

Craig, Hardin. *An Interpretation of Shakespeare*. New York: Doubleday, 1948.

David, Richard. Ed. Arden Edition of Shakespeare's *Love's Labour's Lost*. 5th edn. London: Methuen, 1951; repr. 1980.

Dean, Paul. 'Tudor humanism and the Roman past: a background to Shakespeare'. *Renaissance Quarterly* , 41 (Spring 1988) 84–111.

—'Dramatic mode and historical vision in *Henry VIII*'. *Shakespeare Quarterly*, 37 (Summer 1986) 175–89.

Dekker, Thomas. *The Whore of Babylon*. London, 1607.

Derrida, Jacques. *Marges de la philosophie*. Paris: Minuit, 1972.

Doran, Madeleine 'Some Renaissance "Ovids"'. *Literature and Society*. Edited by Bernice Slote. Lincoln, Nebra.: Nebraska University Press, 1964. 44–62.

Edmunds, John. 'Shakespeare breaks the illusion'. *Critical Inquiry*, 23 (1981) 3–18.

Edwards, Philip. *Shakespeare and the Confines of Art*. London: Methuen, 1968.

Egan, Robert. *Drama Within Drama: Shakespeare's Sense of his Art in 'King Lear', 'The Winter's Tale', and 'The Tempest'*. New York and London: Columbia University Press, 1975.

Elam, Keir. *The Semiotics of Theatre and Drama*. London and New York: Methuen, 1980.

Ellrodt, Robert. 'Shakespeare the non-dramatic poet'. *The Cambridge Companion to Shakespeare Studies*. Edited by Stanley Wells. Cambridge: Cambridge University Press, 1986. 35–48.

Erasmus, Desiderius. *Collected Works*. Edited by Craig R. Thompson. Toronto: Toronto University Press, 1974 – . Vols. 23 and 24 (1978).

Faas, Ekbert. *Shakespeare's Poetics*. Cambridge: Cambridge University Press, 1986.

Felperin, Howard. *Shakespearean Representation: Mimesis and Modernity in Elizabethan Tragedy.* Princeton, NJ: Princeton University Press, 1977.

Galinsky, Karl. *Ovid's 'Metamorphoses': An Introduction to the Basic Aspects.* Oxford: Basil Blackwell, 1975.

Gent, Lucy. *Picture and Poetry 1560–1620: Relations between Literature and the Visual Arts in the English Renaissance.* Leamington Spa: James Hall, 1981.

Goldman, Michael. *Shakespeare and the Energies of Drama.* Princeton, NJ: Princeton University Press, 1972.

Gosson, Stephen. *Playes Confuted in Fiue Actions.* London, 1582.

Greene, Thomas M. *The Light in Troy: Imitation and Discovery in Renaissance Poetry.* New Haven and London: Yale University Press, 1982.

Gruber, William E. 'The actor in the script: affective strategies in Shakespeare's *Antony and Cleopatra'. Comparative Drama*, 19 (Spring 1985) 30–48.

Hagstrum, Jean H. *The Sister Arts: The Tradition of Pictorialism and English Poetry From Dryden to Gray.* 1958. Chicago and London: University of Chicago Press, 1965.

Hakewill, George. *The Vanitie of the eie.* 1st edn Oxford: Joseph Barnes, 1608.

Hall, Edward. *The union of the two noble and illustre famelies of Lancastre & Yorke,* London, 1548.

Halliday, F. R. *The Poetry of Shakespeare's Plays.* 1954. London: Duckworth, 1964.

Hammond, Antony. Ed. Arden Edition of Shakespeare's *King Richard III.* London and New York: Methuen, 1981.

Hawkins, Harriet. *Likenesses of Truth in Elizabethan and Restoration Drama.* Oxford: Clarendon Press, 1972.

Hayward, John. *The first Part of the life and raigne of Henry IIII, Extending to the end of the first yeare of his raigne.* London, 1599.

Heywood, Thomas. *Apology for Actors.* London, 1612.

Hofstadter, Albert. *Truth and Art.* New York and London: Columbia University Press, 1965.

Holinshed, Raphael. *The Chronicles of England, Scotlande and Irelande.* London, 1577.

—*The First and Second Volumes of Chronicles.* London, 1587.

Honigmann, E. A. J. 'Secondary sources of *The Winter's Tale'. Philological Quarterly,* 34 (1955) 27–34.

Ingram, W. G. and Theodore Redpath. Eds. *Shakespeare's Sonnets.* London: Hodder and Stoughton, 1964; repr. 1982.

Johnson, Samuel. *Selected Writings.* Edited by Patrick Cruttwell. Harmondsworth: Penguin, English Library 1968; repr. 1982.

Jones, Emrys. *The Origins of Shakespeare.* Oxford: Clarendon Press, 1977.

Jonson, Ben. *Works.* 11 vols. Edited by C. H. Herford and Percy and Evelyn M. Simpson. Oxford: Clarendon Press, 1954. (First published 1925.)

Kermode, Frank. Ed. Arden Edition of Shakespeare's *The Tempest.* 6th edn. London: Methuen, 1958; repr. 1980.

Kernan, Alvin B. *The Playwright as Magician: Shakespeare's Image of the Poet in the English Public Theater.* New Haven and London: Yale University Press, 1979.

Knights, L. C. 'How many children had Lady Macbeth?: An essay on the theory and practice of Shakespearean criticism'. Cambridge: Minority Press, 1933. Reprinted in *Explorations: Essays in Criticism Mainly on the Literature of the Seventeenth Century.* London: Chatto and Windus, 1946; Harmondsworth: Peregrine Books, 1964.

Lamb, Margaret. *'Antony and Cleopatra' on the English Stage.* Rutherford: Fairleigh Dickinson University Press, 1980.

Lanham, Richard. *Motives of Eloquence: Literary Rhetoric in the Renaissance.* New Haven and London: Yale Universty Press, 1976.

Levy, F. J. *Tudor Historical Thought.* San Marino, Calif: The Huntington Library, 1967.

Lindenberger, Herbert. *Historical Drama: The Relation of Literature and Reality.* Chicago: University of Chicago Press, 1975.

Lindheim, Nancy. 'The Shakespearean *Venus and Adonis*'. *Shakespeare Quarterly,* 37 (Summer 1986) 190–203.

Lothian, J. M. and T. W. Craik. Eds. Arden Edition of Shakespeare's *Twelfth Night.* London: Methuen, 1975; repr. 1987.

Lyly, John. *Works.* 3 vols. Edited by R. W. Bond. Oxford: Oxford University Press, 1902.

McKisack, May. *Medieval History in the Tudor Age.* Oxford: Clarendon Press, 1971.

Marston, John. *Sophonisba.* London, 1606.

Martindale, Charles. Introduction. *Ovid Renewed: Ovidian Influences on Literature and Art from the Middle Ages to the Twentieth Century.* Edited by Charles Martindale. Cambridge: Cambridge University Press, 1988. 1–20.

Meres, Francis. *Palladis Tamia: Wits Treasury.* London, 1598.

Mirror for Magistrates, The Edited by Lily B. Campbell. Cambridge: Cambridge University Press. 1938.

More, St Thomas. Vol. 2 of *Works.* 16 vols. Edited by Richard S. Sylvester. New Haven and London: Yale University Press, 1963 – .

Nashe, Thomas. *The Works.* 5 vols. Edited by Ronald B. McKerrow. 1957. Revised by F. P. Wilson. Oxford: Basil Blackwell, 1966.

Nicholl, Allardyce. *Stuart Masques and the Renaissance Stage.* London: Harrap and Co., 1937.

Nohrnberg, James. *The Analogy of 'The Faerie Queene'*. Princeton, NJ: Princeton University Press, 1976.

Nuttall, A. D. 'Ovid's Narcissus and Shakespeare's *Richard II:* the reflected self'. *Ovid Renewed: Ovidian Influences on Literature and Art from the Middle Ages to the Twentieth Century*. Edited by Charles Martindale. Cambridge: Cambridge University Press, 1988. 137–50.

—*A New Mimesis: Shakespeare and the Representation of Reality*. London and New York: Methuen, 1983.

Oliver, H. J. Ed. Arden Edition of Shakespeare's *Timon of Athens*. 3rd edn. London: Methuen, 1959; repr. 1979.

Ong, Walter J. *The Presence of the Word: Some Prolegomena for Cultural and Religious History*. New Haven and London: Yale University Press, 1967.

Onions, C. T. *A Shakespeare Glossary*. 2nd edn. Oxford: Clarendon Press, 1980.

Ovid. *Heroides and Amores*. Translated by Grant Showerman, revised by G. P. Goold. 2nd edn. Cambridge, Mass.: Harvard University Press, repr. 1986.

—*Metamorphoses*. 2 vols. Translated by Frank H. Justus Miller, revised by G. P. Goold. Vol. 1: 3rd edn. Vol. 2: 2nd edn. Cambridge, Mass.: Harvard University Press, repr. 1984.

—*The Metamorphoses of Ovid*. Translated by Mary M. Innes. Harmondsworth: Penguin, 1955.

—*Ovid's Metamorphoses. The Arthur Golding Translation*. Edited by John Frederick Nims. New York and London: Macmillan, 1965.

Pafford J. H. P. Ed. Arden Edition of Shakespeare's *The Winter's Tale*. London: Methuen, 1963; repr. 1982.

Pater, Walter. 'Shakespeare's English kings'. *Appreciations*. 1889. London: Macmillan, 1944.

Peacham (the Elder), Henry. *The Garden of Eloquence*. London: H. Jackson, 1577.

Pearcy, Lee T. *The Mediated Muse: English Translations of Ovid, 1560–1700*. Hamden, Conn.: Archon, 1984.

Petrarch. *Petrarch's Letters to Classical Authors*. Edited and translated by Mario Emilio Consenza. Chicago: University of Chicago Press, 1910.

Pettet, E. C. 'Shakespeare's conception of poetry'. *Essays and Studies*, n.s. 3 (1950) 29–46.

Pliny. *The Historie of the World, Commonly Called the Natvral Historie of C. Plinivs Secvndvs*. Translated by Philemon Holland. London: Adam Islip, 1601.

Plutarch. Vol. 6 and 8 of *Plutarch's Lives of the Noble Grecians and Romanes*. Translated by Sir Thomas North. 8 vols. Oxford: Basil Blackwell, 1928.

—*The Philosophie, Commonlie Called, The Morals written by the learned Philosopher Plutarch of Chaeronea*. Translated by Philemon Holland. London: Arnold Hatfield, 1603.

Prince, F. T. Ed. Arden Edition of Shakespeare's *The Poems*. London: Methuen, 1960; repr. 1982.

Puttenham, George. *The Arte of English Poesie*. Edited by G. D. Willcock and Alice Walker. Cambridge: Cambridge University Press, 1936.

Rabelais, François. *Gargantua and Pantagruel*. Translated by Sir Thomas Urquhart and Peter le Motteux. 3 vols. New York: E. P. Dutton & Co., 1934.

Rackin, Phyllis. 'Shakespeare's boy Cleopatra, the decorum of nature and the golden world of poetry.' *PMLA*, 87 (1972) 201–12.

Ridley, M. R. Ed. Arden Edition of Shakespeare's *Antony and Cleopatra*. 9th edn. London: Methuen, 1954; repr. 1977.

Schechner, Richard. 'Collective reflexivity: restoration of behaviour'. *A Crack in the Mirror: Reflexive Perspectives in Anthropology*. Edited by Jay Ruby. Philadelphia: University of Pennsylvania Press, 1982.

Sewell, Elizabeth. *The Orphic Voice: Poetry and Natural History*. London: Routledge and Kegan Paul, 1960.

Shapiro, Michael. 'Role-Playing, reflexivity, and metadrama in recent Shakespearean criticism'. *Renaissance Drama*, n.s. 12 (1981) 145–61.

Sidney, Sir Philip. *A Defence of Poetry*. Edited by J. A. Van Dorsten. Oxford: Oxford University Press, 1966; repr. 1982.

Smallwood, R. L. 'Shakespeare's use of history'. *The Cambridge Companion to Shakespeare Studies*. Edited by Stanley Wells. Cambridge: Cambridge University Press, 1986. 143–62.

Smith, G. G. *Elizabethan Critical Essays*, 2 vols. London: Oxford University Press, 1967. (First published 1904.)

Spenser, Edmund. *The Faerie Queene*. Edited by A. C. Hamilton. 2nd edn. London: Longman, 1980.

Taylor, Gary. Ed. Oxford Shakespeare Edition of Shakespeare's *King Henry V*. Oxford: Oxford University Press, 1984.

Thomson, Peter. *Shakespeare's Theatre*. London: Routledge and Kegan Paul, 1983.

Ure, Peter. Ed. Arden Edition of Shakespeare's *King Richard II*. 5th edn. London: Methuen, 1961; repr. 1982.

Viswanathan, S. *The Shakespeare Play as Poem: A Critical Tradition in Perspective*. Cambridge: Cambridge University Press, 1980.

Walter, J. H. Ed. Arden Edition of Shakespeare's *King Henry V* . London: Methuen, 1954; repr. 1983.

Weimann, Robert. *Shakespeare and the Popular Tradition in the Theater: Studies in the Social Dimension of Dramatic Form and Function*. Edited by Robert Schwartz. Baltimore and London: Johns Hopkins University Press, 1978.

—'Mimesis in *Hamlet*'. *Shakespeare and the Question of Theory*. Edited by Patricia Parker and Geoffrey Hartman. New York and London: Methuen, 1985. 275–291.

Wells, Stanley, and Gary Taylor. Eds. *William Shakespeare. The Complete Works*. Modern Spelling Edition. Oxford: Clarendon Press, 1986.

Wells, Stanley and Gary Taylor, with John Jowett and William Montgomery. Eds. *William Shakespeare. The Complete Works: A Textual Companion*. Modern Spelling Edition. Oxford: Clarendon Press, 1987.

Welsford, Enid. *The Court Masque: A Study in the Relationship between Poetry and the Revels*. New York: Russell and Russell, 1962.

Wilbur, Richard. Introduction. 'The Narrative Poems'. *William Shakespeare. The Complete Works*. Edited by Alfred Harbage. 1969. New York: Viking Press, 1977. 1401–5.

Wolf, William D. '"New heaven, new earth": the escape from mutability in *Antony and Cleopatra*'. *Shakespeare Quarterly*, 33 (1982) 328–35.

Worthen, W[illiam] B. 'The weight of Antony: staging "character" in *Antony and Cleopatra*'. *Studies in English Literature, 1500–1900*, 26 (Spring 1986). 295–308.

Young, David P. *Something of Great Constancy: The Art of 'A Midsummer Night's Dream'*. New Haven and London: Yale University Press, 1966.

Index